D0072745

Native Americans in the American Revolution

Native Americans in the American Revolution

How the War Divided, Devastated, and Transformed the Early American Indian World

~

Ethan A. Schmidt

PRAEGER

AN IMPRINT OF ABC-CLIO, LLC

Santa Barbara, California • Denver, Colorado • Oxford, England

Library of Congress Cataloging-in-Publication Data

Schmidt, Ethan A.
  Native Americans in the American Revolution : how the war divided, devastated, and transformed the early American Indian world / Ethan A. Schmidt.
    pages cm.
  Includes bibliographical references and index.
  ISBN 978-0-313-35931-6 (alk. paper) — ISBN 978-0-313-35932-3 (ebook)
1. United States—History—Revolution, 1775–1783—Participation, Indian. 2. Indians of North America—History—Revolution, 1775–1783. 3. Indians of North America—Government relations. 4. United States—Relations—Great Britain. 5. Great Britain—Relations—United States. 6. British—North America—History—18th century. 7. Indians of North America—Wars—1775–1783. I. Title.
  E230.S436 2014
  973.3'43—dc23   2014013335

ISBN: 978-0-313-35931-6
EISBN: 978-0-313-35932-3

18 17 16 15 14   1 2 3 4 5

This book is also available on the World Wide Web as an e-book.
Visit www.abc-clio.com for details.

Praeger
An Imprint of ABC-CLIO, LLC

ABC-CLIO, LLC
130 Cremona Drive, P.O. Box 1911
Santa Barbara, California 93116-1911

This book is printed on acid-free paper ∞
Manufactured in the United States of America

This book is dedicated to my parents,
Tom and Susie Schmidt.

How lucky I am to be their son.

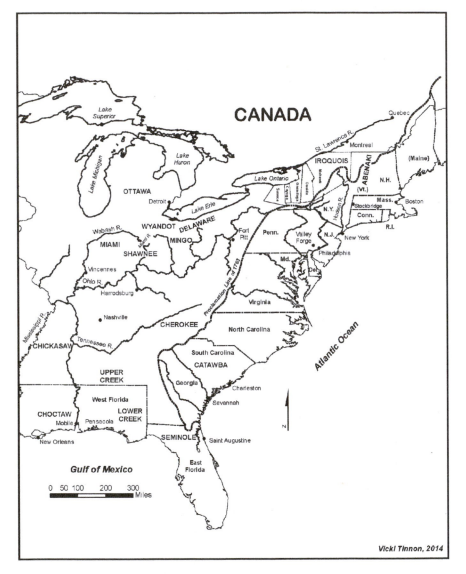

Colonial America on the Eve of the American Revolution

CONTENTS

Acknowledgments ix

Guide to the Principal Native American Groups
during the Revolutionary Era, Grouped by Region xiii

Timeline of the Major Events of the American Revolution,
Including Those Relating to Native Americans xxiii

Introduction: The Great War for Empire and the End
of Triangular Native Diplomacy 1

1 Pontiac's Rebellion, the Proclamation of 1763,
and the New British Indian Policy 11

2 The Collapse of British Indian Policy in the South 25

3 The Collapse of British Indian Policy in the North 47

4 The Collapse of British Indian Policy in the West 67

5 The Revolutionary War in the South 87

6 The Revolutionary War in the North 117

7 The Revolutionary War in the West 139

8 "Like We Should Soon Become No People":
The Assault on Indian Land in the Immediate
Aftermath of the American Revolution 157

Conclusion: The Struggle Continues 177

Notes 181

Bibliographic Essay 205

Index 213

Acknowledgments

So many people beyond me have contributed to this work; I hope the finished product does them credit. My former department chair at Texas Tech University (TTU), Dr. Randy McBee, was generous from the very outset in granting travel funds and time off in order to conduct the research and to write the early chapters. Funds granted me by the office of the vice president for research at TTU also aided in the completion of this project.

The staffs of the Library of Congress, the Missouri Historical Society's Library and Research Center, the Clements Library at the University of Michigan, the Rockefeller Library at Colonial Williamsburg, the British National Archives and Public Record Office, the British Library, the Texas Tech University Library, and the Roberts-LaForge Library at Delta State University provided invaluable assistance to me during the research and writing of this project. I cannot thank them enough for their professionalism and patience. Jack Becker of the Texas Tech University Library was particularly helpful and supportive of this volume and I owe him a great debt.

Many colleagues and associates near and far have been valuable as sounding boards for my ideas regarding this project or simply as providers of emotional and intellectual support. These individuals include my former adviser at the University of Kansas Paul Kelton, Ronald McCoy, Robbie Ethridge, Donald Fixico, Nicole Anslover, Brady DeSanti, Dixie Haggard, Miguel Levario, Karlos Hill, Paul Bjerk, Zachary Brittsan, Emily Skidmore, Sean Cunningham, Manu Vimalassery, Saad Abi-Hamad, Jeff

Mosher, and Jobi Martinez. I would also like to extend a particular thank you to Bruce Johansen of the University of Nebraska-Omaha for his insightful comments on a draft of the project. His thoughts were most helpful to me as I prepared the final manuscript. My colleagues at Delta State University were a tremendous support to both myself and my family as we transitioned from Lubbock to Cleveland and as I worked to finish this book. I am so lucky to have such wonderful people to share my academic life with such as Chuck Westmoreland, Brian Becker, Thomas Laub, Gavin Lee, Lynn Pazzani, James Robinson, Thomas Boschert, Jerry Dallas, Michelle Johansen, Shannon Lamb, Paulette Meikle, Debarashmi Mitra, Leslie Green-Pimentel, Leslie Fadiga-Stewart, David Hebert, Don Allan Mitchell, Mike Smith, Paul Hankins, and Vicky Hartley. Thanks to you all for your support and friendship. My colleague Vicki Tinnon deserves special mention for the excellent map she contributed to this volume. Telling this story would have been infinitely more difficult without it.

I cannot say enough about the people at ABC-CLIO with whom I have worked to bring this project to fruition. Elizabeth Demers took a chance on an unpublished, first-year assistant professor and acquired this project for ABC-CLIO based solely on a proposal and one face-to-face meeting at the Western History Association Conference in 2003. Though she left to pursue other opportunities before the project really got going, I will never forget her faith in me and the idea of this book. James Sherman picked up where she left off and was forced to deal with an extremely lengthy delay as a project I was committed to before this one encountered several setbacks. He stuck by me and the project and it is largely due to his decision not to pull the plug (which would have been entirely understandable) that this volume exists today. It has been a true joy to work closely with Michael Millman during most of the writing of the last half of the book and the entire revision and publication process. His patience, professionalism, and most of all belief in the book, as well as his singular talent for prodding without seeming too pushy or unreasonable were exactly what I needed to bring this project across the finish line. He handled the delays occasioned by my decision to leave Texas Tech and take up my current position at Delta State University with tremendous patience. Words cannot express the full measure of my gratitude to him, but they are all I have, so thank you Michael!

I also owe a debt of gratitude to two scholars whom I have never met, but without whose work this volume would not have been possible. Gary Nash's entire career and most recently his book *The Unknown American Revolution* have been an inspiration to me both in my teaching of the American Revolution as a "many-sided struggle to reinvent America" and to this project. I first bought Colin Calloway's *The American Revolution in Indian Country* as a freshman at Emporia State. Little did I know back then that Calloway's work in that book and his many others would become so important to my life and career. I hope that this book does some small part to answer the call he sounded in 1995 for a synthesis of the Indian experience in the American Revolution. While he would have done a much better job of it than I, hopefully my work will be sufficient for now.

My wife, Elizabeth, and our three children, Connor, Dylan, and Brianna, put up with so much more than they should have in order to allow me to research and teach my passion. They have borne it all with such grace and forbearance. I do not deserve them. Nonetheless I cherish them. Elizabeth, ever since I met you at a fraternity party on the campus of Emporia State University nearly 20 years ago you have enriched my life and inspired me to do my utmost to be as good a husband and father as I can. It has been a long journey to this point for us full of twists, turns, and surprises, but through it all nothing was insurmountable because you were with me, by my side, always encouraging me. Thank you! I love you! As for Connor, Dylan, and Brianna, you three came along and made what was already a great marriage and life even better! I love you all more than you know and now that this project as well as others have come to fruition, there will be even more time for trips, walks, ball games, stories, card games, Legos, video games, swimming, movies, snuggles, and hugs than before. I can't wait!

Cleveland, Mississippi
November 2013

GUIDE TO THE PRINCIPAL NATIVE AMERICAN GROUPS DURING THE REVOLUTIONARY ERA, GROUPED BY REGION

SOUTHERN INDIAN GROUPS

Cherokees. While there is debate as to when exactly the Cherokees arrived in the southeast, most scholars agree that they were originally Iroquoian speakers who migrated to the area from the Great Lakes region. Regardless, the introduction of eastern flint maize during the Mississippian culture period (800 to 1500 CE) provided the basis for their development into one of the largest and most powerful Indian polities in North America by the dawn of the 18th century.

At that time, the Cherokees had organized themselves into two primary semiautonomous divisions. The Overhill Cherokees lived in villages along the lower Little Tennessee, lower Tellico, and lower Hiwassee rivers in what is today the state of Tennessee, while the Lower Town Cherokees were located on the upper Savannah River in present-day South Carolina and Georgia.

Having been staunch allies of the English since 1715, the Seven Years' War opened fissures in the Anglo-Cherokee friendship that would ultimately spark an open war between the two in 1759. The settlement of this war in which older Cherokee political leaders bought peace by ceding large amounts of territory to the English created deep divisions among the

Cherokee which the outbreak of the American Revolution would ultimately widen to the point of Civil War.

Creeks. Unlike the Cherokees, the Creeks, who presently refer to themselves as the Muskogee in recognition of the language family to which they
belong, represent the direct descendants of the Mississippian mound
building culture, which dominated the southeastern region until the eve of
the arrival of Europeans in the area.

In the chaos of both the breakup of Mississippian society and the disease
epidemics initiated by the European invasion in the 16th century, surviv-
ing groups of Muskogean peoples began to reorganize themselves into
what eventually became the Creek Confederacy. By the beginning of the
18th century, the Creeks had organized themselves into a very large and
powerful polity, but one which operated in a very decentralized fashion.
Unlike Europeans and many of their other Indian counterparts, individual
towns and clans constituted the primary units of political and social
organization among the Creeks.

Despite this, the Creeks were grouped into two geographic divisions,
which often served as the primary nodes of contact for European traders
and diplomats. The Upper Creeks occupied territory in central Alabama
along the Coosa, Alabama, and Tallapoosa rivers, while the Lower Creek
villages were located along the lower Chattahoochee, Ocmulgee, and Flint
rivers in southwestern Georgia. Having maintained a policy of neutrality
since 1718 in the imperial wars fought by the British, Spanish, and French,
the removal of the latter from North America as a result of their defeat in
the Seven Years' War made it impossible for the Creeks to continue playing
the English and French off against one another as they had for decades.
Additionally, the growing encroachments of British colonists from Georgia
and South Carolina, hungry for Creek land, combined with the new reality
of British control of most of North America to create an extremely uncertain future in Creek country.

Choctaws. Having come together as a distinct people during the
17th century, the Choctaws were descended from both the Hopewell,
a northerly located mound building culture, as well as from the
Mississippians. By the 18th century, the Choctaw homeland was located
between the Yazoo River in the north and the Natchez Bluffs to the south
in present-day Mississippi.

Located at a strategic crossroads in relation to the French in Louisiana,
the Spanish in Florida, and other native groups such as the Chickasaws to
the north, three separate semiautonomous geographic divisions eventually
developed among the Choctaws all headed by a principal chief. The
Western division of the Choctaws, located near present-day Vicksburg; the

Eastern division near the upper Chickasawhay River and lower Tombigbee River watersheds along the lower Alabama-Mississippi border; and the Southern or "Six Towns" division located in southeast Mississippi all at different times favored trade with all three of the colonizing powers, although prior to the Seven Years' War the entire group tended to associate with the French more than the other two.

When the French were defeated in the war and forced to abandon their American possessions, the Choctaws were forced into a much closer relationship with the British; however, intertribal warfare, internal division, and their previous support of the French complicated their relationship with their new British allies. The growing dispute between Great Britain and her American colonies further complicated these matters.

Chickasaws. Much like the Choctaws, the Chickasaws also formed into a distinct cultural and political entity sometime during the 17th century out of migrants from western regions who had recently congregated east of the Mississippi River in present-day northeast Mississippi. By 1670, the Chickasaws were trading with British colonists in Carolina. Increasingly, they became an important provider of Indian slaves whom they captured in raids on their traditional enemies and then delivered to traders in Charleston in return for guns.

This relationship with the British led the Chickasaws to fight alongside the English in the Imperial Wars of the 18th century against the French; however, in a series of events experienced by many Native American peoples after the end of the Seven Years' War, the penetration of American colonists into Chickasaw country threatened their independence. Additionally, unlicensed traders who increasingly ignored British regulations diminished the authority of traditional Chickasaw leaders who to that point had been the only pipeline for the distribution of trade goods. The increasing numbers of mixed-blood individuals who embraced a more Anglicized lifestyle bred additional conflict among Chickasaws on the eve of the American Revolution.

Catawbas. By all credible accounts, the Catawbas have lived near the Catawba River on the present-day border of the states of North and South Carolina for as long as recorded history and anthropological evidence can pinpoint. As early as 1567, they were recorded as living in that area. The effects of years of warfare with the Seneca and Delawares to their north as well as the ravages of colonialism brought on by the increasing settlement of North and South Carolina eventually took their toll on the Catawba's population. Specifically, a smallpox epidemic which struck their homeland in 1738 severely affected their warrior base and by the end of the Seven Years' War their numbers had declined to the point that their only recourse lay in allying themselves with the colonies of North and South Carolina. In 1763, the South Carolina legislature granted them a small reservation on both sides of the Catawba River. As the dispute between Great Britain and the colonies widened in the 1760s and 1770s, it was no secret that the Catawbas, who had come to depend upon their relationship with the Carolinas, would support the revolutionaries.

NORTHERN INDIAN GROUPS

Abenakis. One of the many Algonquian-speaking peoples of New England at the time of the arrival of English colonists there in the early part of the 17th century, the Abenakis found themselves increasingly surrounded by the English in Massachusetts on one side and the French province of Quebec on the other. Initially, they allied themselves with the French and even joined King Philip and his Wampanoags against the English colonists of New England in 1675 and further supported their French allies against the English during Queen Anne's War from 1702 to 1713. After being defeated by the English in the conflict known as Greylock's War in 1725, many Abenakis moved to Canada, but still others maintained a significant Abenaki presence in New England.

The defeat of their French allies in the Seven Years' War both deprived the Abenakis of a valuable trading and military partner, but also earned them the enmity of the English government and the settlers of New England. Those colonists long remembered the punishing joint French-Abenaki raids, which often punctuated the peace of the New England frontier in the years of Imperial Warfare during the 18th century. On the eve of the American Revolution, the Abenakis had largely dispersed in an effort to avoid both having to ally themselves officially with the British and confrontation with New England colonists.

Stockbridge. The Stockbridge and other praying Indians of New England were the result of the late 17th century missionary efforts of the Puritan clergy. Praying towns were originally established as communities reserved exclusively for Indian converts and the missionaries who attended them; however, over the course of the approximately 100 years between their establishment and the outbreak of the American Revolution, they had also come to serve as refugee centers for native peoples whose original communities had either been destroyed by warfare or succumbed to disease epidemics. During the 18th century, the various Indian peoples living in the praying towns began to fuse their cultures and traditions together, eventually forging new Indian identities tied to the particular praying town in which they lived.

At the outbreak of the American Revolution, the many years of religious interaction with New Englanders had created, in some cases, close personal relationships between the two groups; therefore, the praying Indians of Stockbridge and other praying towns were all very sympathetic to the colonists in their dispute against the English. At the same time, New England settlers were increasingly violating the rules against settling within the bounds of the praying towns. Drawn there in hopes of obtaining Indian land, settlers and speculators were closing in on the praying towns, taking up the land of peoples such as the Stockbridge at breakneck pace. The decision of the Stockbridge to fight for the Americans during the American Revolution would only exacerbate this situation.

THE SIX NATIONS OF THE IROQUOIS CONFEDERACY

There is considerable debate among scholars as to when the Iroquois League (the forerunner of the Six Nations Confederacy) originally formed. Some scholars place its origins as far back as the 11th or 12th centuries while others cite the mid-15th to 17th centuries as the likely beginning of Iroquois political unity. Regardless, all scholars agree that the League arose to end long-standing enmity between the Iroquoian-speaking Senecas, Mohawks, Cayugas, Onondagas, and Oneidas, the Iroquois Confederacy eventually added a sixth nation when the Tuscarora fled war in North Carolina to join their brethren in New York during the early 1720s. By that time, they had already established themselves as the most powerful Native American group in the northern colonies.

Throughout the 17th century, the Iroquois Confederacy engaged in a series of devastating wars against the French-allied Indians of Canada, the Great Lakes, and the Ohio Valley over control of the lucrative fur trade. Known as the Beaver Wars, these conflicts ended in 1701 through a treaty with the French. After this, the Iroquois remained largely neutral in the imperial wars between the English and the French, preferring to play both parties off against one another. They finally ended this policy of neutrality and sided with the English during the Seven Years' War; however, throughout the entire 18th century the Iroquois consisted of both Anglophile and Francophile factions located among the six constituent nations that contested with one another for supremacy in the group's foreign policy, while neutralist Iroquois endeavored to cleave to the group's long-standing policy of favoring neither side.

In the years between the Seven Years' War and the commencement of the American Revolution, the Six Nations of the Iroquois Confederacy sought to arrest white settler encroachment upon their territory via a strategy in which they used their long-standing position as the English government's favored Indian spokesmen to protect their own lands by signing away those of other Native American groups. This strategy not only earned them the animosity of the groups whose lands they bartered away, but also led to chaos in the Ohio Valley as American settlers, armed with Iroquois and British permission to settle there, invaded the lands of the Shawnees, Delawares, Miamis, and Mingos who lived there. Despite their official declarations of neutrality at the outset of the American Revolution, internally, the Six Nations were deeply divided over what course of action to take. Those divisions would eventually widen to the point of civil war as the conflict wore on. The entries for the individual Six Nations below provide insight as to each group's position on the question of how best to deal with the American Revolution.

Mohawks. The Mohawks represented the easternmost member nation of the Iroquois Confederacy. Their territory stretched from the Mohawk Valley to present-day Quebec. Though they originally were first encountered by the Dutch and the French during the early 17th century, by the era of the American Revolution they were the closest of the Six Nations both in terms of geography and sentiment to the English. Additionally, they enjoyed an extremely close relationship with Sir William Johnson, the British superintendent of Indian Affairs for the northern department from the end of the Seven Years' War until his death in 1774, just before the outbreak of the American Revolution. That relationship and the large number of Mohawks who belonged to the anglophile faction in the long-running debate over which European power with whom the Iroquois Confederacy should ally itself predisposed the group to favor the British in their dispute with the American colonies.

Oneidas. The Oneidas were the closest neighbors of the Mohawks. Their territory lay immediately west of the Mohawk homeland near Oneida Lake in what is today Oneida and Madison counties. Because of both their proximity and close friendships with New York frontier settlements, many of which supported the Patriot cause, and their long and close relationship with the Presbyterian missionary Samuel Kirkland, the majority of the Oneida favored the colonists in their growing disputes with England during the 1760s and 1770s. This predisposition placed them among the minority in the councils of the Iroquois Confederacy.

Onondagas. Immediately to the west of the Oneidas lay the territory of the Onondagas, who, since the founding of the Iroquois Confederacy, had kept the sacred council fire at the Iroquois capital village from whence they took their name. At the beginning of the American Revolution, the Onondagas opted for neutrality and attempted to convince the rest of the Iroquois to follow suit.

Cayugas. The Cayuga occupied the Finger Lakes region along Cayuga Lake, in the areas between their Iroquois neighbors, the Onondaga to the east and the Seneca to the west. As the Revolution approached, the situation among the Cayuga epitomized the potential the conflict possessed to divide native peoples against themselves. Advocates for both sides as well as neutrality could be found among them as the Imperial Crisis deepened.

Senecas. The Senecas represented the westernmost of the confederacy's constituent nations. As such, they represented the most avowedly Francophile of all six of the member groups during the Imperial Wars, though they eventually allied themselves with the English when French power faltered during the Seven Years' War. Their relationship with British officials and colonists was always an uneasy one and as a result they attempted to cling to neutrality as long as they could when the American Revolution broke out. They would soon find that such a policy was useless.

Tuscaroras. After suffering defeat in North Carolina during the Tuscarora War between 1711 and 1713, most of the Tuscarora left North Carolina and relocated to New York. Because New York had been their original homeland, they were accepted as one of the Six Nations in 1722. Because of a close relationship with the Oneidas, the Reverend Samuel Kirkland also exhibited considerable influence in the councils of the Tuscaroras and this relationship predisposed them as well to look favorably upon the Americans in the growing dispute between them and the English crown.

OHIO VALLEY INDIAN GROUPS

Shawnees. Most scholars now believe that the Algonquian-speaking Shawnees descended from the mound building Fort Ancient complex in what is today southern Ohio rather than from the Mississippians. In either case, from their Ohio origins they then embarked upon a migratory journey, which eventually took them to Virginia, Maryland, South Carolina, Kentucky, Illinois, Indiana, and Pennsylvania; however, due to white settler encroachment and Six Nations military expansion, they largely returned to the Ohio Valley by the beginning of the Seven Years' War in 1754. From their primary settlements along the Scioto River in present-day central Ohio, they became close allies of the Delawares and Mingos.

After originally allying with the French during the Seven Years' War, their defection to support the British in 1758 represented a major factor in the eventual British victory; however, by 1763 many Shawnees joined in the war against the British, and their colonists most often associated with the Ottawa warrior Pontiac. Despite the end of that conflict and the issuance of the Proclamation of 1763, designed to keep white settlers from overrunning Ohio Valley Indian land, the Shawnees entered the era of the American Revolution determined to arrest the ever-advancing line of white settlement and force British officials to treat them as sovereign allies rather than as subjects.

Delawares. The Delaware, also known as the Lenape, were one of the largest and most powerful Algonquian-speaking Native polities in North America at the time of European contact. When first encountered in the late 16th and early 17th centuries, their territory included parts of what is today eastern Pennsylvania, much of southern and central New York, and almost all of modern-day New Jersey.

In 1682, the Delawares entered into a treaty with Pennsylvania proprietor William Penn, granting him their permission to settle his colony in the midst of their homeland. Despite his efforts at peaceful coexistence with the native people of the colony, Penn could not stop the eventual disruptions to the Delaware subsistence cycle and displacements that the growing population of his colony created.

These problems only worsened after Penn's death in 1718 when his heirs, much less interested in peaceful relations with Indians, took over the running of the colony. In 1737, John and Thomas Penn executed the infamous Walking Purchase agreement, which fraudulently deprived the Delawares of over 1.2 million acres of land and forced them to relocate their settlements to the western portions of the colony away from their traditional homeland.

The refusal of both the Iroquois and the British government to heed Delaware requests for help in resisting the Walking Purchase drove them into an alliance with the French during the early phases of the Seven Years' War; however, due to the combined effects of increasingly imperious demands on the part of French officials, the growing inability of the French to supply their native allies, and the increased diplomatic efforts of the English to win Indian allies to their side, the Delawares eventually abandoned the French and actively supported the English. Despite this, British colonists continued to drive them from their lands, thus forcing them to agree to the Treaty of Easton in 1758, which drove the remaining Delawares living in New York, New Jersey, and eastern Pennsylvania to the western half of the colony and the Ohio Valley beyond. Once there, many Delawares joined the Pontiac War against Britain and her colonists in 1763 and even after the end of that conflict they increasingly aligned themselves with the Shawnees and Mingos in a coalition determined to arrest the tide of white settlement in the west.

Mingos. In response to the trade abuses, debt, disease, and loss of lands initiated by the arrival of whites in their territories starting after the end of

Queen Anne's War in 1713, many members of the Six Nations Iroquois, mostly Senecas, began a significant migration to the Ohio Valley beginning in the late 1730s and early 1740s. Once there, they became known as Mingos. They participated in the Pontiac War against the British and their colonists and entered the era of the American Revolution united with the Shawnees and Delawares in their desire to prevent further settlement of the Ohio Valley by whites.

Miamis. An Algonquian-speaking people descended from the mound building Mississippian culture, by the eighteenth century the Miamis were primarily located in present-day western Ohio and Indiana between the Miami and Wabash rivers. As another group that had experienced considerable dislocations as a result of European colonialism, they too were determined by the end of the Seven Years' War to impede white settlement of the Ohio Valley and the Illinois country beyond.

Timeline of the Major Events of the American Revolution, Including Those Relating to Native Americans

1754–1763:

The French and Indian War

1758–1761:

The Anglo-Cherokee War

1758:

Oct. 26   Treaty of Easton signed between the colonies of New
            Jersey and Pennsylvania and representatives of the
            Iroquois Confederacy, Shawnees, and Delawares

1759:

Oct.   British major Robert Rogers burns the Abenaki village of
            Odanak to the ground

Nov.   The British begin constructing Fort Pitt on the site of the
            recently destroyed French Fort Duquesne

1763:

April 19	Arson fire claims the life of the Delaware leader Teedyuscung
May 9	Pontiac War begins when Pontiac and his followers besiege Fort Detroit
May 16	Fort Sandusky falls to supporters of Pontiac
May 25	The fall of Fort Joseph
May 27	The fall of Fort Miami
June 1	The fall of Fort Ouiatenon
June 2	The fall of Fort Michilimackinac and capture of Major Etherington
June 16	The fall of Fort Venango
June 17	The fall of Fort Le Boeuf
June 19	The fall of Fort Presque Isle
June 22	Delaware supporters of Pontiac attack and besiege Fort Pitt
July 31	Pontiac and his warriors defeat the British army in the Battle of Bloody Run
Aug. 5	Supporters of Pontiac defeated by British troops at the Battle of Bushy Run
Aug. 20	Siege of Fort Pitt ends
Sept. 14	Seventy British soldiers killed in "Devil's Hole Ambush"
Oct. 7	Proclamation of 1763
Oct. 31	Pontiac lifts the Siege of Fort Detroit
Nov. 5	Augusta Conference between representatives of Virginia, North Carolina, South Carolina, and Georgia, and the Creeks, Cherokees, Chickasaws, Choctaws, and Catawbas
Nov. 10	Treaty of Augusta signed. Cedes largest amount of Creek territory since the creation of the Georgia colony 30 years prior.
Dec. 14	Paxton Boys attack the Susquehannock village of Conestoga
Dec. 27	Paxton Boys kill 16 Susquehannocks placed in protective custody in Lancaster, Pennsylvania

1764:

Jan.   Paxton Boys march on Philadelphia, but disband upon
                    reaching an accord with city and colony leaders

1765:

March 22   Passage of the the Stamp Act

Oct. 7   The Stamp Act Congress convenes

Nov.   British Indian superintendent John Stuart negotiates
                    the Treaty of Picolata with the Lower Creeks to establish
                    boundary between East Florida and Creek territory

1766:

March 18   Repeal of the Stamp Act and Passage of the Declaratory Act

May 25   Congress of Pensacola between British Indian
                    superintendent John Stuart and the Creeks convenes

1767:

June 29   Passage of the Townshend Revenue Act

1768:

Aug. 1   Boston Non-Importation Agreement

Oct. 17   British Indian superintendent for the southern colonies
                    agrees to the Treaty of Hard Labor, which grants the
                    Cherokees sole possession of the lands that now make up
                    the present state of Kentucky

Nov. 5   British and colonial representatives agree to the Treaty of Fort
                    Stanwix in New York with representatives of the Iroquois
                    Confederacy. Effectively opens up the lands of the Shawnees,
                    Delawares, Mingos, Miamis, and others in the Ohio Valley to
                    settlement by American colonists despite the fact that the
                    Ohio Valley Indians had not been party to the treaty
                    negotiations. The Treaty of Fort Stanwix directly contradicts
                    the Treaty of Hard Labor agreed to just two weeks prior.

1770:

March 5   The Boston Massacre

1773:

May 10	Passage of the Tea Act
Aug. 1	Creek headmen cede an additional 2.1 million acres to Georgia, angering young Creek warriors who advocated armed resistance to white land encroachment
Sept.–Oct.	Shawnee emissaries arrive in Creek and Cherokee towns with war belts requesting aid in their war against American settlers
Dec. 16	The Boston Tea Party

1774:

March 31	Passage of the Boston Port Act
April	Outbreak of Lord Dunmore's War in Virginia and murder of the peaceful Mingo chief Logan's family
May 20	Passage of the Administration of Justice Act
May 20	Passage of the Massachusetts Government Act
June 2	Passage of the Quartering Act of 1774
June 22	Passage of the Quebec Act
July 11	Death of British Indian superintendent for the northern colonies Sir William Johnson
Sept. 5	The First Continental Congress Convenes
Oct. 10	Battle of Point Pleasant, Virginia ends Lord Dunmore's War

1775:

March 23	Patrick Henry's "Give me liberty or give me death" speech
Apr. 19	Battle of Lexington and Concord, or "The shot heard 'round the world"
May 10	The Second Continental Congress convenes in Philadelphia
June	British superintendent for Indian Affairs in the South John Stuart driven from Charleston. Takes refuge at St. Augustine
June 15	George Washington named commander in chief
June 17	The Battle of Bunker Hill
July 3	Washington assumes command of the Continental Army

| Aug. 25 | Albany Congress between American representatives and the Six Nations of the Iroquois Confederacy convenes |
| Dec. 30–31 | Benedict Arnold's invasion of Canada fails at Quebec |

1776:

Jan. 15	Thomas Paine publishes "Common Sense"
March 17	The British evacuate Boston
May	Six Nations unity destroyed when Oneidas and Tuscaroras defy the confederacy's neutrality policy and begin actively supporting the Americans
June 12	The Virginia Declaration of Rights
July 1	Cherokee militants eventually called Chickamaugas, under the leadership of Dragging Canoe, begin attacking western American settlements. Cherokee War of 1776 begins.
July 1	The Cherokee begin attacks along the southern frontier
July 1–4	Congress debates and revises the Declaration of Independence
July 4	Congress adopts the Declaration of Independence
July 8	The Declaration of Independence is read publicly
Aug. 27	British defeat Washington in the Battle of Long Island
Sept. 15	The British occupy New York City
Sept. 16	The Battle of Harlem Heights
Oct. 11	Benedict Arnold defeated at the Battle of Valcour Island
Nov. 20	British general Cornwallis captures Fort Lee from Nathanael Greene
Dec. 26	Washington crosses the Delaware and defeats the Hessians holding Trenton, New Jersey

1777:

Jan. 3	Washington defeats the British garrison at Princeton, New Jersey
May–June	Mobile Conference held between Choctaws, Chickasaws, and Superintendent John Stuart. Choctaws and Chickasaws agree to patrol the Mississippi River on behalf of the British.
May 20	Treaty of DeWitt's Corner, South Carolina ends Cherokee War. Cherokees lose nearly all of their remaining land in South Carolina. Dragging Canoe and his Chickamauga followers move to Tennessee and continue their resistance.

July 5	American general Arthur St. Clair surrenders Fort Ticonderoga to the British
Aug. 6	Battle of Oriskany, New York
Sept. 11	The Battle of Brandywine, Pennsylvania
Sept. 19	Burgoyne defeated at Freeman's Farm, New York, in the first of the Battles of Saratoga
Sept. 26	British under Howe occupy Philadelphia
Nov. 10	Murder of the Shawnee leader Cornstalk at Fort Randolph
Oct. 4	The Battle of Germantown
Oct. 7	Burgoyne defeated at Freeman's Farm, New York, in the second and final of the Battles of Saratoga
Oct. 17	Burgoyne surrenders to Gates at Saratoga, New York
Nov. 16	British capture Fort Mifflin, Pennsylvania

1778:

Feb. 6	The United States and France sign the Franco-American Alliance
March 7	British general William Howe replaced by Henry Clinton
June 18	British abandon Philadelphia and return to New York
June 28	The Battle of Monmouth Courthouse ends in a draw
July 3	Loyalists and Mohawks destroy the Patriot settlement of Wyoming on the Susquehanna River in Pennsylvania
July 4	George Rogers Clark captures Kaskaskia in the Illinois country
Aug. 8	French and American forces besiege Newport, Rhode Island
Oct. 9	Patriot militia and Continental Army troops destroy the Mohawk village of Onoquaga in New York
Nov. 11	Loyalists and Iroquois warriors destroy the Patriot settlement of Cherry Valley in western New York
Dec. 29	The British occupy Savanna

1779:

Feb. 23–24	American George Rogers Clark captures Vincennes in present-day Indiana
March 21	Death of Southern British Indian superintendent John Stuart

June–Sept.	John Sullivan conducts a scorched earth campaign throughout the Mohawk Valley in New York aimed at weakening or eliminating Indian resistance there
June 21	Spain declares war on Great Britain
Sept. 23	John Paul Jones, aboard the *Bonhomme Richard,* captures British man-of-war *Serapis* near English coast
Oct. 9	American attempt to recapture Savannah, Georgia, fails

1780:

March 14	Spanish forces capture Mobile from the British
May 12	British capture Charleston, South Carolina
May 29	British crush Americans at Waxhaw Creek, South Carolina
June 20	Patriots rout Tories at Ramseur's Mill, North Carolina
July 11	French troops arrive at Newport, Rhode Island, to aid the American cause
Aug. 6	George Rogers Clark burns the Shawnee village of Chillicothe in the Ohio Valley
Aug. 8	Clark's forces surprised at Piqua. Despite winning the battle, Clark is forced to call off his campaign due to the heavy losses he suffers.
Aug. 16	British rout Americans at Camden, South Carolina
Sept. 23	British spy John André arrested
Oct. 7	Battle of King's Mountain, South Carolina
Oct. 14	Washington names Nathanael Greene commander of the Southern Army

1781:

Jan. 1	Mutiny of unpaid Pennsylvania soldiers
Jan. 17	Battle of the Cowpens, North Carolina
March 9	Spanish besiege the British at Pensacola
March 15	Battle of Guilford Courthouse, North Carolina
April	Dragging Canoe and the Chickamaugas defeat American settlers at the Battle of the Bluff near present-day Nashville, Tennessee
May 8	Pensacola capitulates to the Spanish

June 6	Americans recapture Augusta, Georgia
Oct. 19	Cornwallis surrenders at Yorktown, Virginia

1782:

March 8	American militia massacre 96 pacifist Delawares at the Moravian mission village of Gnadenhutten, Ohio
July 11	British evacuate Savannah, Georgia
Aug. 19	Kentucky militia routed by Ohio Valley Indians at the Battle of Blue Licks in Kentucky
Nov. 30	British and Americans sign preliminary Articles of Peace
Dec. 14	British leave Charleston, South Carolina

1783:

April 19	Congress ratifies preliminary peace treaty
Sept. 3	The United States and Great Britain sign the Treaty of Paris
Nov. 1	Pro-American and neutralist Creeks sign a peace treaty with Georgia representatives agreeing to a land cession of over 800 square miles
Nov. 25	British troops leave New York City
Dec. 23	Washington resigns as commander

Introduction: The Great War for Empire and the End of Triangular Native Diplomacy

In 1784, an Indian emissary, speaking to the Spanish governor at St. Louis, summed up his views on the American Revolution. He referred to this period so cherished and celebrated by Americans then and since, as "the greatest blow that could have been dealt us, unless it was our total destruction." The speaker went on to describe the results of the American Revolution for the Cherokee, Shawnee, Chickasaw, and Choctaw people he represented in even greater detail. "The Americans, a great deal more ambitious and numerous than the English, put us out of our lands . . . extending themselves like a plague of locusts in the territories of the Ohio River which we inhabit."[1] The speaker had much cause to characterize the native experience in the American Revolution this way. The 20 years from the end of the Pontiac War to the conclusion of the War for American Independence witnessed the disintegration of the delicate balance of power that had allowed many native peoples to enhance their wealth and prestige as well as to retain some measure of control over their land base. The departure of the French from North America combined with the weakened state of the Spanish Empire to end the ability of many Native American groups in both the northern and southern colonies to play European powers against one another as they had done since the inception of the imperial wars in the late 17th century. As the new era of British unilateral control of North America dawned, Native Americans faced an uncertain future. That uncertain future gave way to a disastrous present as colonists eventually rebelled against the British, whom, among other things, they accused of standing between them and the Indian lands to the west the Americans so coveted.

Like so many pivotal events in history, to understand the Native American role in and experience of the American Revolution, one must begin years before its outbreak. Specifically, several events from the waning days of the Seven Years' War that ravaged colonial America and much of the globe from 1754 to 1763 serve to illustrate the profoundly altered world that Native American groups up and down the eastern seaboard and throughout the trans-Appalachian hinterland confronted.

By the late 1750s, the large Cherokee Confederacy had managed to maintain their position as one of the most powerful polities in the southern colonies via their ability to exploit their geographic position between the English settlements of the Carolinas and Virginia to the east, and the French settlements in Louisiana and Illinois to the west. Realizing that both the English and French desired at most their trade and military support, and at least deprivation of the other of those prizes, the Cherokees skillfully played the two against one another. As the Seven Years' War dragged on and French military fortunes began to decline, the English and their colonists began to bristle at the idea of respecting Cherokee neutrality. In the face of this growing pressure, the British recruited nearly 300 Cherokees under the leadership of Attakullakulla, or the Little Carpenter, to assist in a 1758 campaign against the French Fort Duquesne in the Ohio country. In return for their service, John Forbes, the British general in charge of the expedition, went to great lengths to inform the Cherokees of his dislike for Indians and his displeasure at the Cherokees' failure to join the British cause earlier in the war. On one occasion, he referred to Attakullakulla as "a consummate dog." When Attakullakulla attempted to leave rather than abide Forbes's insults, the British commander had him imprisoned.[2]

If Forbes's high-handed treatment of the Little Carpenter and his warriors were not enough to convince the Cherokees that the British and their colonists now felt little reason to respect either them or their sovereignty, several encounters that same year between Cherokees and their supposed British colonial allies drove the point home. In the fall of 1758, near Winchester, Virginia colonists murdered a group of 30 Cherokees on their way back from participating in the Forbes expedition. In another incident, this one across the border in North Carolina, colonists fired upon a group of Cherokees after the Indians had complied with a request to lay down their guns. Another group of Virginians, this time rangers from

Mayo Fort on an expedition to collect French-allied Indian scalps to exchange for bounties, happened upon a group of Cherokees near a place called Draper's Meadows. Since the Cherokees were allied to the British, their scalps held no value for the Virginians. According to the account of John Echols, a member of the Virginian band, this hardly represented much of an obstacle. When the opportunity presented itself, the Virginians simply "fired at them and followed them up 'till [they] killed 4 of them and wounded the other." The Virginians then swore an oath "not to tell that [they] ever heard them say that they were Cherokees."[3]

Not surprisingly, the Cherokees responded by raiding backcountry Carolina settlements in the fall of 1759. South Carolina's governor, William Henry Lyttelton, responded by preparing to "go in person to the Cherokees as well to humble our perfidious enemy."[4] By the end of what the South Carolinians referred to as the Cherokee War in 1761, several Cherokee towns as well as their accompanying fields and peach orchards lay in smoldering ruin. While the Cherokees managed to avoid large numbers of casualties by abandoning their towns in the face of the advancing colonial troops, the destruction of their crops and towns took its toll and they sued for peace in 1761. In that peace, the Cherokees agreed to allow the British not only to retain Fort Loudon (which the Cherokees had subsequently captured during the Cherokee War after giving the British permission to build it earlier in the decade) but also to build a string of other forts in Cherokee country. Whereas they had once boasted as many as 22,000 people earlier in the century, the Cherokees' defeat at the hands of the British and their colonists hastened a population decline already under way due to disease epidemics and the destruction of their subsistence practices. By 1775, the Cherokee Confederacy consisted of only 12,000 people. Without a reliable French presence with which to successfully countermand British power, the Cherokees had no choice but to accept increasing British and colonial penetration of their country.[5]

The year 1758 also brought ominous events to the Delawares of western Pennsylvania and their allies in the Ohio country beyond. These groups, which had proven themselves indispensable allies to the French during their string of victories early in the war, had by the latter years of the 1750s begun to make peace overtures to the British. Whether out of a long-standing desire to rid the Ohio Valley of both imperial powers or simply a reaction to declining French power and the concomitant failures of the French to live up to their obligations to them, the Ohio groups began meeting with English and colonial representatives as early as 1756. By 1758, the Ohio country Indians found themselves negotiating a treaty that would critically alter the balance of power in the Ohio country.[6]

The negotiators to the Treaty of Easton allowed the Western Delawares to believe that the English would respect their desire that English colonists abandon their settlement activities in the Ohio Valley. It took less than one month for the Western Delawares to discover otherwise. Instead of leaving the area as the Western Delawares had requested, the English decided to build a massive fortification on the site of the recently destroyed French Fort Duquesne. What had begun as an attempt to rid their country of both French and English interlopers had ended with the removal of the French, but at the cost of a powerfully entrenched English military presence. Certainly, hordes of colonists could not be far behind.[7]

Like their brethren in the west, the Eastern Delawares likewise sought to hold back the tide of land-hungry colonists that the removal of the French would most assuredly unleash. In November of 1762, Eastern Delaware leader Teedyuscung went before the governor of Pennsylvania in Philadelphia to protest the settlement activities of the Susquehanna Company, which had been founded in the early 1750s in Connecticut for the purpose of land speculation in the Susquehanna Valley. Teedyuscung professed that he could not fathom "what the White People meant by settling in their Country unless they intended to steal it from them." Unlike the concerns of his Western Delaware brethren five years earlier, Teedyuscung had the power of the crown, the ministry, and the military on his side. In early 1763, Lord Egremont, secretary of state for the Southern Department, wrote the governor of Connecticut to express the king's displeasure at the activities of the Susquehanna Company. Furthermore, Jeffrey Amherst, commander of all British forces in North America at the time, also forbade the Susquehanna Company from continuing settlement in the region. Finally, Superintendent of Indian Affairs Sir William Johnson expressed his displeasure as well, stating that he foresaw grave consequences should the company's activities continue. None of it made any difference.[8]

By the late spring of 1763, Teedyuscung was dead—the victim of arson as he lay asleep in his cabin near present-day Wilkes-Barre, Pennsylvania. Later that year, Pennsylvania militiamen, reportedly drunk, murdered Teedyuscung's nephew and his family in retribution for Teedyuscung's son, Captain Bull, attempting to bring his father's murderers to justice. In the meantime, even the powerful Six Nations of the Iroquois Confederacy could not get the Connecticut Assembly to do anything other than shake their heads in disapproval of the activities of the Susquehanna Company while simultaneously protesting their inability to do anything about it.[9]

For their part, the Iroquois, the seemingly most powerful native group in all of North America, found themselves ignored not only by the government of Connecticut, but by the British military as well. Despite promises to abandon the forts the Six Nations had allowed them to build in their country, the British were now reoccupying and refortifying them. The Iroquois pleaded with British representatives to demolish the forts immediately. "[I]nstead of restoring us to our lands, we See You in possession of them, & building more Forts in many parts of our Country, notwithstanding the French are dead."[10] Their complaints fell on deaf ears. The world had irrevocably changed for native people in Colonial British North America. The French no longer acted as a check on the imperial designs of the British government, and even more alarming for native leaders, the British government seemed no longer to have any means of controlling their land-hungry colonists. The plague of locusts, to borrow the phrase used by the Ohio Valley Indian emissary in 1784, had indeed arrived. The colonists' desire for western Indian land and the strategies those native groups employed to combat them would play a pivotal role in driving the British government and the American colonies toward an irrevocable rupture.

Fifteen years ago, noted ethnohistorian Colin Calloway observed that "in general, historians of the Revolution have not been particularly interested in Indians, and scholars of Indian history have not paid much attention to the Revolution."[11] In *The American Revolution in Indian Country: Crisis and Diversity in Native American Communities,* he sought to begin the process of correcting that omission by detailing Indian experiences in the American Revolution rather than simply their participation as auxiliaries or adversaries of the various combatants involved in it. Calloway did not write a comprehensive synthesis of the revolutionary experiences of Native Americans, but rather he presented a series of eight case studies, each focusing on a particular Indian community. Citing the need for more scholarship on specific native groups during the period, he limited his study to what he called "small patches of a huge tapestry." However, he ended the book's preface by expressing his hope that future scholars might fully piece that tapestry together. In the years since Calloway wrote those words, both revolutionary scholars and ethnohistorians have indeed uncovered many more individual pieces of the tapestry he spoke of. However, as of this writing, no one has undertaken the task of stitching them together. As recently as 2011, historian Woody Holton, in an excellent summation of the state of Revolutionary historiography, commented upon this situation:

We are still waiting for a comprehensive survey of Indian involvement in the American Revolution. That none has yet appeared can no
longer be ascribed to a lack of scholarly interest. Rather, Indians'
experiences in the Revolution were so diverse—some Indians were
loyal allies of the British, others enlisted in the Continental Army,
while still others stood neutral or switched sides as circumstances
dictated—that no one has tried to encompass all of them within the
covers of a single volume. In 1995, Colin G. Calloway published *The
American Revolution in Indian Country,* but he would be the first to
admit that it was really a series of case studies aimed at casting a few
flashes of light into the gloom. Other scholars of the topic have
specialized to an even greater extent, producing biographies of individual Native Americans. But volumes devoted to Indians' involvement in the Revolutionary War are vastly outnumbered by those that
barely mention it.[12]

This work proposes to attempt such a synthesis. Specifically, I seek to
answer the call Calloway issued in that volume by incorporating his work
with those of other scholars in the field who have covered native peoples in
areas beyond those mentioned in *The American Revolution in Indian Country.* As such, this volume represents not so much an attempt to create new
knowledge on Native Americans in the revolutionary era, but instead to
combine as many of the pieces we already know into one comprehensive,
yet succinct and readable volume. I have relied heavily upon the work of
several scholars, some of whom I know, and all of whom I respect
immensely. They will no doubt recognize their interpretations in the pages
that follow and I have given them credit in the notes and in the text for
their extremely important contributions. To paraphrase Sir Isaac Newton,
whatever heights this book achieves, it does so by standing on the shoulders of giants.
    My desire to undertake this task stems from multiple sources. As an
instructor for an upper division course on the American Revolution, I have
always sought to give my students as broad a picture of the event as possible. Rather than simply picking one angle of analysis such as politics, military affairs, social history, and the like, I have found it more useful to ex-
pose my classes to as many of these viewpoints as possible. While I have
had no problem over the years finding texts which provide an excellent
overview of the experiences of women, African Americans, the urban la-
boring classes and debtors in the colonial south among others, I have always been frustrated by the lack of a comprehensive treatment of Native
Americans in the Revolutionary Era.[13]

Additionally, two articles I read, in different classes, during my doctoral work impressed upon me the need for practitioners of social and ethnohistory such as myself to endeavor to inject the results of their research into the larger narrative of American history. Consequently, I have had the words of Thomas Bender and James Merrell in my head constantly as I have engaged in this project. It is my hope that it contributes in some small way to Bender's goal of re-envisioning national history as "the ever changing, always contingent outcome of a continuing contest among social groups."[14] Likewise, I would like to think that this volume does something to further the project that Merrell outlined in 1989, which was to demonstrate not just to others interested in Native American history, but to all historians of the colonial and Revolutionary Era that "Indians were very much a part of the early American scene."[15]

In general, this work proposes three broadly defined frameworks within which to examine the Native American experience in the American Revolution. The first will outline the ways in which the very presence of Indians in certain areas of colonial America contributed to a desire on the part of colonists to break with Great Britain. Instead of serving as bystanders only marginally connected with the genesis of the revolutionary movement who were eventually drawn into participation in the war spawned by it, native people occupied a pivotal role as actors in the complex dramas of the 1760s and 1770s that produced the American Revolution. American Revolution historians generally refer to the 1760s and early 1770s as the period of the "Imperial Crisis" that ultimately led to the American Revolution. During this period, native people experienced their own imperial crisis in which their relationship with the British Empire initially dissolved into open rebellion. The settlement of that rebellion, while repairing the rift with the crown, placed the interests of many Native Americans in direct opposition to the designs of American colonists. Eventually, the pressure brought to bear on native communities by individual colonists, land companies, and colonial governments forced many native groups to sacrifice the interests and land base of their neighbors and allies in order to preserve their own. Additionally, attempts by the British government to avert another general Indian war disrupted the expansion plans of many colonists to the point that they began to advocate separation from Great Britain as the only means of achieving those plans.

The second framework addresses the role of native people in the Revolutionary War itself, but in keeping with the already stated goal of presenting a more nuanced portrayal of native participation in the Revolution, this section will focus on explaining how differing native groups came to very different decisions about how, when, and to what extent to participate.

None of the three choices facing native people (join the British, join the Americans, or attempt to remain neutral) turned out well for most of the groups in the east, and the very difficulties in deciding which of those paths to take led to either the complete dissolution or factionalization of such heretofore united native polities as the Iroquois, Creek, and Cherokee confederacies. West of the Appalachian Mountains, the Revolution spawned a very personal and brutal war between colonists and Native Americans that stretched into the first third of the 19th century.

Finally, the third section will focus on the consequences of the American Revolution for the native people who survived it. This section will demonstrate the very precarious position in which the American Revolution placed Indians. Whether they sided with the British, the Americans, or attempted to maintain neutrality, the Peace of Paris left them to the mercy of land-hungry settlers who moved quickly to appropriate native land and disrupt their cultural, political, and economic systems. Additionally, those who survived both the Revolution and the onslaught of white settlement in its wake found themselves forced to watch as Americans appropriated the artifacts, names, and symbols of now dispossessed native peoples to carve out a national identity. While the Treaty of Paris may have ended the American struggle against foreign empires, the Indian struggle against empire continued. In addition to the more tangible fight to stem the ever-increasing tide of settlement unleashed by independence, those American Indians who survived the war now found themselves locked in a psychological struggle with whites over the very possession and definition of their own Indian identity. That struggle continues even to this day.

Writing in the midst of the 200-year anniversary of the Declaration of Independence in the mid-1970s, the Native American scholar Vine Deloria Jr. remarked, "The frightening thing about the celebrations of the bicentennial is that we are tempted to simply increase the velocity with which we manipulate the familiar symbols of our past without coming to grips with a more profound understanding of our history."[16] Until recently, nowhere have those manipulations clouded our vision more than in the historiography of the American Revolution. As many individual historians have demonstrated in several localized studies over the past 20 years, Indian people served as key actors in the events that led to the American Revolution. They also sought to weather the tremendous upheavals and take advantage of the opportunities the Revolution produced. Finally, they have engaged in a centuries-long fight to preserve their identity in the midst of a culture that has tried repeatedly to force them to adhere to an imagined notion of Americanness that came about largely due to the needs of the founding generations to create nationalism in order to win the

American Revolution. In light of these realities, a historiography that relegates them to a secondary role as simple military auxiliaries can no longer be allowed. Instead, a profound understanding of the Native American experience in the American Revolution is critical to understanding the entire Revolution itself as well as the resulting history of Native Americans in the United States.

1

PONTIAC'S REBELLION, THE PROCLAMATION OF 1763, AND THE NEW BRITISH INDIAN POLICY

Looking out over the Ojibwa/Sauk baggatiway game (often confused with lacrosse) unfolding before him on June 2 of 1763, British major George Etherington had every reason to be on his guard, yet somehow, he was not. In the two weeks prior, British forts at Sandusky, St. Joseph, Ouiatenon, and Miami all fell to a combination of Ottawa, Wyandot, Ojibwa, Potawatomi, and Miami warriors. Despite these incidents (which, given the communication barriers of the day, he might not have been aware of) and warnings that a "renewal of the Indian war," was at hand, Etherington seemed oblivious to it all.[1] On that hot June day he attended the ball game occurring outside the gates of Michillimackinac, the fort commanded by the 30-year-old American-born officer, with only a member of his staff as an escort and with no clue that he was walking into a very cleverly laid trap. As Etherington and his escort, Lieutenant Leslie, were observing the game, they were "suddenly Seized, and Carried into the Woods."[2] The Jesuit missionaries who delivered news of the events from the hand of the now captured Etherington also delivered his version of events that occurred nearly simultaneously back at the fort:

> the Savages having purposely thrown their Ball into the Fort, to make it appear as if it happened by Accident, and followed it in directly, when a Number of their Women had Tomahawks and Spears concealed under their Blankets which they delivered them, and put the whole Garrison to Death except 13 Men.[3]

In his official account of the events at Michilimackinac, Etherington provided more specifics regarding whom it was that the attackers targeted. "They made prisoners of all the English traders and robbed them of everything they had, but they offered no violence to any of the persons or properties of the French men."[4]

Similar incidents occurred all across the western reaches of Britain's newly won North American empire after the taking of Michilimackinac. By the middle of that summer, the allied Indian groups of the Great Lakes, as well as the Ohio and Illinois countries, had driven the British from eight of their western forts, forced the abandonment of two others, and besieged several more including the key strongholds of Fort Pitt and Fort Detroit.[5]

The events commonly and somewhat misleadingly referred to as Pontiac's War often serve as the prelude to discussions of the period of "Imperial Crisis" that led to the American Revolution. As such, Native Americans play a tertiary role in the events that led to the American Revolution. In this rather myopic conception, early historians of the revolutionary era relegated native people to a status equal to that of tax stamps, tea, and luxury goods. In other words, Indians represented simply another inanimate thing over which the British government and American colonists argued their radically diverging conceptions of each other's role in the empire; however, if we conceive of Pontiac's Rebellion as the result of a Native American imperial crisis a new paradigm takes shape. In this native imperial crisis, the groups of the Great Lakes, as well as those of the Ohio and Illinois countries attempted to manage the end of their century-old relationship with the French and the imposition of English control as well as the arrival of American colonists to their best advantage. From this vantage point, native perspectives, choices, and actions occupy an integral role in explaining the coming of the American Revolution. Whether their motivations were to realize a religious vision of a world without whites, or an attempt to restore a more accommodating imperial power with which to trade and ally, the actions of the Native American groups that participated in Pontiac's War put Americans on the path to revolution. They altered

British colonial Indian policy and, by doing so, created a situation in which many colonists saw independence as the only answer.

THE MIDDLE GROUND

For some native people west of the Appalachian Mountains, Pontiac's War constituted an effort not to restore the world to a pre-1492 state, but instead to re-establish a system of accommodation that had undergirded their interactions with the dominant European power of the area for over a century. That system, best described by the term "Middle Ground," first appeared in the mid-17 century as a way for the Indians of the Great Lakes to coexist with the French in a manner that brought wealth, power, and peace to all sides. For these groups, the goal of the Pontiac War was either to help bring about a situation in which the French could reclaim their North American possessions or to force the newcomers to the area, the English, to adhere to the rules of the Middle Ground.[6]

As opposed to the notion of acculturation, the Middle Ground represented a process of accommodation in which, "diverse peoples adjust their differences through what amounts to a process of creative, and often expedient, misunderstandings."[7] In other words, when the Indian peoples of the Great Lakes and the emissaries of New France first encountered one another neither side possessed the ability to make sense of the other's customs, worldview, and motivations. However, through this process of trial and error, the two cultures agreed on new practices designed to bridge the gap between the two while still allowing each to retain those lifeways unique to their particular culture when not interacting with one another.

This phenomenon can best be visualized via the example of murder. Many Indian communities of the colonial era, including those of the northeast and Great Lakes, adhered to practices known as "raising up the dead," or "covering the dead," in the case of murders committed by Indians with whom they were at peace.[8] Essentially, the social unit (family, village, or band) from whence the murderer hailed had a duty to the victim's family to restore the person back to life by providing one of their own members as a captive to take the victim's place or to provide such an amount of trade goods as deemed necessary to replace the loss of the person. Of course, French society approached the subject of murder from a decidedly different perspective. Rather than holding the family of a perpetrator responsible, French justice focused on finding the actual culprit. Additionally, the society in general through the organs of the state, rather than the relatives of the victim, took charge of punishing the offender. Finally, they did so most often by killing the individual deemed responsible. However, when these cultures encountered one another in Northeastern North America several factors prevented each from imposing their will on the other. They therefore, over the course of several years, developed a ritualized system for dealing with murder that was neither Indian nor French, but instead incorporated elements of both. Specifically, they created a "ritual of surrender and redemption," that required native groups to surrender up the individual perpetrators of murderers, who would then be incarcerated until they could be brought to trial in the French fashion. However, once the facts of the case were determined, French officials would then allow the Indian groups involved to provide captives or goods in order to raise or cover the French murder victims.[9]

This same process repeated itself countless times in almost every French-Native interaction in the west during the latter half of the 17th century and the first half of the 18th. Due to each side's mutual need for the other (the French as well as their native partners profited greatly from the fur trade, yet both needed the other's cooperation in order to make the trade work), as well as the relative weakness of the French in North America both in terms of military might and number of colonists, accommodation and reciprocity permeated all aspects of French-Native relations in the west. According to historian Richard White, "the fur trade could not be completely separated from the relationship of French fathers to their Algonquian children, that is, from relations of political and military alliance, a straightforward domination of the local Algonquian village by the market never emerged."[10] From their perspective, the French viewed the fur trade as a typical market exchange in which the ultimate goal was to give up the very least amount possible while maximizing one's economic gains. In this basic capitalist formulation, the more desire the buyer has for one's goods the higher the price the seller can demand. Conversely, from the perspective of the Algonquian-and Iroquoian-speaking peoples the French most often traded with in North America, trade represented the exchange of personal belongings required of kin. In this formulation, the goal was not the maximization of individual profit, but a desire to meet the needs of all parties involved and to demonstrate the high regard in which one held one's kin. Therefore, high desire for the goods in question on the part of one trading partner required the other party to deliver them sufficient quantities to satisfy that need regardless of cost. From the native viewpoint, meeting the needs of others in the community and thus ensuring the community's stability and survival trumped ideas of personal aggrandizement.

Though the amplification of both individual profit and French power likely constituted the primary motivations for their engagement in the

Middle Ground relationship, their participation nonetheless set the French apart from the methods utilized by the other major colonial powers of the time. While the particular rituals and protocols developed by the French and the native peoples of the Great Lakes contained elements recognizable to both cultures, the syncretistic process that produced them sprang entirely from Great Lakes and Ohio Valley Indian cultures. Between 1630 and 1650, the Beaver Wars between Iroquoian-speaking groups from New York and Canada and the Algonquian-speaking groups to the west over access to prime beaver hunting grounds and control of the fur trade with European powers made cultural syncretism a necessity for the Indian peoples of the Great Lakes. Iroquois raids, originally confined to the Ottawa and St. Lawrence River valleys, eventually spread as far south as Lake Erie and as far west as the Mississippi River. In their wake, Iroquois warriors left a trail of smoldering Indian villages and French missions from which survivors fled in all directions seeking refuge from the devastation.[11] In describing the destruction of the villages and mission at St. Joseph during the summer of 1648, Father Paul Ragueneau painted the picture of the burgeoning refugee crisis which the Beaver Wars had created in the Great Lakes.

> A part of those who had escaped from the capture and burning of that Mission of Saint Joseph came to take refuge near our house of Sainte Marie. The number of those who had there been [17] killed or taken captive was probably about seven hundred souls, mostly women and children; the number of those who escaped was much greater. We tried to assist them out of our poverty,—to clothe the naked, and to feed those poor people, who were dying of hunger; to mourn with the afflicted, and to console them with the hope of Paradise.[12]

The attack on St. Joseph was only the beginning. By the 1650s, Iroquois raids and the epidemic diseases that ran rampant through tightly clustered and poorly sanitized villages full of malnourished and injured peoples drove most of the remaining Huron into refugee villages with the equally dispossessed peoples of the Great Lakes. The Great Lakes and Illinois country, or the Iroquois "shatter zone" as White has termed it, became a refugee country home to Iroquoian speakers who were not part of the Iroquois Confederacy, various Algonquian-speaking groups as well as some Muskogean and Siouan speakers who lived on the margins of the area.[13] In order to survive, these diverse peoples created new languages, new cultures, new traditions, and new polities through a process of cultural borrowing and adaptation, which ethnohistorians refer to as ethnogenesis.[14] Shortly thereafter, when French missionaries and traders arrived in the area in desperate need of Indian allies with which to advance their respective quests for souls and furs, they were willing to engage in the exact same processes of accommodation that were already under way there.[15]

As mentioned previously, the Middle Ground relationship manifested itself in other areas of French-Native interaction in the Great Lakes beyond cases of interethnic murder and the fur trade. The alliance between the French and native groups of the Great Lakes and the Illinois country represents the most important of these in regard to the coming of the American Revolution. Richard White refers to the alliance as full of tension stemming from the desire of Great Lakes peoples for "Onontio" (an Algonquian term, which described the French governor in Montreal as literally their father) to behave in the manner of an Indian father. In this native conception of fatherhood, the father figure mediates and keeps the peace between his children in a reciprocal relationship whereby both father and child owe one another certain duties. On the other hand, the French never stopped hoping that one day, they might have sufficient power to dispense with the Middle Ground entirely and simply force the Indians of the area to their will. Given the Indian need to keep their fragmented and still very heterogeneous villages from splintering into rival factions and the continued demographic weakness of the French both in the face of their native allies and their English enemies, neither group could afford to alienate the other.[16]

The precarious alliance between Great Lakes Indians and the French emerged from the decades of imperial warfare between the French and the English battered, but intact. From the War of the Spanish Succession in the first two decades of the 18th century through to the end of the War of the Austrian Succession in 1748, Indian communities throughout North America in general and the Great Lakes in particular, played pivotal roles in the outcomes of these imperial struggles. Native people "fought for their own reasons as their own interests and goals intersected with or jarred against those of the European powers, they participated in colonial systems when they chose to or when they had no choice, and they resisted amalgamation when they had the option or the power to do so."[17] Despite their best efforts, Great Lakes and Illinois country Indians found themselves in an increasingly unstable position by the 1750s. English colonists from Virginia, Pennsylvania, and the Carolinas streamed into their country in increasingly large numbers and threatened to displace Indian communities in the same violent fashion as their colonial forebears had destroyed the Indians' coastal brethren during the previous century. At the same time, enterprising traders from the English colonies began to offer a serious and

potentially lucrative alternative to their traditional French trading partners. Thus at the same time, western Indian communities found themselves
caught between the harsh push of land-hungry English colonists and the
enticing pull of English traders eager to gain their business. While this situation presented difficulty enough for the Franco-Indian alliance in the
area, the decision by the British and the French to fight their next imperial
contest over control of the Ohio country spelled the doom of the Middle
Ground and with it, the French presence in North America.[18]

In an effort to counter growing British strength in the Ohio country, the
French responded with a show of force designed both to deter their English
enemies and cow their Indian allies into obedience. In 1749, the French
embarked upon a strategy designed to secure their claim to the area via the
planting of lead plates in strategic locations bearing French emblems. They
then followed this campaign with the erection of a string of defensive forts
in the area, most notably Fort Duquesne at the strategic junction of the
Allegheny and Monongahela rivers. The act of formally claiming dominion
over the Ohio country and then enforcing it via the construction of forts
represented a grave repudiation of the Middle Ground in that the French
no longer approached the Indian peoples of the Ohio country as equals,
but instead as subjects. In doing so, they sent a very strong message to Ohio
country Indians that the alliance forged via the Middle Ground was dead.[19]

Despite this alarming change in the nature of their relationship with
the French, most Ohio country Indians threw their lot in with them when
hostilities finally broke out in 1754. Some did so out of a conviction that
the French were the militarily stronger combatant, while others did so
based upon the belief that stopping the flow of British colonists to their
lands represented the most immediate danger. Whatever the case, Great
Lakes, Ohio country, and Illinois country Indians played pivotal roles in
early French successes such as the 1755 rout of British general Edward
Braddock as he attempted to drive the French from Fort Duquesne. As the
tide of the war turned toward the British in the late 1750s, however, the
French found themselves unable to supply their Ohio country allies with
the gifts and supplies required of a reciprocal alliance such as the Middle
Ground. At the same time, smallpox tore through the villages of the Ohio
country. For their part, the English simultaneously launched both military
campaigns into the Ohio country designed to dislodge the French and
embarked upon a trade and diplomatic effort designed to win either the
agreement of French allied native people to cease fighting or to ally with
the British. The English used none other than the previous French alliance
based upon gift giving and reciprocity as a model for this campaign. The
combination of French inability to live up to their reciprocal duties,

the increasing haughtiness of French officials in their dealings with Ohio country Indians, as well as the growing power and hospitality of the English proved the turning point in the war. By 1759, many former French allied native groups had deserted them; some were even actively fighting for the English. Duquesne fell to Anglo-American troops in 1758 and Quebec and Montreal followed in 1759 and 1760, respectively. For all practical purposes, the French were driven from North America and the Franco-Indian Middle Ground lay dead. Many western Indians hoped either to keep the English from their country entirely, or at the very least force them to adhere to the reciprocal tenets of a new Middle Ground. It did not take long for the English and their colonists to disappoint them.[20]

PONTIAC'S WAR

The oft-misnamed conflict referred to as Pontiac's War grew from multiple strands, some related and some not, of Indian disaffection both with official British Indian policy and unofficial colonial persecution. Specifically, the failure of the British to live up to their role as the new father in the Middle Ground relationship and the flood of white colonists streaming into the Ohio country to take up Indian land constituted very powerful external stimuli for conflict; however, native people in 1763 also revolted for internal religious reasons. These three forces often worked independently, yet they drove many native groups to the same ultimate conclusion: that a war against the English and their colonists prosecuted by a united coalition of heretofore separate Indian entities represented the best course of action.[21]

Not long after defeating the French at Quebec in 1759, the English began to demonstrate their disinterest in living up to their Middle Ground responsibilities toward the Indian groups of the Great Lakes. Lord Jeffrey Amherst, now in command of all British forces in North America, moved quickly to demonstrate to western Indians that at best he viewed them as subjects to be commanded and at worst as nuisances worthy of extermination. Pressure from Whitehall to drastically cut budgets in the face of the massive debt left over from the war, combined with Amherst's own disgust for Indians and their diplomatic rituals, made the Middle Ground the first casualty of his administration. He moved to end the practice of annual gift giving that represented the ceremonial reforging of the reciprocal alliance. By refusing to do so, Amherst sent the message that he no longer considered the Indians of the Ohio country to be kinsmen of the English.[22] When pressed by both Indians and more sympathetic officials alike as to what he expected the Indians to do now that they had been cut off from the source of the guns, ammunition, blankets, and tools that guaranteed their subsistence every winter, Amherst chided them for growing remiss in their ancient methods of hunting and complained, "purchasing the good behavior, either of Indians or any others is what I do not understand; when men of what race soever behave ill, they must be punished but not bribed."[23]

In addition to Amherst's refusal to engage in ritualized gift giving, the English demonstrated their unwillingness to uphold the Middle Ground in several other ways. As early as the first few weeks of 1759 (several months before the British victory at Quebec effectively ended the French and Indian War in America), English officials began to demand the return of hundreds of white captives living among the Indians of North America, primarily in the Great Lakes and the Ohio country. As they solidified their victory over the French in the first two years of the 1760s, English requests for the return of prisoners quickly transformed into demands. The treatment and role of captives represented another issue in the long list of cultural matters upon which Native and European culture diverged and which neither side fully understood. From the English perspective, captives constituted simply prisoners of war whom combatants were duty-bound to return at the cessation of hostilities. Therefore, when many of the Ohio valley groups left the orbit of the French to ally with the English, they were required (in the eyes of the English) to deliver up those English colonists whom they had taken during the years of open hostility. From the Indian perspective, captives could occupy any category along a very complex continuum of statuses. While some captives were used in a manner akin to slave laborers, most Native American groups in North America took captives as a way to replace lost members of their village. Thus, usually after a kind of probationary acculturation period, most captives were then formally adopted and integrated into the village. Obviously, participation in imperial wars such as the French and Indian War increased the frequency and scope of such captive taking. Hence, by the late 1750s, the native groups who fought on both sides of the war had taken hundreds of white captives.[24]

Since most captives (usually women and children) were quickly incorporated into the political and family structures of the village, they often came to prefer life among their captors to that of colonial society. This of course caused considerable consternation on the part of colonial observers who struggled to understand why one would willingly shed whiteness to live as an Indian. Benjamin Franklin remarked as much in 1753:

> when white persons of either sex have been taken prisoners young by the Indians, and lived a while among them, tho' ransomed by their Friends, and treated with all imaginable tenderness to prevail with

them to stay among the English, yet in a Short time they become dis-
gusted with our manner of life, and the care and pains that are necessary to support it, and take the first good Opportunity of escaping
again into the Woods, from whence there is no reclaiming them. One
instance I remember to have heard, where the person was brought
home to possess a good Estate; but finding some care necessary to
keep it together, he relinquished it to a younger Brother, reserving to
himself nothing but a gun and a match-Coat, with which he took his
way again to the Wilderness.[25]

For their part, Indians did not seek to impede adopted captives who
wished to return to their former lives from doing so. As far as they were
concerned, the former captive had become a full-fledged member of their
village with the same free will to determine his or her own comings and
goings. Therefore, when the English began to request the return of captives
taken during the early years of the French and Indian War those who
wanted to return did just that. The Quaker trader James Kenny wrote of
one such voluntary return of a white captive by her now Indian husband.

Having obtained a white woman and boy, he kept the woman as his
wife, using her kindly; on finding she inclined to return to her own
people he brought her and the boy with the amount of his estate to
our store and told the woman notwithstanding he loved her, as she
wanted to leave him, he would let her go, so he divided his substance
equally with her, giving half the remainder to the boy and set them
both free and went with the woman home giving her a horse to ride;
an instance of more self-denial than many men of great Christian
professions show their poor negroes.[26]

Just as native groups did not prevent former captives from returning to
their families, they also did not force those adoptees who preferred life
among them to leave. Indeed, many did want to remain among their former captors. By 1762, as many as 200 to 300 such captives still lived in the
Indian villages of the Ohio country, and British demands that they be returned began to sound increasingly like threats to those Indian emissaries
to whom they were addressed. Additionally, the Shawnees and Delawares
had come to believe that their refusal to release white adoptees was the
only thing preventing the British and their colonists from invading their
lands entirely.[27]

Ohio country Indians had very concrete and immediate reasons for believing such a thing. Fort Pitt, completed by 1762 and ten times larger than

its French predecessor Fort Duquesne, stood as a constant reminder to the native inhabitants of the Ohio country that the British did not intend to leave as they had originally promised. Instead, Fort Pitt was, in the words of one historian of the period, "a symbol of domination, an emblem of empire."[28] By itself, the fort would have been troubling enough, but combined with Amherst's refusal to live up to the requirements of the Middle Ground, demands for the return of white adoptees, South Carolina's defeat of the Cherokees, and the failure of the English to establish trade anywhere near as beneficial to Indian interests as their former trade with the French, western Indians had a considerable amount of tangible evidence upon which to base their fears. Then, there were continual swarms of white colonists arriving in their country.[29]

The smoke had barely cleared from John Forbes's victory over the French at Fort Duquesne when George Washington, then an aide to Forbes, wrote home to Virginia governor Francis Fauquier encouraging him to immediately take steps to secure Virginia's title to the Ohio country. Quick action, Washington urged, would prevent the benefits of the Ohio country's land and Indian trade from falling into the hands of Pennsylvanians, whom Washington referred to as "a set of rascally fellows divested of all faith and honor."[30] Washington, an investor along with his brothers in the original Ohio Company whose land speculation in the area had helped to spark the French and Indian War, was extremely anxious to restake the company's claims to the area. For their part, so were Pennsylvania land speculators. Within three years of Forbes' victory, the area around Fort Pitt as well as at other western posts such as Fort Stanwix and Fort Niagara in New York were so choked with settlers that at least one fort commandant took to burning illegal settlements to try and stem the tide. Likewise, British and native diplomats alike tried to stop illegal settlements by the Connecticut-based Susquehanna company in central and western Pennsylvania, but nothing worked. When Indians such as Tamaqua and Teedyuscung objected to such settlements, they found themselves assaulted and robbed as in the case of Tamaqua, or burned to death in their homes as in the case of Teedyuscung. Those that sought to negotiate with colonial governments and settlement companies found themselves losing power in their home villages to more militant factions. By late 1762, Indians throughout North America in general and the Ohio country in particular faced a decidedly grim situation. The supplies they had counted on through both ritualized, Middle Ground gift giving and a robust trade with the English had not materialized. What trade there was often brought conflict, fraud, abuse, and alcohol, but little profit. Furthermore, the influx of colonists drawn to their lands by the removal of the French and the erection of British forts created intense competition for the area's natural resources. Their subsistence, and by extension their very existence, hung in the balance. In similar situations, human societies have in the past turned to the solace of religion or to the empowerment of violent resistance. In 1763, the Indians of North America chose both.[31]

On October 15, 1762, James Kenny, the Quaker trader operating out of Fort Pitt, remarked upon the religious influence of what he termed an "imposter" among the Delaware. After explaining that this religious leader's message blamed the desperate state of affairs in Indian country on the corrupting influence of whites as well as explaining that this prophet called for an end to all contact with whites, Kenny then described what in his mind had to have been the most distressing facet of this religious message. "It's also said that the imposter prognosticates that there will be two or three good talks and then war; this gains amongst them so much that mostly they have quit hunting anymore then for to supply nature in that way."[32] The "imposter" to whom Kenny referred was a Delaware holy man called Neolin, but while Neolin was credited by Pontiac as his inspiration, he represented not the originator, but an inheritor of a religious tradition, which historian Greg Dowd has referred to as "nativism."[33]

Simply put, nativism represented a strategy that called for Indians to resist rather than accommodate the arrival and continuing encroachments of white Europeans. Furthermore, the specific brand of nativism preached by Neolin and others like him infused a religious and prophetic element into the mix that promised divine assistance in ridding native lands of white interlopers if Native Americans adhered to the religious demands of the Master of Life. The first stirrings of this pan-Indian theology appeared during the 1730s in the villages along the Susquehanna River that housed the refugee Shawnees, Delawares, and Mingos. While the religious dimension of this message is generally attributed to the Delawares, the Shawnees exhibited just as much devotion to this new faith. When asked by the Pennsylvania Indian agent Conrad Weiser why their lands had become uncharacteristically unproductive, the Shawnee assigned the cause to their articulation with the Atlantic Market economy and its accompanying inducements to greed, sloth, and internecine violence.

> They answered . . . that the Lord and creator of the world was resolved to destroy the Indians. One of their seers, whom they named, had seen a vision of God, who said to him the following words: —You inquire after the cause why game has become scarce, I will tell you. You kill it for the sake of the skins, which you give for strong liquors, and drown your senses, and kill one another, and carry on a dreadful debauchery.

Therefore have I driven the wild animals out of the country, for they are mine. If you will do good, and cease from your sins, I will bring them back; if not, I will destroy you from the end of the earth.[34]

Previous indigenous religion-based explanations for the oft-disastrous effects of contact and trade with Europeans would have focused on the displeasure of a Manitou or spirit particular to the native group in question. This new pan-Indian religious movement stressed the unity of native peoples under one very angry creator. The fact that the group from whom Weiser learned this consisted of both Shawnees and disaffected Onondagas (themselves members of the Six Nations) demonstrates the power of such a philosophy to bridge the tremendous cultural, spiritual, and linguistic gap that had previously divided heretofore opposing groups.[35]

As mentioned previously, Neolin's message was in many ways consistent with nearly 30 years of such religiously inspired nativism. However, Neolin preached his message in the midst of an Indian country crying out for just such a native-based explanation for the troubles that seemed to leer at them on all fronts. Game had all but disappeared. American colonists flooded the Ohio Valley and Susquehanna Valley homes of many native groups. New disease epidemics were rolling through many native communities, and the British were both refusing to act as proper kin under the terms of the Middle Ground and demanding that Ohio country Indians relinquish former captives who, in Indian eyes, were now family members. For many native people, the world now spun dangerously out of control. For some of them, the religious explanation offered by Neolin and other prophets like him provided a very real chance at reversing it.

Whether western Indians found themselves heeding the call of the Ottawa war leader Pontiac and others like him for reasons tied to land, trade, and subsistence, for issues related to prophetic religion, or even as a precursor to modern-day disputes over indigenous sovereignty, by the summer of 1763 these myriad peoples and forces had coalesced into an extremely powerful movement that nearly drove the British and their colonists from their recently won western territorial acquisitions. In addition to the successful attack on Michilimackinac, pan-Indian war parties defeated the garrisons at eight other British forts and laid siege to Fort Detroit and Fort Pitt. In the process, native forces killed approximately 450 British soldiers and forced nearly 4,000 backcountry settlers to flee Indian country. In the end though, the combination of discord among the native allies, the failure to take the two key posts of Fort Pitt and Fort Detroit, the effects of smallpox, and British army counterattacks brought Pontiac's War to an end. While they did not drive the British and their colonists from the west, nor restore the French as the colonial power in the region, Pontiac and his followers did succeed in changing the nature of their relationship with the British. The British government restored the old Middle Ground practices of ritualized gift giving and once again supplied western Indians with guns and ammunition for their hunting and military activities. Additionally, Pontiac's War forced the British to recognize that the only way to prevent another such costly struggle was to use British military and political power to protect Indian interests in the west. In other words, the British would have to make an effort to stem the tide of American settlers in the west and take steps to ensure fair trading practices between colonists and Indians.[36]

THE ROYAL PROCLAMATION OF 1763

Near the close of Pontiac's War, one British official advised Secretary of State Lord Egremont that the surest way to prevent another general Indian war from occurring was to forbid Native Americans and white colonists from mixing with one another.

> The vast intermediate tract of country which lies between the limits to which I would confine the old colonies on this side of the Allegheny Mountains, and the boundaries which the new colonies on the other side of those mountains should have prescribed them, I should wish to see reserved to the Indians, and every white person restrained from killing game beyond the limits prescribed the settlers . . . Such an instance of our goodwill to the Indians, would fix them more firmly in our Interest, than all the talks we can give them, or all the presents we can bestow upon them.[37]

In October of 1763, George III heeded this advice and issued the Royal Proclamation of 1763, which prohibited white settlement west of the Appalachian Mountains. King George's proclamation, along with the British return to the precepts and ritualistic forms of the Middle Ground, assuaged the immediate fears of some western Indians, but failed to address many of the underlying causes of their displeasure; however, the proclamation did just as much or more to raise the ire of King George's American subjects, who now felt that he favored the rights of "savages" over their own. Additionally, many of the most elite colonists believed that the British government's new Indian policy had effectively sentenced them to bankruptcy.[38]

THE COLLAPSE OF BRITISH INDIAN POLICY IN THE SOUTH

During the spring of 1776, just a few weeks before the Second Continental Congress declared American independence, Henry Stuart, the British deputy superintendent for Indian Affairs in the Southern Department, visited the Cherokee town of Mussel Shoals in an attempt not only to shore up Cherokee support for the British against their rebellious American colonies, but also to encourage them to act only when sanctioned by the British. While he lingered there, a delegation made up of representatives from northern Indian groups such as the Shawnee, Ottawa, and Mohawks also arrived to request that the Cherokees go to war against the American rebels immediately. According to Stuart, the Shawnee representative spoke last and displayed "a War Belt about 9 feet long and six inches wide."[1] As he brandished the belt he admonished the neutral-leaning Cherokee headmen that the American colonists meant to destroy all Indians.

> He complained particularly of the Virginians who after having taken away all their Lands and cruelly and treacherously treated some of their people, had unjustly brought war upon their Nation and destroyed many of their people; that in a very few years their Nation from being a great people were now reduced to a handful; that their

Nation possessed Lands almost to the Sea Shore and that the red people who were once Masters of the whole Country hardly possessed
ground enough to stand on; that the Lands where but lately they
hunted close to their Nations were thickly inhabited and covered
with Forts & armed men; that wherever a Fort appeared in their
neighbourhood, they might depend there would soon be Towns and
Settlements; that it was plain, there was an intention to extirpate
them, and that he thought it better to die like men than to diminish
away by inches.[2]

Whether he knew it or not, this Shawnee emissary had arrived among
the Cherokee villages at a time of tremendous division and conflict. While
the peace agreed to at the Augusta Conference in 1763 had largely prevented further bloodshed between American colonists and the Cherokee,
the pressure brought to bear by ever-increasing numbers of settlers was
beginning to take its toll on the internal cohesion of Cherokee politics.
Accommodationist leaders such as Attakullakulla, or the Little Carpenter
as he was known among whites, had, for over a decade, bought peace for
their villages by ceding ever-increasing amounts of land to the Carolinas.
When in March of 1775 they attempted to utilize this strategy once again,
younger warriors desirous of enforcing Cherokee sovereignty began to
oppose them. Specifically, the catalyst for this rift occurred when a group
of North Carolinians under the leadership of Richard Henderson attempted to purchase a large swath of Cherokee lands for nearly £10,000
worth of trade goods. Attakullakulla and other Cherokee headmen approached the purchase as another necessary sacrifice to be made in the
interest of protecting their crops and villages from the kind of devastation
wrought by the Carolina troops during the Anglo-Cherokee War. While
the majority of the Cherokee leaders agreed to the cession, Attakullakulla's
own son, Tsi.yu Gansi. Ni, or Dragging Canoe, arose and, referring to the
piece of land under consideration as "the bloody Ground," promised
the Carolinians it would be "dark, and difficult to settle it."[3] Incensed at the
idea of ceding one more inch of ground to whites, Dragging Canoe stormed
out of the treaty negotiations, which did eventually end with Cherokee
approval of the land deal.[4]

Dragging Canoe's actions at the Sycamore Shoals conference, as historians have come to refer to these negotiations, represented both a significant deviation from the norm in relations between the Carolinas and the
Cherokees since the end of the Anglo-Cherokee War in 1763 and a troubling sign of future strife within the Cherokee world. If Dragging Canoe
had simply represented a lone pariah among the Cherokee, his opposition

to increasing land cessions would have been little more than a footnote to Cherokee history and his calls for resistance would have gone unheeded by his fellow Cherokees, thus ostracizing him from the rest of the people; however, during the period between the end of the Sycamore Shoals Conference and Henry Stuart's visit to Mussel Shoals, Dragging Canoe gained hundreds of followers among younger Cherokees dependent upon hunting grounds not only for their survival, but also for their social and political advancement. The popularity of his opposition to further land cessions underscores the extent to which Cherokees had become divided between young men who hunted for a living and favored resistance to white encroachment and older men who, being better established as political and social leaders, did not have to rely on hunting. Since older men such as Attakullakulla had little use for hunting grounds, they found it easier to give them away in an attempt to satiate the voracious appetite of white colonists for land. In so doing, they placed younger men in an untenable position in which their choice was either to risk group cohesion and white enmity by resisting the land cessions or see their subsistence system and by extension their paths to power destroyed.[5]

A few months after Henry Stuart's visit to Mussel Shoals, Dragging Canoe gave voice to the generational and occupational split among the Cherokees as well as his views on white settlers at another visit with British Indian superintendent John Stuart in Pensacola. According to Stuart, Dragging Canoe "said that they were almost surrounded by the White People, that they had but a small spot of ground left for them to stand upon and that it seemed to be the Intention of the White People to destroy them from being a people." In the words of Stuart, Dragging Canoe went on to lay the blame squarely at the feet of Cherokee elders. "He made answer that he had no hand in making these Bargains but blamed some of their Old Men who he said were too old to hunt and who by their Poverty had been induced to sell their Land." Dragging Canoe ended this meeting with Stuart by promising that he and his followers intended to use whatever force necessary to resist settlement by whites. Once again according to Stuart's account of the conversation, Dragging Canoe promised that "for his part he had a great many young fellows that would support him and that were determined to have their Land."[6]

The arrival of the northern delegation and their war belt in April of 1776 provided Dragging Canoe with the opportunity to make good on his promise. While the elder Cherokee leaders either sat in silence or rejected the proposed alliance with the Ohio country Indians, Dragging Canoe, now the recognized leader of a group of militant young Cherokee warriors, stepped forward and took the war belt from the Shawnee emissary. Two days later, Dragging Canoe appeared before Stuart painted entirely in black. There was no mistaking the meaning of his appearance. He and his warriors, against the wishes of his father and the elder Cherokee leadership, planned to go to war against the Americans, an act that would drive the Cherokees into a full-scale civil war.

The American Revolution not only brought internecine conflict to the white communities of the British colonies, but also to Indian country. The collapse of British Indian policy during the 1760s and early 1770s created difficult choices such as those faced by the Cherokees, for nearly all Indian communities in colonial British North America. As they had responded to colonialism since its inception three centuries before, different native communities adopted various strategies for dealing with this crisis. In the end however, nearly all options available to the Indian peoples of North America brought internal conflict, increased white hostility and tremendous upheaval.

THE IMPERIAL CRISIS IN CREEK COUNTRY

The Revolution also brought similar divisions between young and old to the peoples of Creek Nation, and it hastened the already growing autonomy of a group mainly headed by Oconee Creeks who had left the towns of the Lower Creeks to settle in Florida in the early 18th century. By the end of the American Revolution, both the British and the Americans had begun referring to these "runaway" Creeks as a separate people, known as "Seminoles."[7]

Less than 15 years before the outbreak of the Revolution, the Creeks represented a considerable obstacle to the both the settlement plans of southern American colonists and the imperial designs of British officials. In 1763, at the close of the Seven Years' War, a report on the status of relations with the Southern Indians warned that the Creeks "have been informed the French and Spaniards are to evacuate . . . they [the Creeks] declare they will not suffer them to depart." The same report went on to state that the Creeks believed "we have no right to possess the lands that were never given to us, and they will oppose all our attempt that way."[8]

Over the next few weeks, older Creek leaders began to demand that colonial officials respect their sovereignty while younger warriors went on the attack against both illegal Georgia settlements and traders whom they saw as simply the first wave in an all-out colonial assault on their land base. In doing so, they caught the British military and colonial establishment in an extremely difficult position. With Pontiac's uprising now in full swing in the northern colonies, the best the British could do was to try and bring the

Southern Indian groups to peace. To do so they empowered John Stuart, the newly appointed superintendent of Indian Affairs for the Southern Department, to call a general congress to meet at Augusta in the fall.[9]

The Congress of Augusta in 1763 marks a turning point in Creek relations with both the British and their American colonists. From that point on, the Creeks found themselves unable to enforce their demands and negotiate agreements with the British and Americans that could prevent the loss of significant amounts of their homeland and stem the tide of colonial settlers. The removal of the French and the Spanish as counterweights to British influence had much to do with this outcome as well as the fact that the Creeks, divided as they were into Upper and Lower Creek towns, often worked toward different and sometimes conflicting goals. This was very much the case at Augusta in 1763. In addition to the royal governors of Virginia, North Carolina, South Carolina, and Georgia, approximately 600 Indian representatives from the Choctaws, Cherokees, Chickasaws, and Creeks attended. However, the 150-member Creek delegation was evenly split between Upper and Lower Creeks. For their part, the Lower Creek delegation, desirous of maintaining access to English trade at nearly any cost, expressed their willingness to cede land in return for the forgiveness of all past attacks by Creeks against white settlers and traders. The Upper Creeks, who, rather than sending headmen to the meeting as the Lower Towns had done, sent only representatives whose job was to monitor the proceedings and represent their interests, never agreed to this proposal. In fact, at roughly the same time as the Congress of Augusta, an Upper Creek headman delivered just the opposite message to the British outposts at Pensacola and Mobile. Settlement beyond the military outposts to the west of Florida would be resisted. In the end, the Treaty of Augusta signed on November 10, 1763, without Upper Creek support, ceded the largest swath of Creek territory to Georgia since the creation of the colony in 1733. In fact, according to Governor James Wright of Georgia in his 1773 "Report on the Condition of the Province of Georgia," the total amount of the 1763 cession exceeded 2 million acres.[10]

Despite their anger over the Lower Creeks' unilateral cession of territory to Georgia, the Upper Creeks realized that without the aid of the French or at least the Cherokees (neither of which were available in 1763), they could not hope to stand against the English militarily. Therefore, they were forced to eventually ratify the agreement in the spring of 1764. Approximately one year later, the Creeks found themselves once again negotiating a cession of land to the English, this time in the colony of West Florida, in the hopes that by so doing they could stem the tide of white settlement and keep the supply of English trade goods, now a major part of their subsistence system, flowing. Only this time, the Upper Creeks agreed to the cession as well.[11]

In May of 1765, at what would become known as the Congress of Pensacola, representatives from both the Upper and Lower Creek towns gathered once again to treat with Superintendent John Stuart as well as Governor George Johnstone of West Florida. The official result of that conference, a land cession ten miles wide stretching from Pensacola to Mobile Bay, was less important than its other less formal outcomes. In preparation for the conference, Stuart reached out to a group of "runaway" Creeks living northwest of St. Augustine at a place called Latchaway. While he learned very little useful information from them, being as they were, somewhat outside the regular workings of Creek politics, his decision to do so and their decision to accept his presents and hospitality were an important step in the process by which the British and Americans eventually came to see the Latchaway Creeks as a wholly separate people whom they eventually termed "Seminoles." Additionally, in order to win approval of the Pensacola to Mobile Bay land cession, Stuart had to overcome the opposition of the very important Creek headman Yayatustenuggee, or The Mortar. In order to do so, Stuart both discouraged his opposition by employing former French officials still living in the area to demonstrate to the recalcitrant Creek leader that the French were never coming back to reignite their old alliance with the Creeks, and bought The Mortar's loyalty with presents and created in him one of the so-called great medal chiefs. The concept of creating medal chiefs represented a British strategy to interrupt the normal processes by which native leaders were determined and, in their place, insert mechanisms designed to cultivate and install leaders loyal to British interests. The Mortar, despite a long history of anti-English sentiment and active plotting, capitulated at Pensacola in 1765. While for the rest of his life, Yayatustenuggee was far from the puppet the British had hoped to create, Stuart's success with him prompted the superintendent to attempt similar conversions with other less stalwart Creek opponents.[12]

In November of 1765, Stuart, having successfully negotiated boundaries between the colonies of Georgia and West Florida and the Creeks, invited the headmen of the Lower Towns to meet with him at Picolata near St. Augustine to establish a firm boundary between the new British colony of East Florida and Creek territory. The events of the meeting vividly demonstrate the tremendously diminished bargaining position to which the removal of the French and Spanish had now relegated the Creeks. At the outset of the meeting the Creek representatives delivered Stuart an ultimatum: either force colonial traders to lower their prices or they would only agree to a minimal land cession. Stuart responded with his own ultimatum: either the Creeks would agree to his enlarged definition of British territory or he would supply them with no presents. He further hinted that failure to agree to his proposal would lead to violent attacks from colonial settlers in the area. Two days later, alarmed at the prospect of a cessation in British gift giving, the headmen agreed to all of Stuart's demands. Additionally, they allowed Stuart to establish even more medal chiefs among them. In so doing, they surrendered a tremendous amount of their previously famous autonomy in dealings with the British. The Seven Years' War had ended just over two short years before, and since that time, the Creeks gave up over 2 million acres of land, and at least some of the leaders of the Lower Creek towns had done so simply for the chance to be designated a British medal chief. Additionally, the propensity among the British and the Americans to consider the "runaway" Creeks as not Creeks at all, but instead Seminoles, had been encouraged considerably by the events of the immediate postwar era. While the older headmen and hereditary leaders mutely acquiesced to these changes, younger warriors did not and in the next decade their vocal opposition turned to violent defiance.[13]

Before the ink was dry on the Treaty of Picolata in the fall of 1765, the differences between Creek leaders and the younger warriors of their towns revealed themselves in dramatic fashion. In October, just before the treaty negotiations began, a group of young Creek warriors murdered three whites who had ventured across the boundary into Creek lands on a hunting expedition. Both the murders and the disputes that arose afterward reveal the unevenness of both sides' adherence to the agreements they had made with one another. The Creeks who murdered the hunters felt completely justified in doing so as the whites were in clear violation of the established (at the time) boundary line. On the other hand, colonial officials including Superintendent Stuart and Governor Wright of Georgia, demanded that the Creeks adhere to provisions in their treaties, which called for Indian murderers to be dealt with by Indians, and whites who committed murder to be dealt with by white mechanisms of justice. Specifically, they called for the Creeks to apprehend and execute the warriors for the murders. However, as many of the Creeks who had participated in the killings were members of influential clans and as, in the face of tremendous anger on the part of many of the people they governed over English failures to keep trade prices equitable and trading practices fair, Creek leaders instead opted for banishment rather than execution. The English medal chiefs among the headmen had proven either unwilling or powerless to enforce English demands in this case. It was becoming increasingly clear that both traditional leaders and/or English medal chiefs were losing their hold on the leadership of Creek society.[14]

The fact that anger over trade practices lay at the root of this situation points to one of the fundamental issues underlying the developing impe- rial crisis both among colonists and Southern Indians. While the Procla- mation of 1763 had forbade colonial settlement in Indian country, it had at that same time opened up trade with Indians to any colonist who could manage to obtain a government license. With no restrictions on the num- ber of such licenses that could be issued, colonial governments licensed nearly all comers. Whereas the Indian trade prior to 1763 had been con- ducted by a very small group of traders well versed in the gift giving and exchange rituals upon which the trade had been originally established, the postwar era witnessed a massive influx of "Unruly, Bad White People," in the words of one Creek leader.[15] This new sort plied their clients with liquor, often in the hopes of indebting them to the point that only transfer of their lands could settle their accounts. The new traders often abused Indian women and took every opportunity to fleece their trading partners, while completely disregarding traditional exchange practices and bypassing native distribution systems that almost always ran through traditional leaders in favor of trade with any Indian, anywhere so as to increase their chances of successfully defrauding them.[16]

This situation also represents the first signs that the unity between the British Crown and the people of her southern American colonies was be- coming more and more fragile as the decade wore on. Specifically, during the 1760s, the twin issues of trade abuses and land acquisition increasingly served to pit British colonial administrators against their southern colo- nial subjects. Furthermore, this served to increase settler hatred of Native Americans to the point that many colonists often took matters into their own hands with extremely bloody consequences. This in turn provoked equally bloody reprisals from Southern Indians. In the words of Governor Wright of Georgia, "almost every disturbance & injury that has happened from the Indians has in great measure, if not totally Proceeded from the Great Misconduct & abuses Committed Amongst them by the Traders & Pack- horsemen Employed there."[17]

The situation in Creek territory powerfully demonstrates the quag- mire in which the British found themselves in regard to colonial Indian policy in the south by the late 1760s. In the spring of 1767, Stuart's com- plaints about the activities of backcountry traders and illegal settlers brought a response from Whitehall. In short, he was empowered to call a meeting of all Southern Indian nations in May of that year for the specific purposes of addressing abusive trading practices and adjudicating boundary disputes between colonists and Indians. All of this, he did in as good a faith as could be expected from British officials at the time;

however, in so doing, he unwittingly stoked southern colonial hatred of Indians even higher. The very idea that British government officials would take the part of Indians against whites incensed backcountry settlers and unscrupulous traders alike. Herein lies one of the principal disputes that underlay the imperial crisis in the south (and elsewhere in colonial America), which ultimately brought on the American Revolution there. The British government remained willing to conceive of Native Americans as subjects of the crown, similar to colonists. American colonists, in this case those living in the southern colonies, refused to see Indians as fellow subjects. Instead, they viewed them as obstacles in the way of their dreams of land ownership and trading wealth. This reality then only reinforced the animosity white colonists felt toward young Indian warriors in the south.[18]

An incident on the Oconee River in July of 1767 demonstrates this precarious situation perfectly. A Creek man named Houmahta had set up a base at that location from which to raid white frontier settlements for horses, which he and his followers could then trade to the Cherokees. When the settlers of the area raided his village and burned it to the ground, Houmahta appealed to Governor Wright and Superintendant Stuart for protection, but also admitted that his people's horse raiding had sparked the incident. Stuart and Wright, always more focused on the larger imperial picture rather than protecting the property of a few lowly backwoodsmen, issued warrants for the arrest of the whites who had burned Houmahta's village. They did so out of a desire to prevent white settlers from undertaking such vigilante action in similar situations in the future. At the same time they called on the Upper and Lower Creeks to prevent such renegade settlements as Houmahta's. Only by controlling the rebels on both sides could the treaties be preserved; however, the response of the Creek leader Tallachea reveals the difficulties involved for both whites and Creeks. He protested that the current generation of Creek leaders had much less control over the activities of individuals than had previous leaders, but promised that they would try to prevent such activities if possible.[19] He went on to point out that British leaders such as Stuart and Wright suffered from a similar weakness.

> When our people tell the Virginians [the name by which the Creeks referred to all white frontier settlers] they are over the line and if they don't keep in bounds they will burn their houses, they make answer they [the white settlers] will burn their governor's house over his head. If the governor cannot keep these Virginia people under how can we keep our people under?[20]

In addition to the burgeoning differences between backcountry colonists and British officials regarding Indian relations, this period also widened the conflicts between younger and older Creeks as to how to respond
to white encroachment and questionable trading practices. In late 1767,
Roderick McIntosh, Stuart's representative to the Creeks, wrote the superintendent that, "their young men are become so boisterous and wanton
that without a hearty drubbing such as the Cherokees had they will never
be a tractable people." Both Indian hatred among backcountry colonists
and generational conflict among the Creeks only worsened when young
Creek warriors plundered two illegal white trading posts during the spring
of 1768; and a meeting that summer to officially demarcate the boundary
between Creek territory and the line of white settlement ended in bitter
disagreement between the parties involved.[21]

In the midst of these mounting tensions came an announcement from
Whitehall that promised to exacerbate tensions between colonists and Indians over trade. Colonial governors had finally succeeded in wresting
complete control over the Indian trade from the Indian superintendents.
Citing the impossibility of applying uniform trade regulations to all Indian
groups as well as the cost of enforcing such a policy, Lord Hillsborough, the
newly appointed secretary of state for the Southern Department under
whose jurisdiction the colonies lay, effectively repudiated a key provision
of the Royal Proclamation of 1763. Colonial governors set all terms of
trade and had the power to adjudicate all disputes arising from trade in
addition to their previous power over who received trading licenses. The
colonial governors were almost always more responsive to the colonial
populations they governed than to Indian communities hundreds of miles
away. By taking this step the government at Whitehall virtually destroyed
what little hope there was that groups like the Creeks could regain the favorable trading terms they had enjoyed when the British and French had
competed against one another for their commerce. With no one empowered to at least attempt to look out for Southern Indian interests in these
trading exchanges, southern traders were free to use alcohol, fraud, and
other unsavory methods to encourage Indians to rack up massive debts,
which could then only be settled by large land cessions.[22]

In the summer of 1773, this strategy bore tremendous fruit. In five years
of unregulated trading since Hillsborough's decision, backcountry traders
had succeeding in enticing the Creeks to rack up an enormous amount of
debt. The debts were so high that the Creeks could never pay them down
with trade goods or any other form of currency. The only way to get out
from under them was to cede land. At Augusta on June 1, despite tremendous division among the Creeks over the cession, Creek headmen ceded

another 2.1 million acres to the colony of Georgia. Now nearly all of the land over which Creeks and Georgians had disagreed for nearly 50 years fell under Georgia's control. Even among the Lower Creeks, who had run up by far the highest debts and therefore benefited most from the clearing of those debts, there existed tremendous bitterness and division over the cession for many years.[23]

Since the arrival of the English in their lands in the mid-1730s, the Creeks had ceded over 5 million acres to them, yet the Georgians' hunger for more never ceased. This cession only widened the conflicts between young warriors and older headmen regarding the proper response to English encroachment. Additionally, the fall of 1773 brought Shawnee emissaries from the north seeking to gain both Creek and Cherokee support for a unified Indian response to colonial settlement. While Creek headmen officially rebuffed these overtures, young Creek warriors voted with their feet and their weapons. In a series of attacks on settlers near the Savannah River in December of 1773, Lower Creek warriors killed 17 Georgians including 4 members of the local militia. One can only imagine the dramatic scene as the warriors, one of whom, Ogulki, kinsman of the accommodationist Cherokee headman Escochabey, returned to their home village of Coweta displaying the trophies of their raid and boasting of their exploits. More than likely nervous and saddened, headmen would have looked upon this scene and struggled to find a way to smooth over the attack with the English without executing those involved.

In the end, they could not. Georgians demanded vengeance for the killings and held up previous treaty agreements in which Creeks agreed to punish those Creeks who murdered whites, as a means of forcing crown officials to assist the Georgians in seeking satisfaction. In April of 1774, Governor Wright of Georgia officially informed a Creek delegation in Savannah that all trade would be cut off until those responsible for the killings were put to death. Six weeks later in late May the Upper Creeks, whose warriors had not participated in the killings but who were suffering from the cessation of trade all the same, demanded that the Lower Creeks give satisfaction for the murder by executing the perpetrators. Finally, after another month of deliberation and intense negotiation, the Lower Towns met (without representatives from the town of Coweta from whence the attackers had come) and decided to put the three leaders of the attack, including Ogulki, to death. As he died, he reportedly cried out for his countrymen to exact vengeance on the "Virginians" or the backcountry settlers and traders whom he blamed for his demise. In doing so, Ogulki seemed to see beyond his death to the struggle looming before his unsuspecting people in the coming decade. While there exists no evidence from which to conclude that Ogulki was aware of the now gaping rift between England and her colonies, we do know that it was during the latter months of 1774 that the Creeks in general learned of the events being played out mostly to their north. Over the next nine years they would first try to maintain neutrality, and, only after events forced them to, take up arms with the British against the so-called "Virginians."[24]

CHICKASAW INDEPENDENCE

Even those groups most closely allied to the British throughout most of the colonial period still found themselves at least partially divided by the events of the 1760s. The Chickasaws located between the Yazoo and Tombigbee rivers in what is today northern Mississippi and western Tennessee represent one such group. Throughout the 18th century the Chickasaws allied themselves with the English (and conversely aligned themselves against the French) more closely than any of their southern neighbors.[25] Their staunch support of the British throughout the various imperial wars of the 18th century prompted the Irish trader James Adair to dub them "our friendly gallant Chikkasah."[26] Small (they consisted of approximately 2,300 people of whom no more than 450 were warriors on the eve of the Revolution) but with a reputation as very skilled in battle, the Chickasaws' ultimate goal remained the same throughout the century. According to Piomingo, chief of the principal Chickasaw town of Tchoukafala, the Chickasaws always endeavored to live as "a people to ourselves."[27] In other words, they valued the independence of the Chickasaw people above all else.

Why then would a people so fiercely jealous of their independence cling to the British for so long? The answer to that question lies in the lucrative trading relationship the Chickasaws enjoyed with the English since the earliest days of their contact in the latter half of the 17th century. By allying with the English, the Chickasaws were able to gain the tremendous amounts of guns and goods necessary to maintain their independence in the face of various threats, most notably from their Choctaw neighbors and their French allies. Starting as early as the 1660s and lasting well into the 18th century, Virginians, followed shortly thereafter by Carolinians, extended the Atlantic market economy from their initial settlements along the Atlantic coast as far west as the Mississippi River. In return for deerskins as well as Indian slaves captured in raids on neighboring villages, the English provided groups like the Chickasaws with an enormous amount of guns, ammunition, metal weapons, and utensils as well as other items desired by these native groups. For their part, the Chickasaws, being smaller in number than most of their neighbors and placing such an emphasis on maintaining independence, leapt at the chance to provide the English traders with plenty of deerskins and captives in order to gain sufficient arms with which to defend themselves from their much more populous enemies.[28] This strategy worked so well for the Chickasaws over the years that in 1759, Jean-Bernard Bossu, a French official in Louisiana remarked, "All the northern and southern tribes, as well as the French, have waged war against them without being able to drive them from their lands."[29]

By the end of the Seven Years' War in 1763, the influx of settlers and independent traders into Chickasaw country posed a serious threat to the Chickasaws' cherished independence. Whites began to squat on Chickasaw land in numbers heretofore unseen, placing tremendous pressure on that land to produce the necessary yields of both plants and animals to enable the Chickasaws to subsist as they had in the past. Furthermore, unlicensed traders operating outside the orbit of British regulations undercut the authority of traditional leaders who until then had served as the only conduit for the transmission of British trade goods. By 1772, the Chickasaws complained to British officials bitterly of the ill effects of unregulated trade. "Their little nation is distracted and split in parties by the jarring interest of traders as well as the number of vagabonds that resort to it. . . ."[30] Additionally, the growing numbers of mixed-blood individuals who shed traditional cultural practices in favor of a more Anglicized lifestyle increasingly bred conflict among the once largely homogenous Chickasaw population.[31]

By the eve of the American Revolution, Chickasaws not only found themselves wracked by internal conflicts, but also facing serious external threats to their physical survival and position as a British favorite. Growing Spanish penetration into the region led those few Chickasaws who had favored alliance with the French during the Seven Years' War to openly advocate allegiance to the Spanish. This of course alarmed British officials in the area. Furthermore, Illinois country Indians began to raid south into Chickasaw territory, and in retaliation for these incursions the Chickasaws murdered a group of French hunters allied to the Illinoisan groups despite British assertions that the hunters were now British subjects and therefore under their protection. The situation threatened to completely derail the long-standing Anglo-Chickasaw friendship and might have done so had the outbreak of Lord Dunmore's War not occurred. This conflict between the Shawnees and Virginians over control of Kentucky, now offered an opportunity for the Chickasaws to demonstrate their loyalty to the crown. While Chickasaws were now firmly back within the orbit of British friendship, the seeming willingness of the British to discard that friendship in order to protect Frenchmen and formerly French-allied Indians in the Illinois country seems to have caused much bitterness among the Chickasaws. While the British entered the war with their former American subjects confident that the Chickasaws would once again place their warriors at their disposal, the Chickasaws would initially demonstrate a new-found reluctance to blindly do the redcoats' bidding.[32]

CHOCTAW TRANSFORMATION

For at least one Southern Indian group, the growing rift between Great Britain and the American colonies actually brought peace and a return to relatively normal trading relations. Unlike the other major Southern Indian groups, the Choctaws maintained virtually no relationship with the British before 1763. Located in the eastern Mississippi Valley, northwest of present-day Mobile, Alabama, the Choctaws were shielded from prolonged contacts with the British colonies to their east by the presence of the Creeks, with whom they often warred during this period. While this location precluded the development of a significant relationship with the British, it nevertheless placed the Choctaws at a strategic crossroads in relation to the French in Louisiana, the Spanish in Florida, and other native groups such as the Chickasaws to the north. Their relationship with the French gained considerable importance for the Choctaws as the imperial wars of the 18th century increasingly drew the Native Americans of the colonial south into the military contest for control of the continent. Therefore, when the French were driven out of North America as a result of their defeat in the Seven Years' War, Choctaws faced an uncertain future replete with intertribal warfare, internal division, and a very rocky relationship with their new British allies. That future grew all the more tenuous as the rift between Great Britain and the American colonies flared into open rebellion.[33]

The end of the Seven Years' War and the imperial crisis that presaged the American Revolution occurred in the midst of a long period of tremendous cultural transformation among the Choctaws. According to Choctaw historian Greg O'Brien, during the 18th century "the Choctaw people transformed their notions of power and authority as a result of decades of contact with Euro-Americans, and from the beginning they struggled with the implications of that transformation." Specifically,European contact gradually altered Choctaw notions of power to the point that leaders derived their authority from their ability to gain trade goods and favorable relations from European and eventually American representatives instead of their control of spiritual sources of power. In fact, by the end of the 18th century, spiritual power and political authority were completely separate spheres of activity no longer conjoined as they had been in Choctaw society since long before contact with whites. It was in the midst of this decades-long transformation that the upheavals wrought by the departure of the French and the outbreak of the American Revolution occurred, and it is against this backdrop that the events of the 1760s and 1770s must be understood.[34]

Most Choctaw leaders first set eyes on representatives of the British crown during the general Indian conference held by John Stuart at Mobile in 1765. The Choctaw leaders who addressed Stuart at the meeting assumed that their new relationship with the British would operate in exactly the same manner as their previous relationship with the French. One Choctaw speaker informed the Indian superintendent that they expected to receive even more trade goods from the British as a sign of the strength of the newly forged friendship between the two. He went on to warn Stuart, "if we do not, it must proceed from want of affection . . . not from want of ability." The Choctaw speaker ended his address by saying that his reason for needing an increased amount of gifts stemmed not just from the traditional belief that reciprocal gift giving denoted the strength of the friendship between two peoples, but also from the fact that without goods to distribute to his warriors he could not control their behavior toward English traders and outlying settlements.[35]

Since the beginning of their relationship, the French supported traditional Choctaw social relations by distributing presents to recognized Choctaw leaders who then distributed them to their families and supporters in such a way as to increase those leaders' prestige within the group. Additionally, the French utilized the Middle Ground framework in their relations with the Choctaws just as they had with the groups of the Great Lakes. Under this paradigm, trade was seen as an outgrowth of diplomatic relations rather than a strict economic exchange. Once again according to O'Brien, "trade took the form of an elaborate, ritualized gift-exchange that bolstered chiefly power through their control of goods which they redistributed according to the demands of kinship responsibilities and political needs."[36] For their part the British did not see their relationship with the Choctaws in the same light. The British largely eschewed the idea of trade as a ritualistic exchange designed to demonstrate the level of esteem with which each side regarded the other. Instead, most British and colonial leaders saw the Indian trade as a private activity subject to market forces and into which any individual could enter. Therefore, the British abandoned the

French practices of licensing a small number of experienced traders in favor of allowing nearly anyone interested to enter into the trade. In turn, the new traders ignored previous prohibitions on the use of alcohol and on trade with individual Choctaws rather than tribal leaders. Furthermore, these tremendous changes to trade policy resulted not simply from British ignorance or even disinterest in native trading customs, instead they represented part of a concerted strategy on the part of British officials to bring groups to heel whom they felt the French had imbued with too much obstinacy and independence.[37]

Accordingly, these fundamental changes in their trading relationship with the new European power in the area brought serious consequences for Choctaw society. Non-elite Choctaw males began to challenge the authority and position of traditional leaders. More Choctaw hunters than ever before roamed their hunting grounds in competition with one another for the precious animal skins required to trade with English and colonial traders. As a result, the availability of those animal skins began to decline precipitously. In response, many young Choctaw men intent on proving their worth to the community and to their families as either hunters or warriors then turned to raiding outlying British settlements as a way of both obtaining goods and being recognized as warriors. This of course brought with it the potential to spark a war with the British and colonial governments. [38]

The prospect of such a war worried British civil and military officials alike. Since a war with one Southern Indian group would more than likely also involve several others, the British realized that the small force they had posted to east and west Florida would be no match for the combined strength of an alliance between the Creeks and Choctaws, the two groups that had been the least friendly to British occupation of the area. British and colonial leaders therefore decided to divide and conquer. In 1764, General Thomas Gage began to order his subordinates as well as the various governors of the southern colonies to do all in their power to foment a war between the Creeks and the Choctaws. For their part, the Choctaws were more than happy to oblige the British for two reasons. First of all, they and the Creeks had often been enemies in the past and there was plenty of lingering animosity on both sides from these previous conflicts. More specific to the Choctaws was the fact that many of the Choctaw leaders saw such a war as the perfect way to draw their young men's focus away from raiding British settlements and/or competing with elders for British trade goods.[39]

Despite attempts at peace in the late 1760s, the war raged on for over 10 years as both British officials and Choctaw headmen continued to believe that the Choctaw-Creek war was in their respective best interests. Eventually, the growing likelihood of war between Great Britain and the American colonies forced the British to seek a peaceful resolution to the conflict which would bind both the Creeks and Choctaws to the English side should a revolution indeed break out. The only way to do that was to return to a trade and gift-exchange system much more like the old French one and to greatly increase the amount of goods distributed. Therefore, despite the increased warfare, increased internal strife, and decreased access to European goods that the early years of the Imperial Crisis brought to the Choctaws, the period ended in relative prosperity and harmony as the British actively sought to buy their allegiance in the coming internal imperial struggle.[40]

CATAWBA SURVIVAL

The downward spiraling relationship between Great Britain and the American colonies brought tremendous change and upheaval to both large and small Indian communities. Much of the relevant scholarship focuses on groups still quite well known today such as the Cherokees and the Creeks; however, the experience of the Catawbas, a much smaller polity located in close proximity to North and South Carolina provides a particularly compelling example of the circumstances facing Indian people during the era of the Imperial Crisis.

If one were to survey the Indian peoples of eastern North America on the eve of the English arrival at Jamestown in 1607, one would find no group either referring to themselves or being referred by others as Catawbas. Instead, one would find several autonomous Siouan-speaking groups in the Piedmont areas of what would eventually become North and South Carolina. In fact, according to Catawba historian James H. Merrell, these Siouan-speaking groups were less homogenous at the time of first European contact (the DeSoto expedition of 1540) than they had been when they arrived in the area, thanks to their relative isolation from and infrequent contact with one another.[41] After the arrival of Europeans, these various groups chose to coexist with the invaders rather than resort to outright resistance. Whether this was due to the tremendous damage to their fighting strength caused by European diseases or for economic and/or spiritual reasons is unknown. Whatever the case, up to the dawn of the 18th century the groups that eventually coalesced into the Catawba Nation still lived separate from one another and in relative peace with the growing numbers of European invaders who in the early 1660s founded the colony of Carolina— a colony that eventually became two in 1712. At roughly the same time that Carolina was divided, the autonomous Siouan groups in the colony, driven by the need to replace those members of their villages killed or carried off by the deadly combination of slave raids and epidemic diseases that ravaged the southeast during the late 17th and early 18th centuries, began to coalesce into a single polity in the Catawba River Valley, which eventually became known as the Catawba Nation.[42]

Coalescing into a larger unit only provided security for so long. By the mid-18th century, observers ranging from South Carolina governor James Glen to traders such as Matthew Toole and John Evans agreed that the Catawbas were on the verge of extinction. Specifically, the recent peace between the Cherokees and the Six Nations of the Iroquois Confederacy as well as the Catawbas' past rejections of French offers of an alliance had created a situation in which the Catawbas found themselves under attack from all sides. Now, without fear of Cherokee reprisals, Six Nations warriors were free to raid smaller southern groups such as the Catawbas. At the same time, in retaliation for the Catawbas' refusal to join them, the French encouraged their native allies in the Ohio and Illinois countries to raid Catawba villages as well. These constant raids as well as the continuing effects of disease and increased white settlement in the area were responsible for the precarious state the Catawbas found themselves in by mid-century.[43]

Yet unlike so many similar stories of Anglo-Indian contact in Colonial North America, Governor Glen did not view the prospect of Catawba destruction with glee. Instead, he dedicated himself to preventing it. Glen, in the midst of the on-and-off imperial contest between Great Britain and France for control of the continent, could not afford to lose any Indian allies, no matter how few in number. Realizing this, the Catawbas decided that the only way to ensure their continued survival as a cohesive polity was to draw themselves into a much closer relationship with the colonies, South Carolina in particular. Stressing their importance as a defensive barrier against the French and other Indian groups as well as their willingness to serve as runaway slave catchers for the colony, the Catawbas managed to survive the deadly attacks of enemies both human and viral as well as to reorient their economy around their diplomatic rather than trading alliance with South Carolina. Instead of trading skins and other commodities (which the Catawbas were too small to effectively obtain) to the South Carolinians, the Catawbas now depended upon South Carolinian gifts given in return for their diplomatic and military loyalty to support the group throughout the year. What once had been symbolic exchanges divorced from the economic well-being of the community represented the most critical piece of the group's subsistence system. Eventually, much like the Choctaws, only those Catawbas with access to Europeans and colonial officials had a chance to become leaders.[44]

Initially, this system worked quite well for the Catawbas and at first they entered into similar trade for diplomatic loyalty arrangements with Virginia and North Carolina as well. With the outbreak of the Seven Years' War, the loyalty of the Catawbas became an even more highly sought after commodity to the point that colonies actually competed with one another to see who could gain the greater share of Catawba loyalty. This was not lost on the Catawbas and they used this fact to their advantage as they played various colonial officials against one another in an effort to gain the maximum amount of benefits possible for themselves; but even as this strategy seemed to be paying dividends for them, it also contained within it the seeds of its own demise. As the Catawbas drew closer to the Carolinas and Virginia, what had once been a relatively steady trickle of white settlers into their Piedmont homeland exploded into a massive flood. The end of the Seven Years' War in 1763 unleashed a torrent of western settlement in Catawba country, as in so many other locations in Colonial North America By the late 1760s, the Catawbas were completely surrounded by settlers. According to one observer, one of the settlements closest to the Catawba villages was "settled beyond any spot in England of its extent."[45]

Despite their numerical disadvantage, the Catawbas steadfastly refused to vacate their lands in the face of the oncoming rush of white settlement. Violent episodes between western Carolinians and Catawbas became increasingly common throughout the entire decade of the 1760s. Given their relatively small population (most contemporary estimates placed Catawba strength at approximately 300 warriors in 1759), it seemed a foregone conclusion that the advancing tide of colonists would soon wipe them out, but still they refused to budge. According to John Evans, a South Carolina trader who had lived and worked among the Catawbas since the end of the Yamasee War in 1715, "Dayly New Animosities Doth a rise Between them, [white settlers and Catawbas] which In my Humble oppion will be of Bad Consequence In a Short time, Both Partys Being obstinate."[46]

In the end, disease more than conflict with settlers forced the Catawbas to abandon all but their most remote settlements. A particularly virulent epidemic struck the Catawba homeland in late 1759 that, within a very short period of time, cut the effective warrior strength of the Catawbas from the aforementioned 300 warriors to below 100, and cut their total population from well over 1,500 to approximately 500.[47] According to historian James Merrell, however, such a disaster may have been what saved the Catawbas as a people for two reasons. First, the disastrous impact of smallpox on their warrior base now ruled out a direct military challenge to white settlement in the Carolinas. Therefore, their eradication via a military conflict with the Carolinians never happened. Secondly, in response to the smallpox epidemic the Catawbas abandoned five of their six previously occupied villages and the one they retreated to was located well away from the prime lands near Sugar Creek, which were so coveted by settlers. In Merrell's words, "Why bother to drive Indians from some place nobody wanted. . . . 'Harmless and friendly' Indians were replacing 'proud and devilish' ones."[48]

Not long after they abandoned the majority of their villages, the Catawbas negotiated an agreement with Superintendent of Indian Affairs Edmund Atkin in which they agreed to relinquish their claims to a vast tract of land 60 miles wide in return for a much smaller section on which North Carolina was to build a fort. In effect, the Catawbas agreed to move to a reservation. Despite our modern tendency to see all such reservation agreements as a negative outcome, in this case (and in others) both the fort and the reservation represented a long-term strategy for survival on the part of the Catawbas. The fort, although it was never actually manned by North Carolinians and quickly fell into disrepair, represented a stronghold which the Catawbas could relocate to in times of danger. By getting the North Carolinians to agree to their reservation boundaries, the Catawbas were creating the western legal means by which they could evict settlers who would encroach upon their lands. Whereas before, their title to their lands had always been largely ignored by whites since it did not originate in and was not delineated with white legal strictures, this new reservation was laid out by whites and agreed to in accordance with English and colonial legal norms. This new legal relationship not only attempted (of course it was not always successful) to keep out trespassers and squatters, it also foiled at least one large land scheme fomented by the colonial elite. In so doing, however, the Catawbas' new legal relationship with the English crown exposed the potential for Indian affairs to cause rifts between crown and colonist. It also demonstrated to the Catawbas that their standing as key allies to the leading men of the colony had deteriorated to the point that they were now only valued for their land.[49]

In 1772, a member of South Carolina's governor's council, William Henry Drayton, attempted to lease the entire Catawba reservation for himself and the rest of the governor's council, promising to look after the Indians' interests in return for permission to rent out his portion of the lease to colonial settlers. When John Stuart, the newly appointed superintendent of Indian Affairs for the south, caught wind of the scheme he immediately took steps to defeat it, and, as representative of the crown, his opposition caused enough of the governor's council to backtrack on their support for Drayton's plan that he was forced to withdraw it. For South Carolinians eager to gain even more Indian land, here was a sure sign that the English crown did not have their best interests at heart. Taken together with similar actions of the British government and its agents, such as the Proclamation of 1763 and the Treaty of Hard Labor, which guaranteed Cherokee land rights, Stuart's opposition to Drayton's plan more than likely struck many colonists as another sign that King George valued the rights of Indians above those of his white subjects. On the other hand, the whole scheme and the willingness of the governor's council to initially support it had to have signaled to the Catawbas that they were no longer deemed important allies by the South Carolina government. Having seen firsthand what happened to the Westos, the Tuscaroras, and the Yamasees in a similar situation, Catawba leaders had to have been quite concerned about the people's future.[50]

For much of the 18th century the Catawbas had survived by making themselves important to the colonial governments of the Carolinas and to a lesser extent that of Virginia. By the late 1760s, those governments had come to see them as harmless "inoffensive, insignificant people"; however, it was that very insignificance and their inability to prevent it that led the Catawbas to see the growing dispute between crown and colonies as a tremendous opportunity. The outbreak of the revolution arrested much of the growing strength of the Carolina colonies and once again created in them a desperate need for allies, this time against the British rather than the French and Spanish. Having seen their influence in the councils of the Carolinas wane progressively since the end of the Seven Years' War, the Catawbas jumped at the chance to reassert their importance to Carolina leaders. In short, Catawbas had no choice but to join the Americans as a way to try to stay relevant to them, and by the fall of 1775 they were hunting down Tories and runaway slaves at the behest of the Carolinians.[51]

While they by no means represent all of the Indian peoples of the southern colonies, the Creeks, Chickasaws, Choctaws, Catawbas, and those that followed the traditional Cherokee leaders do demonstrate the choices presented by the breakup of the British Empire in North America. Neutrality, alliance with the British, or support for the American cause all seemed to point to a similar outcome for native people: more land cessions, increasing settler encroachment, population loss, and the denigration of their spiritual and subsistence systems. Only the renegade Cherokee under the leadership of Dragging Canoe seemed to sense that the American Revolution held the possibility of more than mere self-preservation. For Dragging Canoe, the conflict between Britain and the American colonies offered an opportunity to make the world anew. In this respect, Dragging Canoe and his followers had more in common with American colonists than either cared to admit.[52]

3

THE COLLAPSE OF BRITISH INDIAN POLICY IN THE NORTH

By all accounts July 11, 1774, was another day in what had been a succession of sweltering days in the Mohawk River Valley of New York. Despite the heat, hundreds of Indian delegates as well as various colonial and local officials crowded onto the grounds of Johnson Hall near Hall Creek. The delegates had come to the home of Sir William Johnson, northern superintendent for Indian Affairs, as they had on numerous other occasions over the past decade, to renew the Covenant Chain system of treaties and agreements between the British government and the principal Indian nations of North America. They had also gathered to negotiate a peaceful resolution to various crises which threatened to derail the Northern Indians' relationship with the British crown. On this particular day, the third since Johnson had opened the council, the superintendent himself delivered an impassioned address in which he pleaded with the Indian representatives to refrain from taking matters into their own hands in order to deal with the gruesome murders committed by Pennsylvania and Virginia frontiersmen looking for an excuse to justify the appropriation of Indian land in the Ohio Valley. He further beseeched the sachems in his audience to give him time to correct unfair trading practices by whites who often defrauded their native clients after intoxicating them with rum.

Finally, he counseled patience and promised justice to those native people who pressed him as to why King George III's white subjects had not abided by either the Proclamation of 1763 or the 1768 Treaty of Fort Stanwix. Visibly frail and obviously affected by the heat, Sir William, now nearly 60 years old, finished his speech just before dusk and retired to his room to rest. Within two hours he was dead and the future of British-Indian relations in the northern colonies was plunged into chaos and uncertainty. Though the relationship limped along for a time without him, Johnson's death signaled the beginning of the end for both the Covenant Chain system of diplomacy and the Six Nations Confederacy and thus led to the overall destabilization of Native American diplomatic and military power in the region.[1]

While the decline of the Six Nations constitutes the largest and most well-known example of the turmoil visited upon Northern Indian communities by the Imperial Crisis of the 1760s and 1770s, it was far from the only one. The growing split between the colonies and Great Britain brought tremendous upheaval to Indian people in New England as well as New York. Specifically, smaller groups such as the Western Abenaki in Vermont and Quebec, and the praying Indians of Massachusetts all faced excruciating choices brought on by the Imperial Crisis that carried the potential to end their existence as unified peoples.

THE DECENTRALIZED RESPONSE OF THE ABENAKIS

In addition to the common problems rooted in land quarrels, trade disputes, and imperial politics, the Western Abenakis of New England and Canada faced the additional issue of religious conflict when approaching the decision of which side to support in the burgeoning conflict between crown and colonies. At the turn of the 17th century, the Western Abenakis occupied an area stretching from what are today the White Mountains in Vermont in the east to Lake Champlain and present-day eastern New York in the west. From north to south their traditional homeland ranged from southern Quebec to Massachusetts. With the advent of European colonialism in the north, most Abenaki bands opted to ally themselves with the nearby French at Quebec for both trade and military purposes. This economic and political alliance soon led to the introduction of Catholicism via Jesuit missionaries by the middle of the 17th century. Due to these economic, political, and spiritual relationships, the Abenakis became staunch opponents of English colonial expansion during the first half of the 17th century, to the point that the American ranger leader Robert Rogers burned their most important settlement,

Odanak, to the ground during the Seven Years' War in 1759. Due to their attachment to the French and their influence among other Canadian Indians, the British military occupied Western Abenaki villages indefinitely after the Treaty of Paris in 1763 in order to hasten their adjustment to British rule. British officials, who no doubt eyed their lands in the St. Lawrence Valley for colonial settlement, encouraged the Abenaki to drastically circumscribe their traditional migratory patterns and settle "together on one Village." However, the Western Abenakis soon realized that the combination of increased white settlement, the refusal of the English to replicate the same reciprocal gift-giving relationship they had enjoyed with the French, and the decline of the fur trade within their homeland made this an extremely difficult proposition. As a result, many Abenaki resorted to an age-old tradition of breaking into small family bands and scattering over a wide swath of territory so as to lessen competition for resources and keep their interactions with the British and their colonists to a minimum.[2]

This strategy of avoidance not only made it difficult for British officials to determine the number of Abenaki people living in the colonies, but also frustrated their efforts to establish a relationship strong enough to bring the Western Abenakis under even nominal British control. Unable to maintain any contact with those family groups who chose to retreat to the hinterlands of Abenaki territory, the British were forced to accept the village of Odanak as their only node of contact with Western Abenakis. This meant that while they could endeavor to tie the fortunes of those families at Odanak to the success of the British Empire (as they had done with groups such as the Mohawks and Cherokees), they were powerless to influence the hundreds of Abenaki families who had retreated to the forests beyond. Both war and political leaders in Abenaki society had never enjoyed the same level of influence as those of groups such as the Mohawks or Cherokees. Additionally, the end of the Seven Years' War and the termination of the gift exchange that went with it eroded the power of Abenaki chiefs even further. Therefore, even those few leaders at Odanak whom the British managed to cultivate possessed very little sway over the rest of their fellow Abenakis. Consequently, this reality made the Western Abenakis an ambiguous ally at best and at worst a potential source of support for those Americans who grew increasingly hostile to the crown as the 1760s and early 1770s wore on.[3] For example, when asked in 1775 by one supporter of the Massachusetts committee of safety which side the Western Abenakis would support in the war with Great Britain, one Abenaki woman responded, "why should we fight for t'other country, for we never see t'other country; our hunting is in this country." Another Abenaki woman, when asked the same question, responded that she planned to convince her brother, apparently a colonel in the local militia, "not to fight for t'other country, but to fight for this country."[4]

Given the situation described, it would seem that the Western Abenakis represented the perfect ally for the American revolutionaries. Yet, despite this obvious predisposition to their cause, Massachusetts revolutionaries were hesitant to embrace the Abenakis. For many of them instances of French Jesuits exhorting Abenaki warriors to raid their settlements remained a particularly alarming memory. Even if the memory of these previous enmities had faded, the 1774 passage of the Quebec Act, which, among others things, granted religious toleration to Catholics in Canada, further stoked the fires of anti-Catholic hatred in New England. For many New Englanders, especially Samuel Adams and his cousin John, the Quebec Act constituted yet another "Intolerable Act." In February of 1776, John Adams, writing under the pseudonym "Novanglus," stated as much: "The port bill, charter bill, murder bill, Quebec bill, making all together such a frightful system, as would have terrified any people, who did not prefer liberty to life, were all concerted at once."[5]

Of the bills mentioned by Adams, none had more potential to unite colonial resistance than the Quebec Act. The closing of Boston Harbor directly affected the economy of Massachusetts and New England and certainly caused reverberations throughout the colonies, but those tertiary effects took time to reveal themselves to colonists as far flung as Georgia, the Ohio Valley, and the western reaches of New York and Pennsylvania. While the revocation of Massachusetts' charter produced an immediate reaction from various colonial elites (the best example being Patrick Henry's "Give Me Liberty or Give Me Death" speech to the Virginia House of Burgesses), it seems to have had much less of an effect on the lower orders of colonial society. Finally, the Administration of Justice Act, which Adams referred to as the Murder Bill once again only affected those people living in places under British military control. Southern and western colonists were certainly upset at the idea that British troops could use any level of force they desired on them without having to face the levers of provincial justice, but since British troops were mainly concentrated in New England at the time, this prospect seemed a remote one.[6] The Quebec Act constituted the thread that could stitch these various constituencies together. While the people of New England hardly needed any more reason to oppose the British government than the revocation of the government of Massachusetts, the toleration of Catholicism only added fuel to an already burning fire and the presence of Catholic Indians formerly allied to the French provided an immediate target.

Finally, since the Abenaki responded to the conflict in the same decentralized manner in which they had previous crises, some family bands made overtures to the British at the very same time that others approached the American rebels. The majority of Abenaki bands favored neutrality. The result of all of this was that neither the Americans nor the British fully trusted them. Furthermore, as the 1775 American invasion of Canada would powerfully demonstrate, neutrality constituted as poor a choice as throwing one's lot in with the losing side, as all three options would inexorably lead to forced relocation and dispossession of Abenaki land.[7]

PRAYING INDIAN PATRIOTS

As hard as it was to determine which side the Western Abenakis would support in the American Revolution, there was little doubt as to whom the various "praying Indian" communities of New England would support. Unlike the Abenakis, the Indians who lived in the New England praying towns were not Catholic, but members of the Congregational Church just like many of the revolutionary leaders in New England. Established during the latter half of the 17th century, praying towns were intended to serve the purpose of bringing New England native peoples to Christianity. Originally, only Indian converts and Puritan clergy were allowed to live there. However, by the middle of the 18th century the rest of New England's nonnative population had begun to encroach upon these Christian Indian conclaves, yet the relationship between the towns and the Puritan clergy remained strong. Though these ties to the New England clergy might make it seem obvious that they would support the revolutionaries, in fact, praying Indians had very powerful reasons to join the British in putting down the American rebellion. Not the least of all was the rapidity with which white New Englanders were appropriating native land on the eve of Lexington and Concord.

Established much later than the 14 praying towns created in the 17th century, the praying town of Stockbridge, chartered in 1736, provides some of the best evidence of the effects of the Imperial Crisis on the Christian Indians of New England. Perhaps nothing best demonstrates this than the brisk rate of land transfer from Indian to white ownership from 1763 to 1774. At the end of the Seven Years' War, Stockbridge Indians still held title to more than three quarters of their land base. Eleven years later, as the colonies stood on the brink of open rebellion, the Indians of Stockbridge retained title to somewhere between 5 and 10 percent. Other praying towns throughout New England seem to have experienced similar upheavals as well.[8]

Given this constant threat to their land base and by extension their very existence, the fact that the overwhelming majority of New England praying

Indians enthusiastically supported the American Revolution takes on a much more puzzling complexity. It would seem that supporting the revolutionaries would only hasten their demise, and in the end that is indeed what happened; however, their decision to offer their services to the American rebels seemed at the time the only viable option for two related reasons. First, colonialism had so altered the Indian people of New England that violent resistance against the colonial leadership of New England constituted an even quicker route to demise. Over the past century, factors such as the devastation of King Philip's War, poverty, homelessness, relocation to inner cities, conversion to Congregationalism, the establishment of a system of white guardianship for many native people, disease epidemics, ties to the regional market economy, and intermarriage with African Americans, had so stripped New England praying Indians of political unity, cultural cohesion, and population that rising up against their neighbors was completely impossible for them. Additionally, the physical distance of the crown necessitated an alliance with colonial leaders rather that with those in Whitehall. Survival for praying Indians was dependent upon creating links to local Anglo-Americans, not distant bureaucrats and functionaries, in the hopes that they would be rewarded for such loyalty. Therefore, when the leadership of the New England colonies steered their respective governments to revolution, praying Indians had no choice but to go along. They would eventually discover that their very decision to support the revolution would lead to their demise as a unified people.[9]

THE IROQUOIS CONFEDERACY IN CRISIS

While New England praying Indians responded to the Imperial Crisis with more or less unanimity and the Western Abenakis responded in their traditional fashion of allowing individual family groups to decide their own course, the deepening conflict between Great Britain and the colonies fatally split the Iroquois Confederacy and destroyed a unity forged long before the arrival of English or even Dutch colonists in what is today New York. The archaeological evidence places the formation of the Iroquois Great League of Peace and Friendship sometime during the late 15th century, or on the eve of the Columbian landing in the Caribbean, while the Haudenosanee, as the Iroquois as well as other scholars, refer to themselves, place the events of the league's founding back to the 11th century. Regardless of the exact date, it was in the midst of a period of intense warfare and feuding among the people that the events known as the Deganawidah epic occurred.[10]

According to the epic, a man named Hiawatha, after losing all of his children to the incessant violence, became almost crazed by his grief and retreated to the forests where he encountered a supernatural being known as Deganawidah, the Peacemaker. There Deganawidah soothed Hiawatha's grief and instructed him in condolence rituals utilizing strings of wampum beads. From there, the two set out to preach a message of peace and reconciliation throughout the Mohawk, Cayuga, Oneida, Seneca, and Onondaga nations and after many struggles to cure the hearts, minds, and bodies of the people of the five nations, the Great League of Peace and Power was formed.[11]

Whether or not the events of the Deganawidah epic occurred in the 11th or 15th centuries, or the epic is literally accurate (in fact there are many conflicting versions), it most certainly expresses a fundamental truth. Specifically, the epic demonstrates that out of bloodshed and chaos the wampum-based rituals of condolence and diplomacy created the fabric of unity from which the Five and later the Six Nations of the Iroquois Confederacy would come to dominate much of the economic, military, and political affairs of an area from the Ohio Valley to the western edge of New England. Its exact origin notwithstanding, the Great League of Peace and Power was well in place by the time the Iroquois entered into the written historical record via a French Jesuit account in 1668:

> Proceeding in a Southwesterly direction, we reach Onnontaé,—a large Village, and the center of all the Iroquois Nations,—where every year the States-general, so to speak, is held, to settle the differences that may have arisen among them in the course of the year. Their Policy in this is very wise, and has nothing Barbarous in it. For, since their preservation depends upon their union, and since it is hardly possible that among peoples where license reigns with all impunity— and, above all, among young people—there should not happen some event capable of causing a rupture, and disuniting their minds,—for these reasons, they hold every year a general assembly in Onnontaé. There all the Deputies from the different Nations are present, to make their complaints and receive the necessary satisfaction in mutual gifts,—by means of which they maintain a good understanding with one another.[12]

Of course, the arrival of European colonialism in the land of the Haudenosanee brought new challenges and opportunities to the league that, much like other native peoples in the Americas, transformed their daily lives. Dealing at first with Dutch and French colonists and eventually the English, the Iroquois, by the early years of the 18th century, had fashioned a diplomatic system in which they were often able to play the

English and French off one another to obtain Iroquois ends. This system allowed Francophile factions usually found among the Senecas in the west, Anglophile adherents from primarily among the Mohawks in the east, and those leaders advocating neutrality who typically hailed from the Cayuga, Onondaga, and Oneida villages, to often seek their own ends—the result of which was that "neither power [the French or the English] knew which way the Iroquois would turn and neither gained ascendancy." Additionally, during a period of Anglophile ascendancy among the councils of the Iroquois Confederacy in the 1670s, the English governor of New York, Sir Edmund Andros, in an effort to stabilize several crises that all involved the Iroquois in some manner, set about creating a system of alliances known as the Covenant Chain, which established them as the primary diplomatic and at times military partner of the English in their dealings with all other northeastern Indian peoples. According to Iroquois historian Daniel Richter, this system created for the Iroquois not so much an empire, "but rather a system of alliances in which, at best, the Five Nations were first among equals by virtue of their ability to serve as brokers between English governments and Indian nations."[14] From this unique position of strength in which the Five, and after 1722, the Six Nations could both claim some degree of leadership over the other Indian peoples of the northeast and avoid having to pick a side in the ongoing imperial struggles between the French and the English, the Iroquois Confederacy managed to avoid the ultimate fate of so many other once powerful native polities like the Pequots, the Wampanoags, the Mahicans, and the Huron. However, the events of the Seven Years' War and its aftermath sealed the fate of this highly effective diplomatic system.[15]

The early years of the Seven Years' War in North America constituted one disaster after another for the British. Edward Braddock's disastrous defeat at the hands of the French and their Great Lakes allies near Fort Duquesne began a two-year period in which they utterly failed to get many of their military expeditions off the ground and suffered crushing setbacks in the face of better organized and executed French campaigns such as at Fort Oswego in 1756 and at Fort William-Henry in 1757. Even before the outbreak of hostilities though, the British suffered a major blow to their ability to check French expansion to the Ohio Valley. Angry at the failure of crown officials to both prevent Canadian agents and traders from enticing factions of the Six Nations to favor France and to stop the encroachment of white English settlers on Iroquois land, the Mohawk leader Hendrick angrily declared to New York governor George Clinton and Sir William Johnson in 1753 that the Covenant Chain was irrevocably broken.[16] The next year at the Albany Congress, called at least partially to repair the damaged relationship with the Iroquois, Hendrick went further by taking a stick and throwing it behind his back, saying to the colonial officials gathered, "you have thrown us behind your back and disregarded us; whereas, the French are subtle and vigilant people, ever using their utmost endeavors to seduce and bring our people over to them." Later in the same speech he directly challenged both the collective military leadership of the English and their individual masculinity: "Brethren, You were desirous we should open our minds and our hearts to you; look at the French, they are men; they are fortifying everywhere; but we are ashamed to say it; you are like women, bare and open, without any fortifications."[17] Despite these harsh rebukes and those of Hendrick's brother Abraham, who declared "the Fire here is burnt out," in reference to the diplomatic relationship between the Six Nations and colony of New York, Sir William Johnson and other colonial officials at the Albany Congress managed to ameliorate the Iroquois representatives enough to maintain the relationship. However, the weaknesses the Six Nations perceived in the English and colonial leadership would complicate future attempts to win the Iroquois as allies against the French and thus contribute to the woes the British experienced during the early stages of the war.[18]

In fact, the combination of their soured relationship with the Six Nations and their distinct lack of military success from 1755 to 1757 fused together in a mutually reinforcing downward spiral that seemed irreversible. Still angered by the inability of English and New York officials to protect their land and with a considerable Francophile faction (particularly among the Senecas) in their midst, the Six Nations declared neutrality upon the outbreak of the war in 1754. Without their support, English forces succumbed time and again to French forces that were both augmented by a considerable amount of native allies and willing to adopt Indian strategies such as in the disastrous defeat of Edward Braddock at Fort Duquesne in 1755. In turn, these defeats only convinced many in the Six Nations who were keenly desirous of attaching themselves only to the eventual winner of the contest, that it most likely would not be the English. In 1757, Sir William Johnson summed up this vicious cycle in a letter to his southern counterpart Edmund Atkin:

Tho' there may be some Foundation for the Fears the Upper Nations have expressed for their own Safety, Yet I am far from believing the Reasons they assign for their Neutrality to be the true Ones. Our ill Success hitherto hath intimidated them. Our Methods of Carrying on the War is not according to their Methods, And the present Prospect of Our Affairs doth not seem to please them. Hence they are not prejudiced in our Favour, but seem to think We are going wrong, and therefore will not go with Us. In short, without some striking Success on our Sides, I believe they will not join us.[19]

Within two years, however, the British war effort had achieved a string of moderate successes. The arrival of a much larger force of British regulars in America commanded by several of the best and brightest young commanders in the army combined with an emphasis on bringing the English colonial population advantage to bear as well as challenging the virtual French monopoly on assistance from Native American allies turned the tide of the war toward the British. These changes in British strategy occurred as a result of the elevation of William Pitt to the de facto leadership of the British government. In July of 1758, the French fortress of Louisbourg on Cape Breton Island fell to British and colonial forces. One month later, Fort Frontenac in present-day Ontario fell to English forces. In November of that same year, Major General John Forbes's expedition managed to drive the French from Fort Duquesne. Duquesne, at the confluence of the Monongahela and Allegheny rivers, had been Braddock's original objective in 1755 and with the French now fled, the British finally possessed the Ohio River Valley over which the conflict had originally flared.[20] At the same time, Pitt's naval blockade of French shipping drastically limited the ability of French emissaries to maintain the reciprocal gift giving that their kinship relationship with their native allies demanded. Additionally, French officers fresh from the continent, including the man in overall command of French forces, the Marquis de Montcalm, understood little of Indian customs and often "attempted to treat Indians as soldiers, bound to military discipline, instead of as warriors who came and went as they chose and who consulted manitous not French officers on the eve of battle."[21] Finally, smallpox epidemics, combined with the French failure to live up to their responsibilities as kin-based allies as noted above, convinced many of their allies to sit out the rest of the war and drove some Indian groups formerly allied to France and some neutral groups such as the Six Nations, into the waiting arms of Sir William Johnson and the English.[22]

The Treaty of Easton, concluded in October of 1758, epitomizes the extent to which the relationship between the crown and northern Indian groups had improved since the early days of the war. Specifically, Pennsylvania returned large swaths of native land they had rather dubiously purchased at the Albany Conference in 1754 and promised to stem white settlement west of the Appalachian Mountains in return for Indian promises to withdraw from active support of the French. While not an active alliance per se, the pledge to desert the French was directly responsible for many of the English military successes mentioned above and would prove to be critical to eventual English victory.[23]

In April of 1759, representatives of the Iroquois Confederacy met with Johnson at the Mohawk town of Canajoharie and pledged the full support of all Six Nations to Johnson's upcoming campaign against the French at Fort Niagara. The participation of Iroquois diplomats and warriors in the successful capture of Niagara in July of that year signaled to all that the confederacy had now fully thrown off its policy of neutrality and was firmly ensconced in an alliance with the English. Despite this, the underlying motive of the Six Nations remained what it had always been: group survival. According to Iroquois scholar William Fenton, "The Iroquois adhered to the policy of neutrality until one side demonstrated superiority. . . . When a British victory became apparent in 1759, they dropped the policy of neutrality and joined Johnson's campaign against Niagara." While this was the wisest course of action in order to ensure their continued existence as a unified polity in 1759, all factions within the confederacy did not support it. Additionally, the early 1760s brought the Six Nations face-to-face with the negative ramifications of such a decision.[24]

The alliance with the English brought new threats to the Iroquois Confederacy from within and without. Internally, the end of neutrality and eventually the defeat of the French created tremendous tension among the various factions within the Six Nations that threatened to boil over into outright civil war. Externally, the end of their ability to use the French as a counterweight to English expansion and imperial hubris endangered their way of life and their land base. Not long after the alliance was cemented, those factions favoring the French (particularly among the Seneca) began to talk openly of repudiating the alliance altogether. Several factors beyond their traditional attachment to the French contributed to the disillusionment of many of the westernmost elements of the confederacy. While they had accompanied Johnson on his campaign to drive the French from Fort Niagara, the garrison the English had left there had refused to offer trade terms similar to those offered by the previous French occupants. Less than hospitable attitudes on the part of many English officers also contributed to the anger simmering among the Senecas and other western Iroquois. In early 1761, two Seneca war chiefs attempted to draw the Wyandots and other Algonquian-speaking peoples to their west into a plot to rise up against the English. Made wise to the scheme by an informant, Sir William Johnson hastily rushed to Detroit in September of 1761 to quell the proposed rebellion. He succeeded in doing so by sowing distrust between the western Algonquian nations and the Six Nations to the point that they both refused to have much to do with one another; but the Senecas would remain a doubtful ally at best and over the next five years would on more than one occasion strike against the English.[25]

The loyalty of the Senecas represented only one of the problems facing Sir William Johnson during the early 1760s. The defeat of the French at Quebec in 1759 and at Montreal in 1760 had all but ended the war in North America; and subsequently British settlers had begun streaming onto Indian lands with no regard to the promises made by Johnson and other crown officials to limit white settlement in the west. Specifically, a settlement made up of farmers from Connecticut in the Wyoming Valley, deep in the heart of the territory promised to the Delawares by the Treaty of Easton, threatened to spark violence not only between the Delawares and the Wyoming settlers, but also between the Delawares and the Six Nations who had actually sold the land to the Connecticut settlement company in the first place. The Mohawks, fearing the loss of what had since become critical hunting grounds, argued that the original Wyoming land sale to the Connecticut settlers and the promise of the land as a refuge for the Delawares should be declared null and void, thus returning control of the area back to them. Additionally, many groups outside the Six Nations proper had begun to lodge complaints regarding Johnson's handling of Indian affairs in general and trade in particular.[26]

Faced with these difficulties, Johnson called for a conference with representatives of the Six Nations at Johnson Hall in April of 1762. While he managed to gain the allegiance of the Senecas for at least the short-term at that meeting, the controversy surrounding the Connecticut settlement at Wyoming still remained. In an effort to settle both this issue and another controversy over the Delaware lands acquired by Pennsylvania in the so-called Walking Purchase of 1737, Johnson was given the power to call a judicial investigation with the purpose to determine whether or not Pennsylvania and the Iroquois had conspired to deprive the Delawares of their lands in eastern Pennsylvania during the Walking Purchase. The understanding was that if Johnson accepted the Delawares' claims that they had been deceived in the Walking Purchase he would award the disputed land in the Wyoming Valley to them as recompense. However, Johnson had never been close to the Delawares and his closest Indian allies, the Mohawks, wanted Wyoming for themselves. Furthermore, given the importance of the Covenant Chain relationship to British-Indian diplomacy neither Johnson nor the crown was about to diminish the power of Mohawks within that structure simply to appease the Delawares. Johnson was also desirous of strengthening his ties to the politically powerful Penn family and was well aware of what a judgment against them in the matter of the Walking Purchase would do to those hopes.

Finally, the Delaware leader Teedyuscung, often drunk, exhibited extremely irrational and erratic behavior throughout the proceedings and therefore lessened the already slim chances that Johnson might find in his favor. In the end, despite the objections of some Quaker observers friendly to the Delaware (on one occasion Johnson even threatened to kill one Quaker who objected to his administration of the proceedings) Johnson forced Teedyuscung and the Delawares to give up objections to the previous land transfers in exchange for 200 pounds worth of goods and a lump sum payment of 400 pounds.[27]

While Johnson's activities in the summer of 1762 did much to restore the internal peace among the Six Nations, their relationships with other representatives of the British government remained tense at best. Colonial governments increasingly skirted the established protocols for dealing with the confederacy. Pennsylvania and its Indian agent Conrad Weiser were particularly guilty of this infraction by favoring direct communication with the leaders of the confederacy at Onondaga rather than initiating diplomacy with either of the two groups, the Mohawks in the east and the Senecas in the west, which represented the traditional entry for such matters.

As troubling as these broaches of protocol were, however, the attitude and actions of British commander in chief Jeffrey Amherst presented by far the greatest obstacle to Anglo-Iroquois harmony. Not long before his death, General John Forbes, the captor of Fort Duquesne, wrote Amherst beseeching him not to neglect good relations with the native peoples of North America. "I beg in the meantime that you will not think triflingly of the Indians or their friendship; when I venture to assure that twenty Indians are capable of laying half this province to waste, of which I have been an eye witness."[28] Amherst, however, was not inclined to take the advice.

In 1760, Amherst needed Indians, specifically the Six Nations, to support him in his campaign against Montreal. But despite the critical role they eventually played in the success of that campaign, his basic attitudes about Native Americans never wavered. In order to gain their cooperation, Amherst had been reluctantly forced to approve Sir William Johnson's request for 17,000 pounds worth of goods and cash payments to the Iroquois. He also complained incessantly of Johnson's offers of trade and amnesty to any Indians formerly allied to the French who agreed to support the expedition. Yet, as historian Fred Anderson has demonstrated, without the participation of the Six Nations warriors and Johnson's offers of peace and forgiveness the campaign against Montreal might very well have failed. According to Anderson:

The most valuable component of Amherst's army was the one that Amherst most despised and distrusted: the seven hundred Iroquois warriors who had accompanied him from Oswego. . . . Whenever his army appeared at a [French] mission village—as, for example, at the mission of La Présentation near Fort Lévis—the mere presence of the Iroquois and their testimony to the benefits of alliance with the British gave enough weight to Sir William's offers of amnesty and trade to procure not only peace but active support for the invaders. Through the whole of Amherst's expedition, therefore, the very Indian villages that had always furnished New France with its most loyal auxiliaries actually expedited the British advance.[29]

None of this changed Amherst's outlook regarding Indians. He repeatedly refused to allow them to participate in the many skirmishes that occurred on the way to Montreal for fear that they would commit "atrocities." Feeling betrayed by Amherst, who had promised them they would have an opportunity to reap the trophies of war needed to prove their fitness as warriors, the Iroquois disobeyed and began to open up graves and scalp the corpses therein. When Amherst finally ordered them to disperse after the campaign, he awarded the individual warriors with silver medals, but refused to provide any of the presents or trade goods culturally required of native allies in eastern North America. It was a sign of things to come.[30]

According to historian Gregory Dowd, Pontiac's Rebellion was less about the preservation of Indian land, trade, or even racial hatred, though those issues were all relevant. Instead, Pontiac's Rebellion represented a "war over status . . . awash in matters of the spirit." In other words, Indian leaders (including those who had helped the British prevail) in the post–Seven Years' War era feared that the British meant to dominate them and rule them as conquered subjects rather than to deal with them as allies. To accept this new reality would be tantamount to Indian leaders "surrendering their standing as the protectors of their followers' autonomy and security, giving up their peoples' independence, perhaps even exchanging it for slavery." Therefore to combat this outcome they turned to both violent resistance and spiritual renewal.[31]

The Six Nations were not spared the disruptions brought on by these fears and the methods some native people chose to combat them. When the Ottawa leader Pontiac, utilizing the religious message of the Delaware prophet Neolin, began to court individual Indian villages to join his coalition against the British in 1763, he found a willing audience among the Senecas, who of course had traditionally aligned themselves with the French. A group of French-leaning Senecas from the village of Geneseo, known as the "Genesees," who had conspired to attack the British at Fort Niagara as recently as the previous year, took up Pontiac's war belts and began to circulate them among the rest of the Six Nations. At a meeting with representatives of the confederacy at German Flats in July of 1763, Sir William Johnson reported that many of the Senecas "were resolved to follow the resolution they had taken, which was to carry on the war against the English, and that those who acted differently might repent it."[32]

In September of that year, the Genesee Senecas made good on this promise. Surprising a supply train on its way to Niagara, Genesee warriors not only killed most of the 30 soldiers guarding it and another 40 soldiers from the two companies sent to reinforce it, they also made off with or destroyed nearly all of the supplies including a considerable number of pack animals. Once again according to Dowd, "British troops around Niagara found their workloads vastly increased as they had to carry supplies on their own shoulders and under guard."[33]

Eventually, Sir William Johnson managed to convince Amherst that the surest way to victory against Pontiac and his allies was to bring the Senecas back into the fold and reunite them with the rest of their Six Nations brethren. He would attempt to do this by stressing the role played by the Shawnees, Delawares, and other Ohio Valley and Great Lakes groups in the outbreak of Pontiac's War by assigning to those groups not only a desire to strike the British, but also the Six Nations. By doing so, Johnson hoped to convince the Senecas that since Pontiac's coalition bore ill will toward both the British and the Six Nations, the two powers must make common cause with one another. Despite Johnson's arguments on this score in both written and oral form and the generous overtures he made to the Genesee Senecas in the first months of 1764, many refused to abandon Pontiac's coalition. Other Senecas urged Johnson to reconsider his designs of punishing the Shawnees and Delawares, but instead to negotiate with them through the Six Nations and the Covenant Chain. Finally, the Cayugas resisted him by offering asylum to Delaware warriors who had participated in many of the coalition's attacks on British positions in the west.[34]

In the end, it was not Sir William Johnson's grand strategy that brought the Senecas back into the fold and reunited the Six Nations, but rather the failure of Pontiac's coalition to sustain its campaign in the wake of his death, British and colonial counterattacks, and internal dissension among the member groups; however, Johnson reaped much of the glory for this turn of events. In the summer of 1764, the Genesee Senecas made peace with the superintendent at Niagara and thus brought Johnson to the high-water mark of his power and standing both with his government in London and with the peoples of the Iroquois Confederacy. Accordingly, Johnson was confident he could use his increased authority and political capital to "advance British dominion in North America." He might have succeeded had it not been for American colonists with very different ideas about the future of the continent. Over the next 10 years, various land schemes and religious missionary efforts carried out by Americans combined to undermine the efforts of Johnson and the British government to fully subject the north to British control and ultimately eroded his power and his health.[35]

Despite King George III's issuance of the Royal Proclamation of 1763, which sought to bar colonial settlement west of the Appalachian Mountains and reserve those lands to the Indians, the issue of white encroachment on Indian land both east and west of the Appalachians continued to threaten the relationship between the Six Nations and His Majesty's government. Since the King's proclamation did not apply to the lands of the Six Nations, which were located east of the Proclamation Line, the issue of a fixed boundary between the territory of the Iroquois Confederacy and that of neighboring colonies occupied a preeminent place in the business of Sir William Johnson between the end of the Pontiac War in 1764 and the Treaty of Fort Stanwix in 1768. At a congress held at his Johnson Hall estate in March of 1768, an Iroquois speaker laid this and other lingering issues before the superintendent, promising that these grievances held the potential to unravel the alliance altogether:

> English promises made at the beginning of the Seven Years War had not been fulfilled and lingered as postwar complaints. Traders continued to abuse the Indians, the speaker said, and rum bottles hung at every door. Would-be English protectors stole their land. The Mohawks were about to lose land at their very doors. "If you wont do justice to our Fathers the Mohawks . . . if you wont keep the people away from the Rivers near Ohio, and keep the Road open making Pennsylvania and Virginia quiet we must get tired of looking to you, and turn our faces another way."[36]

Such exchanges underscored for Johnson his urgent need to settle the Northern Boundary once and for all. He would eventually call for negotiations to determine the Northern Boundary between Indian country and the American colonies to commence in September of 1768 at Fort Stanwix, but during the interlude between the end of the Pontiac War and the Treaty of Fort Stanwix, one other issue increasingly drove a wedge between Johnson and his Iroquois allies.[37]

Calvinist missionaries from New England began making inroads among the Iroquois Confederacy shortly after the end of the Seven Years' War in 1763. Despite his staunch support of the Anglican Church, Sir William Johnson allowed these dissenters to work among the peoples of the confederacy. By the middle of the 1770s, he would come to regret that decision as the influence of dissenting missionaries, most notably the Presbyterian Samuel Kirkland, fostered divisions among the Six Nations that contributed to the confederacy's fractured response to the Imperial Crisis and the American Revolution.[38]

When Kirkland, a graduate of the Reverend Eleazar Wheelock's Indian Charity School and Princeton University, first arrived among the Iroquois in 1764, Sir William readily endorsed the young missionary and supported his first mission to the Seneca villages located at the extreme western door of the confederacy. Two years later, Kirkland moved to live among the Oneidas, where he would spend the remainder of his life and career. There he would increasingly frustrate Johnson by his refusal to recognize Anglican teachings relating to baptism, and by steering both the Oneidas and the Tuscaroras toward an alliance with the Americans as the Imperial Crisis raged on.[39] By 1771, Johnson was actively taking steps to damage Kirkland's mission to the Oneidas, but they ultimately proved futile as Kirkland had managed in only five years to become in the words of one Iroquois scholar, "an indispensable member of the community . . . he had enough friends among them and rendered sufficient service to become a highly respected and necessary part of their life."[40] In so doing, he had also driven a wedge between his adherents and their Iroquoian brethren as well as between them and Sir William Johnson. The first inklings of this fracturing of both Iroquois unity and devotion to Johnson and the English crown appeared at Johnson's 1768 conference at Fort Stanwix to settle the long, simmering boundary dispute.

Throughout the latter days of September and most of October 1768, Indian delegates from throughout the northern colonies descended upon Fort Stanwix near present-day Rome, New York. By October 24 more than 3,000 delegates had arrived and Johnson initiated the proceedings by lighting a ceremonial council fire. In addition to a final settlement of the boundary line ordered by the Royal Proclamation of 1763, Johnson also saw the negotiations as an opportunity to restore the unity to the Iroquois Confederacy that had been frayed by settler encroachment, trader abuses, and the penetration of religious dissenting missionaries. In addition to public rituals designed to refurbish and strengthen the Covenant Chain relationship between the Iroquois, their constituents, and Great Britain, Johnson also worked tirelessly behind the scenes in private meetings designed to bolster the attachment of the confederacy to the crown. For their part the representatives of the Six Nations sought to divert English settlement away from their New York homelands.[41]

Finally, on November 5, 1768, all parties agreed to the Treaty of Fort Stanwix, which ostensibly addressed the issues of all parties. The boundary line between white and Indian settlements was now fixed. It ran south and west to the confluence of the Ohio and Kanawha rivers and then further down the Ohio River to its meeting with the Tennessee River, therefore ceding lands in the west, which ostensibly the Iroquois had no power to give away. In doing so, the Six Nations had not only confirmed the Covenant Chain but also, they hoped, eased the pressure on their own homelands by signing away those of the Shawnees, Delawares, and others in western Pennsylvania, Western Virginia, and Kentucky; however, the negotiations leading to the treaty signing had been contentious, and Johnson's tactics, particularly in convincing the Oneida to agree to it, angered them and drove the Oneidas further into an alliance with Samuel Kirkland and his dissenting coreligionists. Additionally, representatives from another religious dissenting missionary, Eleazar Wheelock, tried to use the treaty negotiations as a vehicle through which to secure a new site for Wheelock's school, angering Johnson to the point that he became convinced of the need to combat their doctrines more forcefully in Iroquois territory. This, combined with Johnson's alarm at the fact that missionaries such as Kirkland were active in spreading opposition to Parliament's passage of the Stamp Act and Townsend Duties, led him to support the establishment of an Anglican episcopate in America. The idea of assigning an Anglican bishop to the colonies had long been a controversial one, particularly in the northern colonies where Anglicanism enjoyed much less widespread support than in the south. Therefore, Sir William's support of the idea served to further alienate him from many revolutionaries in places such as New England and Pennsylvania.[42]

These actions, along with others in which he sought to impede the progress of Kirkland's Oneida mission, seriously damaged Johnson's relationship with the Oneidas and Tuscaroras who were by far the mission's most zealous converts. In 1771, Johnson used every means at his disposal to dissuade the Oneidas from building a new church for Kirkland's Presbyterian mission on their lands. He even went so far as to make reference to the beheading of Charles I at the hands of Puritans during the English civil war nearly a century and a half earlier. In the end, neither this argument nor Sir William's none-too-subtle reminder that disobeying the King's representative (in this case himself) might carry with it unfortunate consequences could deter the Oneidas from building the new meetinghouse. Johnson had succeeded only in inflicting more damage to his already waning influence among the Oneidas. This in turn drove him into an even closer relationship with the staunchly Anglican and royalist Mohawks as evidenced by his close relationship with the Mohawk leader Joseph Brant, himself an Anglican minister. Johnson's relationship with Brant's sister Mary, the mother of several of Johnson's children and his eventual wife, also cemented his ties to the Mohawks. Additionally, Johnson's encouragement of the missionary efforts of John Stuart, an Anglican missionary among the Mohawks, not only further alienated the Oneidas and Tuscaroras from him, but also placed them at odds with their league brethren.[43] In the words of Iroquois historian Barbara Graymont, the issue of the Oneida Church and Johnson's attempts to establish Anglicanism "were a harbinger of a more serious crisis yet to come . . . the sentiments of the missionaries, the influence of the Johnsons, the supply of trade goods, the control of military posts, the old covenants with the whites, the rivalry between warriors and sachems and the structural weakness of a kinship state would all combine to pull apart the famous League founded by Deganawidah and Hiawatha."[44] Whether they be Abenakis in Vermont, Praying Indians in Massachusetts, or members of the once powerful Six Nations Confederacy in New York, all Indian communities in the North experienced a similar crisis on the eve of the American Revolution. The added issue of continued white encroachment on their land base only made their decision about which side to support in that conflict all the more fateful.

4

THE COLLAPSE OF BRITISH INDIAN POLICY IN THE WEST

Before the Western Delawares signed a treaty allying them with the British at Easton, Pennsylvania, in 1758, a treaty already agreed to by the Iroquois and the Eastern Delawares in 1756, one of the negotiators at the treaty conference, King Beaver, or Tamaqua as he was known among his people, arose and spoke directly to the English representatives. His speech made clear that the price the English must pay for the assistance of the Western Delawares and their allies against the French was nothing less than a guarantee that the English and their colonists would abandon their settlement plans in the Ohio Valley. "Brother," he began as he addressed his remarks specifically to the English representative Christian Frederick Post, "I would tell you in a most soft, loving and friendly manner, to go back over the mountain, and stay there; for if you will do that, I will use it for an argument, to argue with other nations of Indians."[1]

At almost exactly the same time that King Beaver spoke to Post, Major General John Forbes and his army succeeded in taking Fort Duquesne, the French outpost at the confluence of the Allegheny and Monongahela rivers that had sparked the war four years earlier. Within weeks, British, colonial, and native diplomats were once again debating what right, if any, the British and their colonists had to the area. In addition to their earlier demands that

the British leave in return for their service, the Indian diplomats also reminded the British that their victory at Duquesne had been made possible
by the withdrawal of western Indians from active support of the French.
Colonel Henry Bouquet, commanding in relief of the terminally ill Forbes,
demanded that the Western Delaware and Ohio Indians acquiesce to his
rebuilding Duquesne (to be renamed Fort Pitt in honor of the architect of
British success in the war) and stationing 200 troops there. In response to
the negotiators Andrew Montour, George Croghan, and Post, the Indian
representatives made it explicitly clear that they would not accept such an
arrangement. For his part, Post planned to inform Bouquet of their answer.
The other two at first tried to avoid delivering the news to Bouquet altogether and finally, when pressed by him, concocted a story that the Indian
representatives had held private discussions without Post in attendance and
had miraculously changed their position. Christian Post then objected, "I
told him [Bouquet] I had already spoke with the Indians; he said it was a
damned lie."[2] In the end, Bouquet, Croghan, and Montour simply ignored
Post and the Western Indian delegates. As one historian has characterized
it, "Ohio leaders learned the hard way that among a go-between's tricks was
making *no* mean *yes* and *yes, no.*"[3]

Yet, the British government didn't allow their colonists the free reign
over the Ohio country that many such as George Washington hoped for
either.[4] Throughout the decade and a half prior to the American Revolution,
the British government and military took multiple steps to enforce and
buttress the Royal Proclamation of 1763. This situation in which the British
sought to exert control over the Ohio Valley and its peoples while at the
same time attempting to protect Indians exposes what historian Patrick
Griffin has labeled "the patronizing logic upon which the [British] myth of
the west had been constructed." Specifically, the British government saw
Indians in the west as inferior people, but people nonetheless who were
capable, with the proper instruction, of ascending to "civilization." At the
same time, British imperial administrators, politicians, and officers also
wholeheartedly believed that the lands of the Indians of the west were
solely the property of the British Empire by virtue of their victory in
the Seven Years' War, so they therefore felt entirely justified in taking possession of the Ohio Valley and in forcing their version of civilization on the
area's inhabitants. In the British imperial view, the Indians of the Ohio
Valley possessed neither civilization nor sovereignty, and the British, by
virtue of their possession of both, would bring Ohio Valley peoples to
civilization.[5]

This plan faced two particularly daunting obstacles. First, the Ohio Valley
Indians considered themselves sovereign. In the words of Sir William

Johnson's deputy George Croghan, Indians "don't look on themselves under any obligation to us, but rather think we are oblig'd to them, for letting us reside in their Country." Despite the prevailing belief among the British imperial policymakers that their taking possession of the Ohio country was in the best interests of the Native Americans living there, the plan would run headlong into violent and entrenched Indian resistance. This resistance would only strengthen the second obstacle standing in the way of the British imperial plan for the Ohio Valley. In order for Ohio Valley Indians to accept the British attempt to "civilize" them, they would have to feel secure in the ownership of their lands, which in turn would allow them to trust the British. However, settlers and speculators from Pennsylvania, Virginia, and other colonies had other ideas about who would determine the future of the west. Once again according to Griffin, "for the plan for the West to work, colonies—and by implication their speculating elite—had to forego claims to the West."[6] American colonists intent on possessing Ohio for themselves of course did no such thing. Instead, they swarmed into the Ohio Valley in such a chaotic and completely defiant manner as to cause British general Thomas Gage to characterize them as "Licentious Ruffians," who could no more be contained than the highwaymen and brigands of England.[7] So in the end the British Empire's Ohio Valley Indian policy completely backfired: it not only alienated the British government from the Ohio Valley Indians, but also from its own subjects east of the Appalachians.

THE PAXTON BOYS

The Paxton Boys incidents of late 1763 and early 1764 in Pennsylvania powerfully demonstrate the potential of such a policy to spawn horrific violence even while trying to prevent it. Having lived on the lands granted them by the Penn family since 1717, the Conestogas (a combined polity of Senecas, Delawares, and Susquehannocks) had maintained a long-peaceful relationship with Pennsylvanians; however, by mid-century a large influx of Scotch-Irish Presbyterians began to settle near the lands of the Conestogas along the Susquehanna River in east-central Pennsylvania. Their desire for Conestoga land combined with the widespread fear spawned by the Pontiac War in 1763 created a situation ripe for violence. Accusing the Pennsylvania Assembly of favoring Indians to the point that frontier settlements that bordered Conestoga lands such as theirs at Paxtang, also along the Susquehanna River, were left to the mercy of war parties, these Scotch-Irish took matters into their own hands. Justifying their decision on the baseless claim that the Conestogas were secretly aiding Delaware war parties during the Pontiac War, the frontiersmen attacked Conestoga Town (near present-day Millersville) on December 14, 1764, killing 20 Indians who were both peaceful and converts to Christianity. Just after Christmas of that year the "Paxton Boys," as they became known, stormed the jail at Lancaster, Pennsylvania, and murdered 14 Indians the local sheriff had placed there in protective custody. Finally, the vigilantes, now nearly 500 strong, marched on Philadelphia in February of 1764 in an attempt to find and kill other peaceful Indians who had sought refuge there. Their design was only thwarted when representatives of the colony's assembly (Benjamin Franklin among them) promised to hear their complaints and exempted them from prosecution for the murders at Conestoga and at Lancaster.[8]

The Paxton Boys episode provides a telling glimpse into the difficulties British Indian policy in the west had the potential to produce on both sides of the equation. Essentially, the British were trying to serve two masters in their Indian policy in the area. On the one hand they sought to reassure and confirm western Indians in the possession of their lands, but on the other they asserted British dominion over those lands and such an assertion of dominion encouraged American colonists to disregard Indian claims to ownership. The situation the British found themselves in with regard to western Indians and American colonists was not unlike one in which someone holds a candle that is burning at both ends, but any attempt to extinguish one end only fans the flames of the other. When, in this case, Pennsylvania attempted to protect peaceful Indians, frontier settlers rose up to murder them and nearly attacked the colony's government itself; however, the Pennsylvania government's response to the Paxton Boys convinced many western Indians that the British government as well as the governments of the colonies would always sacrifice Indian sovereignty in the name of appeasing violent colonists bent on expansion.[9] No one was prosecuted for the murders at Conestoga and Lancaster and in the end Pennsylvania governor and proprietor John Penn gave in to the demands of the frontiersmen and eventually expressed the opinion "that all the Indians should be removed out of the Province."[10] Even in the face of these events the British government failed to recognize the deep flaws in its policies regarding western Indians. A policy with such contradictory purposes could not stand for long, and while the British may not have realized this truth, both American colonists and western Indians were beginning to do so.

REFUGEES NO MORE

The collective historical experiences of the Mingos, Shawnees, and Delawares, the three most powerful Indian groups living in the Ohio Valley, provide a particularly powerful explanation for their resistance to both American settlers and British imperial control and thus a likewise potent explanation of the eventual failure of British policy in the area. All three of these groups were refugees who had been pushed into the Ohio Valley as a result of earlier clashes with European colonialism, and they were determined to retreat no further. The Ohio Valley would be where they would take their stand against the onrushing tide of death and destruction unleashed by the advent of European settlement in the so-called New World that began in the late 15th century.

Of the three Ohio Valley groups that fiercely resisted British and American domination in the late 18th century, the Shawnee are the most difficult to track. Interestingly, one of their most effective strategies for dealing with the upheavals wrought by the penetration of the Atlantic market economy and the diseases that accompanied it accounts for the difficulty in placing all of them in any one location at a particular time. Rather than congregate in one location to meet the oncoming European invaders as one group, the Shawnees often split into new bands and relocated rather than risk complete destruction or subjugation. Therefore, both historical and anthropological evidence of 17th century Shawnee bands exists in various locales ranging from South Carolina to New York and from Virginia to the Illinois country. In the words of Southern Department Indian superintendent Edmund Atkin, the Shawnees were without a doubt, "the greatest Travellers in America."[11] While there exists no unanimous consensus among archaeologists regarding the pre-contact origins of the Shawnee, the majority of scholarship now leans toward their inclusion in what is known as the Fort Ancient complex of the Ohio Valley, near present-day Elizabethtown, Ohio. Furthermore, the earliest historical evidence recorded by early French explorers as well as later statements by individual Shawnees themselves places them in this general vicinity.[12]

During the mid-17th century, the Shawnee were actively opposing western expansion by the Five Nations of the Iroquois Confederacy. A previous trading relationship that had formed between the Susquehannocks and Shawnees eventually morphed into a military alliance against the Five Nations during this period, but the combination of disease outbreaks and Five Nations military strength conspired to wear down the Shawnees and their allies to the point that a Five Nations victory became a foregone conclusion; however, sources disagree on whether the Iroquois vanquished the Susquehannocks or the Shawnee first. The dates for the defeat vary within an approximately 25-year period from the mid-1650s to the late 1670s. The decentralized organization of the Shawnee likely explains this wide variance. The Ohio Valley Shawnees constituted only the northern branch of the group. A nominally separate southern Shawnee polity existed to the south along the Cumberland River. Furthermore, the northern/ Ohio branch consisted of five semiautonomous divisions. It therefore seems likely that these different Shawnee groups experienced warfare and eventual defeat at the hands of the Five Nations at differing times throughout the middle third of the 17th century.[13]

In any case, with most of their Susquehannock allies having accepted Five Nations Iroquois suzerainty and relocated to Seneca and Mohawk villages in Pennsylvania and New York, the Shawnees, as they had on numerous occasions in the past, broke into smaller bands and dispersed throughout North America. Some migrated first to the French outposts of Starved Rock and Fort St. Louis in the Illinois country, while others migrated directly to live in close contact with their defeated Susquehannock allies in Pennsylvania. One group of Shawnees moved south to the Savannah River and for a time occupied the coveted position of most-favored Indian slave trader to Carolina, but by the early 18th century, Carolina no longer needed their services so much as their land. The Savannahs (as they were known) joined a native coalition fighting against further encroachment by the Carolinas and Virginia. By the end of the conflict known as the Yamassee War in 1715, the Savannah Shawnees were forced to migrate once again. While some went south and west to join the Creeks, others migrated back to the north and rejoined their brethren who had resettled in Pennsylvania. Whatever the route they took to get there, the majority of Shawnee bands reunited as refugees among the Susquehannocks (now referred to by Pennsylvanians as Conestogas) in the early 18th century and by the 1750s they had come full circle to their ancient Ohio Valley homelands, where they thought they would at last be free from both the ravages of white colonialism and the interference of the Iroquois Confederacy. When the end of Seven Years' War unleashed thousands of colonists, traders, and a large British army presence upon their homeland, the Shawnees chose to resist rather than relocate as they had in the past. The invaders might have the other places that they had once called home, but they would not give up their ancient Ohio homeland without a fight.[14]

The Shawnees were of course not the only Ohio Valley group to resist the postwar invasion of their homeland. The Delawares and Mingos also left the Pennsylvania/New York orbit of the Five Nations during the first half of the 18th century to move to the Ohio Valley. The Delawares in particular shared the Shawnees' determination never to bow in subordination to the French, the English, or the Iroquois; but unlike the Shawnees, the construction of the village of Kittaning near the Allegheny River in 1724 marked not a homecoming for the Delawares, but an entirely new beginning west of the Appalachians. Having originated in the Lower Delaware

River Valley to the east, the Delawares had, since the establishment of Pennsylvania in 1681, steadily receded in the face of growing English settlement in the area. With increased colonial settlement came less game, diminished agricultural capacity, and of course, disease. By the 1720s, some Delaware leaders had become convinced that to remain east of the Appalachian Mountains would be to sentence their children to a life of poverty and vagrancy. While the Delawares would maintain economic and diplomatic ties to the Pennsylvania colony, Kittaning was to be a new start with, they hoped, enough distance and topographical obstacles to keep white colonists at bay.[15]

No doubt the Delaware leaders suspected that their move would not keep white settlers at bay forever. Even the most pessimistic among them must have been shocked at just how short-lived their respite was from colonial encroachment. Less than seven years after the Delawares removed to the western side of the Appalachian Mountains, English colonial officials grew nervous about the prospect of their falling under the influence of the French, who were also making inroads into the Ohio and Illinois countries. In late 1731, Pennsylvania governor Patrick Gordon wrote the Delawares expressing his fear that they might "fall into the hands of Strangers." He concluded the letter by inviting the Indians to return to the eastern side of the mountains. Specifically, Gordon's fears were driven by Pennsylvania's desire (as well as that of Virginia and Maryland) for the immense natural resources of the Ohio Valley. The Delawares, as well as the Shawnees, sensed these motives and refused to take Pennsylvania up on the offer.[16]

In response to their reticence, Gordon and Pennsylvania proprietor Thomas Penn enlisted the help of the Six Nations Iroquois in an effort to use the system of interlocking alliances known as the Covenant Chain to pressure the Delawares and other western Indians to move back within the orbit of English colonial power centers. The Covenant Chain system of alliances and agreements between the English and the Iroquois Confederacy grew out of attempts by the English to establish at least nominal control over both Indian affairs in their American colonies and internal conflicts among the Iroquois over which of the colonial powers to ally with. Since nearly the beginning of the colonial era in North America, the peoples of first the Iroquois League and later the Iroquois Confederacy had debated among themselves whether to align their fortunes with one colonial power over another or choose neutrality. Anglophile, Francophile, and neutralist factions among the Iroquois sought every opportunity to impose their particular agenda for the future peace and security of the group on the others. By the late 1660s and 1670s, those who favored a closer relationship with France had gained the upper hand among the various villages of the Iroquois League. The arrival of a new English governor in New York, Sir Edmund Andros, offered anglophiles among the Iroquois an opportunity unlike any before to wrest control of the group's diplomatic policies from the hands of the French-leaning faction. Unlike his predecessors, Andros exhibited considerable desire to work with anti-French Iroquois against both their Francophile brethren and New France itself. The diplomatic agreements that ended King Philip's War in New England, Bacon's Rebellion in Virginia, as well as a conflict between Mahicans and Mohawks—all occurring in the late 1670s and early 1680s—afforded both Andros and his Anglophile allies an opportunity to remake both the English relationship with the Iroquois as well as the internal dynamics of Iroquois politics. By the early 1680s, Andros had successfully relocated both the losing native groups from the wars in New England and New York as well as those from Bacon's Rebellion in Virginia to various outposts on the fringe of Iroquois territory or within Iroquois villages themselves. These refugees were now to live as dependents under the protection of the Iroquois; thus began the Covenant Chain.[17]

Over the years and in response to various wars, treaty negotiations, and other events, both the English and the Six Nations Iroquois came to view the Covenant Chain more as a hierarchical relationship in which the Six Nations served as the overlords of the other member nations. This interpretation fit well with English desires to have one native conduit through which to exert control over the various groups within and beyond their colonies' borders. It also coincided with Iroquois desires to exert more power over the other groups such as the Delawares, Mingos, and Shawnees in an effort to steer English colonialism away from their own lands. According to historian Michael McConnell, this development created dire consequences for groups such as the Delaware. He refers to this expanded Covenant Chain as "a blatant tool for provincial expansion," which caught groups like the Delawares "in an Iroquois-Pennsylvania vise . . . they were now viewed as 'dependents' of both the Six Nations and the colony and were expected to live wherever those two powerful partners dictated." Given this reality, both the Delawares' decision to move west and their subsequent refusal to accept Gordon's offer in 1731 make much sense. Once again to quote McConnell, "those who could joined the exodus to the Ohio Country, and it was there that Covenant Chain met its most persistent opposition."[18]

The Delawares refused to even send a delegation to discuss Pennsylvania's invitation to move east until 1740. When they did finally acknowledge the invitation they used the occasion to inform the Pennsylvanians of their position that though they were nominal allies, the Iroquois were not the masters of Delaware lands, and they demanded that Pennsylvania and by extension the English allow the Delawares to determine their own fate. Therefore, despite the fact that they had not originated there, this new Ohio homeland symbolized something more for the Delawares than simply a new locale in which to live, hunt, raise their families, and practice their religious traditions. In the 40 years between 1724 and 1763, the Ohio Valley came to represent a last refuge, a bastion against the ever-increasing threats of colonial expansion, trading abuses, Iroquois imperialism, and the destruction of their ability to live as Indian people according to their own definition of what that meant. The Delawares, like the Shawnees, had no intention of giving it up peacefully.[19]

By the late 1740s a third group of Ohio Indians had entered the picture and though their background and their reasons for calling the Ohio Valley home differed considerably from the Shawnees and the Delawares, this new group of Ohio country refugees was just as determined to maintain their foothold in the region. These Indians, sometimes referred to as Mingos, were former members of the Six Nations Iroquois, mostly Senecas, who participated in a considerable migration to the Ohio Valley beginning in the late 1730s and early 1740s. During the long peace between the French and English in America falling between the end of Queen Anne's War in 1713 and the outbreak of King George's War in 1744, both French and English traders made inroads into the territory of the Senecas in the previously forbidden western reaches of Six Nations territory near Lake Ontario. With them came alcohol, trade abuses, debt, and disease. Within 15 years of the establishment of the British trading post at Oswego, British officials reported disastrous smallpox epidemics. By 1741, western Iroquois villages were so paralyzed by these epidemics that they suffered severe food shortages because of their inability to grow crops or hunt. In the face of these disasters, many Senecas (including many who were very likely the descendants of captives taken from now vanquished Ohio Valley groups during the Beaver Wars of the 17th century) led an exodus to the Ohio Valley so substantial that by the middle of the century Pennsylvania governor James Hamilton remarked that Iroquois in the Ohio Valley had grown "more numerous than in the countrys they left." Having come there to save their communities from the disease, alcoholism, and cultural degradation brought on by increased contact with Europeans, the Mingos were just as determined as their Shawnee and Delaware neighbors to make the Appalachian Mountains an impenetrable barrier beyond which life would proceed according to Indian dictates and not those of white traders, colonists, or imperial officials.[20]

The subsequent attempts of the Ohio Valley groups to cautiously ally themselves with whichever power could offer the best commodities while pledging to respect their land base demonstrate their commitment to playing the major powers against one another to ensure group survival; however, this was more than the realpolitik often associated with the Iroquois, Creek, and Cherokee Confederacies. Many of these new Ohio Valley Indians had come to believe in the nativist religious message of the Delaware prophet Neolin mentioned previously.[21]

Finally, while all three of these groups played crucial roles in the eventual revitalization movement that engulfed the Ohio Valley during the 1760s, such a movement would not have been possible without the Shawnees for two primary reasons. First of all, the Shawnees' desire to return to their ancestral homeland coupled with their nearly 100 years of resistance to both Europeans and the Five Nations gave the movement a core group that had never accepted the culture and leadership of either the Europeans or the Iroquois. Secondly, because of the many years of Shawnee migrations in response to European and Five Nations aggression, there were pockets of Shawnee sympathizers in native communities from the Great Lakes to the Gulf of Mexico. Their shared belief that from time immemorial they had "always been the frontier" against the penetration of European settlers, traders, markets, diseases, and clients such as the Five Nations, which predisposed them to embrace the pan-Indian message of the Delaware Prophet Neolin in the 1760s.

By the end of the Seven Years' War in 1763, the situation in the Ohio Valley was therefore ripe for conflict. Shawnees, Delawares, and Mingos had created communities there which they viewed as either sacred due to their establishment on ancestral homelands, or as a place of ultimate retreat that they were determined to defend to the last. American colonists, particularly those from the Chesapeake and Pennsylvania, believed that the purpose of the Seven Years' War had been to secure the Ohio Valley for them to settle. They were, therefore, just as determined to wrest the Ohio country from Indian control, as the Mingos, Shawnees, and Delawares were to keep it. This situation boiled over in 1763 to produce the Pontiac War, but even after the conclusion of that conflict these animosities continued to roil, and they would come to play an important role in both the coming of the American Revolution and the Ohio Valley Indian response to it.

INDIAN RESISTANCE IN THE WEST

Of course, the diametrically opposed attitudes of white settlers and Ohio Valley Indians placed the British government and the British army in a very precarious position. They responded to it by embarking upon a kind of Janus-faced policy that attempted to impose British sovereignty on the Ohio Valley, bring "civilization" to the Indians there, and simultaneously protect their land base from ravenous colonists intent on settling it. This policy brought with it far-reaching consequences for all involved. In fact, the changing role of the British army in the west constitutes one of the most significant and curious results of this attempt to impose sovereignty and civilization upon Indians in the Ohio Valley while simultaneously protecting them from American settlers. Having as recently as 1763 been at war with many of the Ohio country groups, the British army's mission during the latter half of the 1760s quickly transitioned to one designed to reinforce British imperial control over the region while at the same time enforcing the Proclamation of 1763 and protecting Indian land claims. Of course, key to the first of these objectives was the role of western British army forts as projections of British power and might, and no fort projected such characteristics more so than the massive Fort Pitt built on the ruins of France's Fort Duquesne. Fort Pitt was nearly ten times the size of the French fortification that had previously occupied the strategic junction of the Monongahela and Allegheny rivers. Taking up nearly 17 acres and with room to house over 1,000 troops and more than twenty artillery pieces, the fortification was truly "a symbol of dominion, an emblem of empire."[22] Yet, outposts like Fort Pitt it also served functions aimed at protecting both Indian trade and land from white colonists. In the words of one recent account of Indian/colonial relationships in the west during this period:

> For immovable structures, forts had a dynamic role to play in the system. While ensuring that colonists stayed east of the line, the system of forts, posts, and civilized pockets also created "a Barrier impenetrable to savages." Forts, in other words, enforced the line in two directions. They also served as nerve centers, tying together trade routes and through them connecting subject regions. Finally, they maintained order and the integrity of the line while keeping recalcitrant Indians at bay until the civilizing mission proved successful.[23]

Fort Pitt's history epitomizes this dynamism. Even before its completion, Ohio Valley Indians resisted it. George Croghan warned Sir William Johnson to expect resistance to the construction of Fort Pitt as early as 1759. "The Indians," warned Croghan, "are very jealous seeing a large Fort building here."[24] In 1761, Mingos, Shawnees, and Delaware warriors attempted to slow down construction on the fort by stealing the horses that performed much of the heavy labor associated with construction at that time, but these actions were not enough to prevent either the completion of the fort or the arrival of a large number of settlers, traders, and speculators in its wake.[25] In response to the influx of white colonists, many area Indians escalated their resistance to include violence. Even after Pontiac's War, Fort Pitt continued to be a focal point for warriors intent on violently resisting further English settlement of the Ohio Valley. In early 1764, for example, a group of warriors ambushed a detachment of soldiers gathering firewood in the woods near Fort Pitt, killing two of them including one that they "sclp'd, rip't open his body, and took out his heart." Another victim was "ripped up from the private parts to the throat," and "carried off by the Savages."[26] This enmity over the very presence of Fort Pitt, its garrison, and the swarms of colonists that followed it did not subside as the decade wore on. In 1770, George Croghan attempted to liquidate all of his assets in or around Fort Pitt due to his being convinced that another Indian attack similar to Pontiac's Rebellion was about to occur there.[27]

Resistance to the British occupation of the west was not just confined to the area around Fort Pitt. Major Henry Gladwin, the commanding officer of Fort Detroit complained of "the insults of those villains," the Wyandots, in 1764. Additionally, the further west one went the more volatile the relationship between the British and the area native groups became. For example, George Croghan found the Indians of Post St. Vincent's (Vincennes) in the Illinois country still under the influence of the French. They had "become one people with themselves . . . the French is continually poisoning their minds & seducing them against the English." Finally, in 1764, the conflicts in the Ohio country had become so widespread that Colonel John Bradstreet was dispatched to punish the Ohio River groups that had to that point refused to recognized British dominion over the area.[28]

Of course, while the violent resistance put up by the native people of the Ohio country may have been motivated by lingering animosities from the Pontiac War or the encouragement of French settlers in the Illinois country, the overwhelming explanation for it lay with the English themselves. The ever-increasing waves of white settlers arriving every week, the unscrupulous practices of many Indian traders, and the failure of both the British army and the British government to even recognize, let alone respect Indian sovereignty in the Ohio Valley, all combined to inflame the violent reprisals. Those reprisals did, however, affect British policy significantly. Throughout the latter half of the 1760s and into the next decade, the British government largely maintained a dedication to forcing colonists to obey the Proclamation of 1763; however, their failure to ever completely stop their colonists from encroaching on Indian lands in the Ohio Valley, along with their staunch refusal to recognize full Indian sovereignty, ensured that Ohio Indians would never fully trust them. Furthermore, each subsequent attempt to enforce the Proclamation drove the spike that much deeper into the heart of England's relationship with its colonies, particularly those which bordered the Ohio Valley.

BRITISH ATTEMPTS TO LIMIT WESTERN SETTLEMENT

The Indians of the Ohio Valley exerted extreme pressure on the British government to halt the westward movement of Virginians, Pennsylvanians, and other intrepid mid-Atlantic colonists intent on establishing themselves west of the Appalachians. Their attempts to resist tighter British control of the area such as their attempts to stop the construction of Fort Pitt caused much trepidation in London. When coupled with the fresh memory of the events of 1763, this resistance was beginning to pay dividends for groups such as the Mingos, Shawnees, and Delawares. In particular, the Pontiac War taught the British government that it possessed neither the financial nor the military strength to immediately quell another such rebellion. In light of this, King George III and many of his ministers recognized the dire need to stem westward settlement as a way of minimizing the chances of another major conflict between whites and Indians. Therefore, on multiple occasions throughout the 1760s, various organs of the British government attempted to put teeth into the Proclamation of 1763 by issuing rulings that favored Ohio Valley Indians seeking to cordon their lands off from settler encroachment. For example, the Treaty of Hard Labor, signed in 1768, gave sole possession of Kentucky to the Cherokees. Two years later, Lord Hillsborough, the King's secretary of state for the colonies, refused to agree to a Virginia House of Burgesses petition asking him to nullify that treaty. In 1774, his successor, Lord Dartmouth, prohibited Virginia veterans of the Seven Years, War from claiming bounty land grants for their service, most of which were located west of the Appalachian Mountains.[29] That same year, Parliament attempted to use a bill designed to establish a workable government in the former French colony of Quebec as a means of further discouraging colonial settlement in the Ohio Valley. The Quebec Act extended the boundaries of the province to include nearly all of the Ohio Valley. Americans wishing to violate the Proclamation and settle there would have to abide by the laws of Quebec, not Pennsylvania or Virginia. Additionally, an appointed council and governor, as opposed to a legislature in which the colonists had a voice, would make those laws. Finally, since the act permitted the free exercise of Roman Catholicism, the colonists would have to tolerate its presence in the region.[30]

Upon the introduction of the bill, Benjamin Franklin immediately seized on its possible meaning for American expansion. "I apprehend that one View of the intended Bill may be, the Discouraging of Emigrations," he wrote in March of 1774. Early in 1775, he helped Lord Chatham compose a speech in favor of reconciliation with the colonies. According to Franklin's notes, one of the primary arguments of the speech centered on the notion that Britain had a duty to look after the defense, expansion, and prosperity of the colonies. Therefore, he encouraged Chatham to argue, "the late Canada Act prevents their Extension, and may check their Prosperity."[31]

British officials in the colonies also attempted to block American settlement as well as trading abuses in the Ohio Valley. Even before Pontiac's Rebellion and the subsequent creation of the Proclamation Line, Colonel Henry Bouquet was burning squatters' cabins in an effort to demonstrate the British army's seriousness about protecting Indians from white encroachment.[32] In 1766, General Thomas Gage, now in command of all British forces in North America, blamed much of the difficulty of Indian affairs in the west on settlers, most of which originally hailed from Virginia. He made his position clear in a letter to Virginia governor Francis Fauquier. Gage wrote, "The murders which have been too frequently committed and gone unpunished, and the people settling themselves upon the lands belonging to the Indians. Its greatly feared unless some speedy and vigorous measures are taken to prevent both, will too soon involve us again in all the misery of an Indian War." Yet, despite his insistence that something be done to halt settlement and abuse of Indians by settlers and traders, Gage was largely powerless to stop it. According to historian Fred Anderson, Gage, "could do no more than take note of these impending tragedies because he was preoccupied with disorders that had erupted unexpectedly, literally outside his own front door. The disorders and riots in Boston and other eastern cities associated with the passage of the Stamp Act drew the commander in chief's attention away from the West. Hence, the latter section of this letter to Governor Fauquier simply begged him to deal with the issue. "You will best know what is most proper to be done on such occasions. I can only offer you every assistance in my power that you may have occasion for, either to apprehend and secure the murderers, or to drive the settlers off any lands belonging to the Indians which they may have taken possession of in your province." Throughout the period however, colonial governments would prove themselves at best extremely indifferent and at worst downright hostile to the notion of curbing settler activity in the Ohio Valley.[33]

In seeking to preserve Indian title to land in the Ohio country by denying settler's access to that land, the British government exposed both middling and upper-class Virginians in particular to possible financial ruin. Land represented the best avenue to obtain credit in Colonial Virginia. Since land remained the most stable form of capital, it therefore constituted the principal requirement for the attainment of credit. By depriving both upper-class land speculators and lower-class squatters from western lands, the crown set in motion a series of events that often placed Virginians at the behest of their British creditors. Therefore, Virginians began to seek ways in which they might gain access to western lands and avert financial ruin. As time wore on, they came to see independence as the best means to achieve this goal.[34] Additionally, the notion of protecting Indian rights by limiting the designs and perceived rights of whites had to have incensed white western Virginians who had already been notorious for their racial hatred of Indians for over 100 years by that point.[35]

LORD DUNMORE'S WAR

In 1774, British Indian policy in the west finally imploded in a violent clash involving Ohio Valley Indians, western settlers, and the Virginia government. The 1774 Virginia Anglo-Indian conflict known as Lord Dunmore's War was small in comparison to other similar disputes between colonists and Native Americans such as King Philip's War in 1675 to 1676 and the more recent conflict ascribed to the Ottawa leader Pontiac in 1763. These earlier clashes, and more importantly, the American Revolution itself, which broke out less than a year later, have overshadowed the fighting on the Virginia frontier. While scholars cite various combinations of precipitants and triggers to explain Lord Dunmore's War, its most immediate roots stretched back six years from its outbreak and more than 500 miles to Fort Stanwix near present-day Rome, New York.

The 1768 Treaty of Fort Stanwix, brokered between British Indian superintendent Sir William Johnson and the Six Nations of the Iroquois Confederacy in New York, effectively sold the land of the Shawnees of western Virginia out from under them. According to Native American historian Colin Calloway, the Iroquois delegates wanted "to ensure that white expansion went south, not north."[36] Neither the Shawnee nor any other southern or western tribe was party to the treaty, in which the Six Nations sold all the lands "to which the Iroquois had claim on the south side of the Ohio River as far as the mouth of the Tennessee River."[37] The Iroquois ceded land that was not theirs to dispose of in the first place. The Shawnee inhabited the land covered by the treaty. The Shawnee, like many other southern nations, had for many years recognized the Six Nations as their elder brothers. However, that recognition did not give the Iroquois Confederacy the authority to give away Shawnee land. Regardless of this, the Treaty of Fort Stanwix was justification enough for the hundreds of Virginians and Pennsylvanians who quickly began to establish claims in the area. To land-hungry colonists, it represented the all-clear signal for their planned settlement of the area that became the state of Kentucky among others. George Rogers Clark was one such colonist.

> This country was explored in 1773. A resolution was formed to make a settlement the spring following, and the mouth of the Little Kenaway was appointed the place of general rendezvous in order to descend the river from thence in a body. . . . The whole party was enrolled and determined to execute their project of forming a settlement in Kentucky, as we had every necessary store that could be thought of. [38]

Little did Clark know at the time that his proposed settlement would trigger a bloody conflict throughout the summer and fall of 1774.

According to historian C. Hale Sipe, the Treaty of Fort Stanwix was only one of three principal causes of Dunmore's War. The other two were the massacre of unarmed Indians at the mouth of Captina Creek and the murder of the family of the Mingo Chief Logan. George Rogers Clark played a direct or indirect role in each of these events.[39] In a letter written in 1798, Clark recounted the events of the spring of 1774 that led to hostilities. According to Clark, the party of settlers that he joined that spring consisted of approximately 80 or 90 men. During the journey, an unidentified group of Indians fired upon a party of hunters near the settlers' encampment. This act brought Clark and his companions to the conclusion that "the Indians were determined to war." With the intentions of the Ohio River nations supposedly clear, Clark's party instantly transformed itself from a settlement company to a militia. Clark continued, "An Indian town called Horsehead Bottom on the Sciota . . . lay nearly in our way. The determination was to cross the country and surprise it. Who was to command was the question." The settlers found their answer in another settlement group nearby commanded by Captain Michael Cresap. Cresap, a former merchant from Baltimore, had recently come west to establish a settlement near Wheeling.[40] Since Cresap had more experience with warfare than anyone in Clark's party, they decided to ask him to command their impromptu expedition. Upon hearing of their request, Cresap came at once to the campsite. According to Clark, now that their "army" had a commander, "the destruction of the Indians," would surely follow.[41]

Michael Cresap, however, seemed to be the only cool head among the group. To Clark's astonishment, Cresap did his best to dissuade the would-be raiders from harming the village. He convinced the party that even though the conduct of the nameless Indian assailants was certainly criminal, an attack on a defenseless village would undoubtedly start an all-out frontier war, and he was not about to ignite that powder keg. Instead, Cresap advised that they should all retire to Wheeling and await news from official channels as to whether or not the area tribes were indeed inclined toward war. If a war did break out, they could then join the militia units that would inevitably form to put it down. If the attack on the hunters proved to be the act of only a few individuals, then there would still be plenty of time left for them to continue with their settlement plans.[42] The party agreed to this proposal and within two hours was on its way to Wheeling. They found the settlement in a general state of uproar. Other reports of "Indian aggressions" were flooding the frontier outpost. Some of these reports might have been true, but in reality, it did not matter. Men much higher in the chain of command than either Clark or Cresap had been looking for any excuse to go to war against the Shawnee and their allies for some time and now they had it. In fact, the main architect was John Dunmore, Murray, the Fourth Earl of Dunmore, the royal governor.[43]

In 1771, Lord Dunmore had been named royal governor of Virginia, the most prestigious of colonial appointments. Dunmore's time in Virginia was relatively short and very controversial. Twice in the span of one year, he dissolved the House of Burgesses, first in 1773 for organizing a committee of correspondence, and then again a year later when the House voted to establish a day of fasting and mourning in protest of the Boston Port Bill. At this same time, Dunmore began to take steps to encourage a confrontation with the Shawnee of western Virginia and their leader, Cornstalk. It seems likely that he prosecuted the war with the Shawnee for one of two reasons or perhaps a combination of both. The first possible explanation is that he needed a diversion to draw the public's attention from the revolutionary rhetoric of Patrick Henry and his radical followers. The second is that he quite simply wanted to extend his domain even further to the west. Either way, his pursuit of settlement to the west stood in direct violation of the Proclamation of 1763, which forbade settlement beyond the headwaters of rivers flowing into the Atlantic Ocean. Of course, the Proclamation of 1763 had done very little in 11 years to stop anyone from settling wherever they wished, but it was one thing for an intrepid colonist to violate it and quite another for the representative of the crown in Virginia to set it aside.[44]

To aid in the prosecution of his plans, Dunmore appointed Dr. John Connolly, captain commandant of the district of West Augusta, of which Pittsburgh was the county seat. He also ordered Connolly to reoccupy Fort Pitt, which the King had ordered abandoned a few years earlier. Connolly not only reoccupied it, but renamed it Fort Dunmore.[45] In his capacity as captain commandant of West Augusta, Connolly provided the direction that Michael Cresap and George Rogers Clark sought in Wheeling. According to Clark, within days of their arrival they received a message from Connolly stating that a war with the Shawnee and their allies was indeed imminent. Before Cresap or Clark could respond to this first message, Connolly addressed a second letter to Cresap. This one informed them that the Indians had openly declared war and ordered him to "cover the country by scouts until the inhabitants could fortify themselves." Connolly and Dunmore did not need to say much else. Clark, Cresap, and the Virginians did the rest:

The reception of this letter was the epoch of open hostilities with the Indians. A new post was planted, a council was called and the letter read by Cresap. All the Indian traders being summoned on so important an occasion, action was had and war declared in the most solemn manner; and the same evening two scalps were brought into camp.[46]

Sometime during the last week in April, Cresap's men encountered a party of Indians in canoes on the Ohio River. They gave chase for almost 15 miles until they forced them ashore. They opened fire and wounded some of them. Either that same evening or the next day, depending on which account one consults, Cresap's men attacked an encampment of Indians at the mouth of Captina Creek killing most of them.[47]

On April 28, after the attack at Captina Creek, the party debated whether to attack the camp of the traditionally friendly Mingo Chief Logan some 30 miles up the Ohio. The majority of the men favored it, and they proceeded upriver, but during a halt 5 miles into the march, Cresap argued against such a plan. Upon Cresap's recommendation, the group then decided to call off the attack and headed for the settlement of Redstone below Fort Pitt.[48] The violence they had initiated, however, would only intensify.

By Clark's account, two days later Logan's encampment was indeed attacked with disastrous consequences. The Indians encamped with Logan at the mouth of the Yellow Creek were not hostile. Apparently Daniel Greathouse, a member of Cresap's party who had argued for the attack on Logan's camp, stayed behind with some men when Cresap and Clark left for Redstone. After the two men had departed, Greathouse and 20 men set out for Baker's Bottom, opposite the mouth of Yellow Creek. They arrived there on the evening of April 29. The next morning, Greathouse and some of his men crossed the river and invited the Indians to join them at Baker's tavern. Logan was away on a hunting trip at the time. Several Indians accepted the invitation and went to the tavern. Many of them left their guns behind. While at the tavern, 3 of the Indians got very drunk. The sober ones, including Logan's brother John Petty, "were challenged to shoot at a mark. The Indians shot first, and as soon as they had emptied their guns, Greathouse's band shot down the sober Indians in cold blood." They then quickly executed the remaining Indians, most of whom were too drunk to offer any sort of resistance. Within minutes, 10 Indians lay murdered in the tavern including Logan's mother, brother, and sister.[49]

When Logan discovered the murder of his family near Yellow Creek, he was enraged. According to one account, Logan proceeded to lead raids throughout the summer in which he collected nearly 30 scalps and prisoners.[50] Mistakenly though, Logan blamed Cresap's party for the murder of his family. He had heard that Cresap's party was in the area the day before his family was murdered and that they had attacked the encampment at Captina Creek as well. In Dunmore's report to his superiors in London, he characterized the attack on Logan's family as cruel and inhumane, yet justified it on the grounds that the Indians "had recently repeated their blows, and given too much cause for these People, not much less Savage than themselves to Justify their Sanguinary deeds."[51] The raids continued back and forth throughout May and into June until Dunmore decided that the time was right to personally lead an army west.

On October 10, after much marching and countermarching, 1,100 Virginia militia under the command of Colonel Andrew Lewis came under attack by a Native American force of nearly 1,000 strong composed of Shawnee, Mingo, and Delaware warriors. The Battle of Point Pleasant had begun in earnest. By that evening, the Indians had retreated across the river. When it was over, 3 militia officers and 66 soldiers were dead. The official total of Native American dead recovered stood at 33, but many suspected they had thrown the bodies of their wounded into the river so the actual number may have been much higher. Whatever the case, the Shawnee chief Cornstalk signed a peace treaty with Lord Dunmore in November at Chillicothe, Ohio, and the conflict ended.[52]

Any hopes that the British could maintain their self-contradictory Indian policy in the west now lay smoldering alongside the dead at Point Pleasant. Not only had individual settlers disobeyed the Proclamation of 1763 for 10 years, but the entire government of Virginia had now fought a war in violation of it. Hordes of additional settlers would surely follow in its wake, and given the rapidly deteriorating relationship between Britain and her colonies, any attempt to reestablish imperial control over settlement in the area would more than likely push colonies such as Pennsylvania and Virginia over the edge to full-scale rebellion. For the Shawnees, Delawares, and Mingos, Lord Dunmore's War was only the beginning of a decades-long conflict that would extend for much of the next 40 years as they would continue their fight to maintain control over the Ohio Valley and by extension, their lives.

5

The Revolutionary War in the South

On July 13, 1775, a committee appointed to compose an address intended to be transmitted to the principal Indian nations of North America read a draft of the document to the main body of the Second Continental Congress. Designed to blunt the influence of British Indian agents among the various native societies of the continent, the address made clear in no uncertain terms that the armed struggle then unfolding between Great Britain and her American colonies did not concern Native Americans:

Brothers and Friends!

We desire you will hear and receive what we have now told you, and that you will open a good ear and listen to what we are now going to say. This is a family quarrel between us and Old England. You Indians are not concerned in it. We don't wish you to take up the hatchet against the king's troops. We desire you to remain at home, and not join on either side, but keep the hatchet buried deep. In the name and in behalf of all our people, we ask and desire you to love peace and maintain it, and to love and sympathise with us in our troubles; that the path may be kept open with all our people and yours, to pass and repass, without molestation.[1]

Approximately one month later, John Stuart, British superintendent of Indian Affairs for the Southern Department, sent a message to the Creeks outlining the official position of the British government with respect to the role of Native Americans in the conflict. Stuart argued along similar lines that the American Revolution was likewise a whites-only struggle. "Nothing is meant by it against you or any other nation of Red People," he argued, "but to decide a Dispute amongst the white People themselves."[2] Two weeks later, Stuart echoed these sentiments in an address to the Cherokees, saying, "there is a difference between the White people of America. This is a matter which does not concern you; they will decide it amongst themselves."[3]

On this one issue at least, there seemed to be complete agreement between His Majesty's Government and the leadership of the American Revolutionary effort. The dispute between the 13 colonies and Great Britain did not concern Indians and therefore the native communities of the colonies need not concern themselves with it except insofaras they should pledge not to support the other side of that conflict. Yet, by September of 1775, the Upper and Lower Creeks as well as their Seminole kin were deeply divided about which side of the conflict to support. That same fall saw Catawba war parties patrolling the backcountry of North and South Carolina in search of British loyalists and slaves who had taken advantage of upheavals to make a bid for freedom. By July of 1776, militant Cherokees under the leadership of Dragging Canoe were launching vicious attacks on American settlements in the first blows of what would become known as the Cherokee War of 1776. Finally, by late 1777, the Chickasaws and Choctaws were patrolling the Mississippi River in order to prevent the Spanish at New Orleans from resupplying American rebels in the Ohio and Illinois countries. For a war that both combatants had made clear did not concern Indians, Indians were certainly concerning themselves.[4] In fact, Native Americans seized on the upheaval wrought by the American Revolution to advance their own particular agendas, and it was the attainment of those specific goals, unique to their particular place and time, that determined their decisions as to when, how, and with whom to engage in the conflict. Regardless of their particular decisions concerning whether to support the British, Americans, or to attempt neutrality, Southern Indians chose their respective responses to the American Revolution for their own reasons, which as often as not had little to do with the ministrations and inducements of either the Continental Congress or the British government.

CIVIL WAR AMONG THE CHEROKEES

For the militant faction of young Cherokees led by Dragging Canoe, the commencement of hostilities between American colonists and the British was fortuitous. It provided the perfect opening for them to unleash years of pent up hostility toward both land-hungry colonists and accommodationist Cherokee leaders. Obviously, such a course of action had the potential to tear at the very fabric of Cherokee society as well as at their long-standing relationship with the British. The majority of Cherokee headmen as well as the informally powerful women of the Cherokee towns counseled against such an action for fear that the result would repeat that of the Anglo-Cherokee War of 15 years before. Likewise, John Stuart, the Cherokees' main point of contact with the British government, was categorically opposed to such a course of action—at least, initially. By the early fall of 1775, however, Stuart had stopped actively discouraging Southern Indians from getting involved in the conflict. The explanation for this reversal has less to do with any change of heart or opinion on the part of Stuart himself than upon the evolving strategies of his superiors.[5] As early as June of 1775, General Thomas Gage, overall commander of His Majesty's forces in North America, wrote his superiors at Whitehall that, given the attempts by the American rebels to enlist the aid of Native Americans, the British "need not be tender of calling upon the Savages."[6] By September, Gage was ordering Stuart "when opportunity offers to make them [Indians] take up arms against His Majesty's Enemies, and to distress them all in their power, for no terms is now to be kept with them."[7] For his part, Stuart was still reluctant and resolved only to use Indian warriors as auxiliaries to regular troops rather than to encourage independent raids on frontier settlements.[8] While older Cherokee leaders were receptive to such a strategy, Stuart's newly appointed deputy, his own brother Henry, soon came face-to-face with the extent to which the generational conflict among the Cherokees over the proper course of action had doomed the superintendent's plans from the start. On a visit designed to shore up Cherokee support via the distribution of presents and trade goods including ammunition and firearms, Henry Stuart remarked that when the younger warriors of the towns received the weapons and shot it became extremely difficult for the elders to stop them from marching off immediately to use them against nearby white settlements. It was on this same visit that Stuart witnessed Dragging Canoe's defiance of his father and other Cherokee elders as he accepted the war belt offered by the visiting Shawnee emissaries (as recounted in chapter 2). By this point Henry Stuart, and by extension his brother, must have begun to realize that it would be next to impossible to limit the participation of young Cherokee warriors in the conflict to simply that of auxiliaries operating in support of overall British army strategy.[9]

If the Stuart brothers still needed convincing, the events of early July 1776 would leave no doubt in their minds about the intentions of Dragging Canoe and his followers. Throughout the previous two months, they had taken advantage of their elders' reluctance to openly join the British by feeding American representatives false information about their intentions to support the rebels' cause. According to the prominent South Carolina revolutionary Henry Laurens, "the Cherokees had amused us by the most flattering Talks, full of assurances of friendship."[10] Once this stratagem had lulled the leaders of Virginia, as well as North and South Carolina, into a false sense of security, Dragging Canoe and his warriors struck hard at frontier settlements on and around July 1, 1776. These initial attacks threw the backcountry of the Carolinas in particular into a state of mass panic and confusion. Nearly 60 South Carolina frontier residents died as the Cherokees, in the words of one South Carolinian, "spread great desolation all along the frontiers and killed a great number."[11] In North Carolina, one report cited nearly 50 miles' worth of frontier settlements were abandoned with "thirty houses burned and plantations destroyed hundreds of fields loaded with A plentiful harvest laid waste."[12]

In addition to the fact that the militant Cherokees refused to abide by either the wishes of their elders or of Stuart and his deputies, one other aspect of their campaign during the summer of 1776 supports the conclusion that their decision to participate in the American Revolutionary conflict stemmed from their own internal concerns rather than the designs of British officials. Despite initial American claims that the Cherokees spared backcountry Loyalists, much of the available evidence indicates that the Cherokees attacked backcountry settlements regardless of the sympathies of those living in them. According to one account from a Patriot sympathizer nonetheless, the Cherokees "killed the disaffected in common, without distinction of party."[13] The indiscriminate nature of these attacks further demonstrates that the primary motivation for militant Cherokee involvement in the American Revolution stemmed from a desire to arrest white land encroachment rather than a desire to preserve British control over North America.

Ironically, while Dragging Canoe's attacks during the summer of 1776 signaled to both the British and the Americans that young Cherokee warriors would forge their own path during the conflict, they also sowed the seeds of eventual Cherokee defeat. First, by shedding their neutrality and attacking colonists, Cherokee warriors provided Virginia, Georgia, North Carolina, and South Carolina, as well as the Continental Congress and its army, an excuse to launch an all-out assault on Cherokees lands and villages.[14] Second, by indiscriminately attacking both Loyalist and Whig settlers alike, the Cherokees drove many budding Loyalists into the revolutionary camp and deprived themselves of potential Loyalist allies in their own struggle. Third and finally, the refusal of the Creeks to join them dealt another serious blow to Dragging Canoe's offensive.[15]

These consequences became clear when less than a month after the initial Cherokee attacks on backcountry residents, both Loyalist and Patriot alike, launched a series of vicious counterattacks against the Cherokees—whether or not they were loyal to Dragging Canoe. With the backing of General Charles Lee, commander of the Continental Army's southern forces, militia leaders in the Carolinas and Virginia hatched a plan whereby South Carolina would mount an attack on the Lower Cherokee towns, the combined forces of the Carolinas would be turned against the Middle and Valley Cherokee villages, and Virginia would exact vengeance upon the Overhill settlements located in present-day Tennessee.[16] The first of these militias, a force of approximately 1,000 South Carolinians under the command of Colonel Andrew Williamson set out in early August. Approximately two weeks later he informed his North Carolina counterpart, General Griffith Rutherford, of his progress: "Desolation is spread over all the lower towns, and I hope we shall thro' the divine assistance, soon have the Valley and Middle Settlements in the same situation."[17] By late September Williamson and Rutherford had joined forces and their united army of 3,000 men spent two weeks devastating the Middle settlements of the Cherokee homeland. By the time William Christian and his Virginia forces reached the Overhill towns in present-day Tennessee some two weeks later, only the most militant of Dragging Canoes followers, who soon split from the Cherokees altogether, remained unwilling to surrender. By mid-November 1776, Cherokee resistance had disintegrated. In May of 1777, the Lower Cherokees signed the Treaty of Dewitt's Corner, giving away all but a sliver of their remaining land in South Carolina. In July of that year, the Overhill Cherokees followed suit and likewise relinquished all of their territory to the east of the Blue Ridge Mountains to the Virginians. All told, the Cherokee War of 1776 had cost them over 5 million acres of their territory, which included many of their most ancient and important towns. Additionally, they lost hundreds of lives to battle, hunger, and exposure to the elements. Finally, the settlement of the Cherokee War rent the very fabric of Cherokee society as Dragging Canoe and his followers, in protest over the two treaties, renounced their identity as Cherokees, moved to the area near present-day Chattanooga, Tennessee, and began to refer to themselves as Chickamaugas in honor of the creek they settled on.[18]

From their new location the Chickamaugas continued their armed resistance to the ever-advancing surge of white settlement. Dragging Canoe's warriors continued to raid frontier settlements in late 1776 and throughout 1777. In 1778 and 1779 Chickamauga forces aided the British captures of both Savannah and Augusta, Georgia.[19] Even American attacks on Chickamauga villages left undefended while the warriors were participating in the campaigns in Georgia and South Carolina during the winter of 1778 to 1779 could not dislodge Dragging Canoe and his followers from what they believed to be their sacred duty to arrest the progress of white encroachment on their lands. When Dragging Canoe returned to survey the destruction caused by troops under the command of Evan Shelby and John Montgomery, Shawnee emissaries then visiting his territory inquired as to whether or not the Chickamauga leader and his people still possessed the strength and desire to continue to resist the Americans. In reply, Dragging Canoe is said to have presented the original Shawnee war belts he had accepted in April of 1776 and remarked, "We are not yet conquered."[20]

Any hopes that the Chickamaugas may have held that their former Cherokee brethren might experience a change of heart and join them in their resistance to the Americans were also dealt a serious blow in the spring of 1779. At that time, the Cherokees reached an accord with the Delaware of the Ohio country in which they pledged not to take up arms against the Americans. For their part, these same Delaware had reached an agreement with the Continental Congress for the establishment of an Indian state with representation in the Congress of the new nation. Of course, these agreements on the part of both the Delawares and the Cherokees placed them at odds with many former allies including the Shawnees, the Chickamaugas, and the Mohawks. However, they made these decisions for the same reasons that the Shawnees, Chickamaugas, and Mohawks made their own decisions to fight. Specifically, these groups, like all native people during the American Revolution, decided whom to ally with based upon internal and localized calculations of which path would most effectively assure their people's survival and independence. That the American Revolution forced Native groups to come to divergent answers to this question epitomizes the power the conflict possessed to wreak havoc in Indian country.[21]

Despite these developments, and an outbreak of smallpox in 1779 to 1780, the Chickamaugas pressed on in their campaign to defend their homeland from American settlers while their former Cherokee kin spent most of that time divided among themselves or attempting to play both sides of the struggle against the middle. During the summer of 1780, Chickamauga warriors helped to defend Augusta against an American attempt to retake it. When the war's main theater shifted to the south during 1780, Dragging Canoe launched an ambitious campaign of raids against frontier settlements; however, Virginia governor Thomas Jefferson, convinced that the Cherokees were about to re-enter the war on the side of the British, ordered a series of blistering campaigns against the Cherokee homeland. According to one Cherokee leader who survived the attacks, Jefferson's Virginians "dyed their hands in the Blood of many of our Women and Children, burnt 17 towns, destroyed all our provisions by which we & our families were almost destroyed by famine this Spring."[22] This campaign caused shockwaves that affected the Chickamaugas as well. In the aftermath of these attacks, Virginia representatives demanded large land cessions as the price to be paid for the Cherokee disloyalty. Fearing that if they did not provide the Virginians with some tribute they would be driven completely from their own lands, the Cherokees urged the Virginians to take their payment by attacking the Chickamaugas and helping themselves to their lands instead. By the end of 1780, the Virginia campaigns against both the Cherokees and Chickamaugas had resulted in the destruction of several towns and the deaths of a considerable number in both groups.[23]

The year 1781 would provide both the high-water mark of Chickamauga resistance and also irrefutable signs that their struggle would ultimately fail. At the Battle of the Bluff near present-day Nashville, Tennessee, in April of that year, Dragging Canoe and his warriors inflicted such tremendous damage on the area's defenders that settlement in the area was largely abandoned until 1785; however, the combination of the Spanish (now allied to the Americans) capture of Mobile in 1780 and the vicious attacks of the Virginians caught the Chickamaugas in a rapidly closing vice. Pensacola fell to the Spanish just a few short months after the Chickamauga victory in the Battle of the Bluff. By August of 1781, the Americans had captured Savannah. With these three posts in the hands of their enemies, the Chickamaugas were now effectively cut off from their British allies. They were now left to face the wrath of Virginia and North Carolina militias without the benefit of British arms, ammunition, and military support. By September of 1782, another devastating American invasion of their country forced the Chickamaugas to abandon their towns and seek refuge among the Creeks.[24]

Eventually, Dragging Canoe realized that one Indian people operating independently could not hope to stem the tide of white aggression. The only viable solution for the various Indian nations to maintain their independence was to unite in an alliance against the Americans. Now living among the Upper Creeks, Dragging Canoe worked to increase his ties to the anti-American Creek leader Alexander McGillivray. Additionally, he continued to send his warriors to fight alongside the Shawnee, Choctaw, and Delaware. In January 1783, he travelled to St. Augustine, the capital of East Florida, for a summit meeting with a delegation of northern tribes, and called for a federation of Indians to oppose the Americans and their settlers. Thomas Brown, John Stuart's successor as Indian superintendent, supported the idea. At Tuckabatchee a few months later, a general council of the major southern tribes (Cherokee, Creek, Chickasaw, Choctaw, and Seminole) plus representatives of smaller groups was convened to bring the coalition into existence, but plans for the federation were cut short by the signing of the Treaty of Paris. In June, Brown received orders from London to cease all resistance to the Americans and he informed the Chickamaugas and their allies that he could no longer support their planned federation. Though his plans for a grand Indian federation in the south had failed, Dragging Canoe and his Chickamauga warriors continued their struggle against the United States well into the 1790s. But by defying traditional Cherokee leaders and insisting on armed resistance to the point of seceding from the Cherokee nation, Dragging Canoe and the Chickamaugas had already lost the battle.[25] In the words of historian Colin Calloway:

> The new Chickamauga communities were new in more ways than one, as young warriors acted free from the usual restraint of the beloved old men. Traditional ceremonies virtually ceased as the communities existed in a perpetual war alert. A social structure that had functioned for generations crumbled.

In their uncompromising defense of their Cherokee homeland, Dragging Canoe and his followers divorced themselves from critical aspects of what it meant to be Cherokee and had created an identity and towns devoid of the balance and harmony so central to Cherokee life. Even if resistance had ultimately succeeded, Indian communities still lost. In this respect the experience of the Cherokees in the Revolutionary Era epitomizes one of the many bitter truths wrought by the very existence of European colonialism and American expansion.[26]

THE REVOLUTION COMES TO CREEK COUNTRY

In the same way that the Cherokees made their decisions regarding their participation in the American Revolution based upon their own interests and considerations, the Creek Confederacy likewise approached the conflict from varying perspectives based upon the economic and political goals of the individual towns within the Creek polity, and the desires of individual Creek leaders. Not surprisingly, this rather fragmented approach resulted in a tremendous amount of division within individual Creek communities as well as the confederacy itself; however, the Creeks managed to avoid breaking apart like the Cherokees and to maintain both their sovereignty and their access to trade. The real struggle for the loyalty

of the Creeks commenced in June of 1775, when British Indian superintendent John Stuart was driven from Charleston to St. Augustine. Now too far
removed from Creek country to be able to exercise constant vigilance in
maintaining their allegiance to the crown and with the war limiting his
supply of presents and trade goods, Stuart dispatched his deputy David
Taitt with what supplies were available to encourage the Creeks to remain
within the British orbit. In similar fashion to his early messages to the
Cherokee, Stuart also encouraged the Creeks to stay out of the dispute between the crown and its rebellious American colonies.[27]

While Taitt found the leaders of the Upper Towns almost unanimously
inclined toward neutrality, he found a very different story in the Lower
Towns. Due to the recent arrival of American trade goods and gifts sent by
the South Carolina Council of Safety, American influence was greatest among
the Lower Creeks. Furthermore, Escochabey, kinsman of Ogulki, the man
whom the Lower Creeks had recently been forced to execute for murder in
order for the British to restart the flow of trade goods to the area, remained a
prominent leader among the Lower Towns and refused to meet with Stuart's
representatives. Given these factors, it is no surprise that most of the Lower
Creek headmen leaned toward supporting the Americans in 1775.[28]

Of course, just as they had with the Cherokees, the Americans also
courted the Creeks in order to sway them to neutrality and thus deprive the
British of a potential ally. In the end however, the headmen of the Lower
Towns opted for neutrality (which at the time was what both sides were
asking for) and announced that they would only accept speeches and talks
from crown representatives. However, the Lower Creeks also sent a message to both combatants which made clear that their main goal was to continue receiving supplies from both:

> We hope the path between us and you will remain white and clear,
> and as we are a poor people we hope you will help us with as much
> ammunition as you possibly can and we are determined to lye quiet and
> not meddle with the quarrel.[29]

Not long after this, the Lower Creeks seemed to experience a sudden
change of heart about their earlier pro-British stance. By the early fall of
1775, they expressed their intention to receive messengers and talks from
American officials as well as the British out of a desire to trade with both
sides. This abrupt reversal was caused by the fact that British supply failures
had rendered Stuart and his agents unable to provide the Lower Creeks
with the requisite amounts of ammunition, firearms, and other supplies
needed to see them through the coming winter. In order for their people to

survive the winter relatively intact, those deficiencies had to be made up somewhere, and the Americans represented the only other player in the game. Thus, much like other native people during the American Revolution, the Lower Creeks remained primarily concerned with maintaining access to the European goods, which had over the years become crucial to their subsistence and survival. It was this consideration that shaped their policies rather than the arguments of the combatants in the conflict.[30]

Meanwhile, the staunch British support Stuart had witnessed among the Upper Creeks earlier in 1775 was beginning to erode. Large gifts of powder and shot from the Georgia committee of safety had recently arrived there, and the Upper Towns divided into two factions over the issue of whether to accept or not.[31] At the same time the Latchaway Creeks, or Seminoles as they were increasingly known, were proving themselves quite receptive to the entreaties of Governor Tonyn of East Florida, who in defiance of Stuart was urging them to disregard neutrality and actively support the British. In fact, this particular disagreement between Stuart and Tonyn represents one of the most important steps along the path by which the Seminoles came to be an independent entity. In justifying his course of action, Tonyn and his subordinates argued that the Seminoles were in fact a separate people and not under the jurisdiction of Creek Indian agents. In an effort to solidify this position, Tonyn, made the Seminole leaders Long Warrior and the Pumpkin King "Captains of their Town and East Florida."[32] Thus, by the fall of 1774, the Upper Towns officially declared neutrality but were engaged in a bitter disagreement about which side to favor; the Lower Towns were divided in sentiment, but agreed on neutrality; and Seminoles were largely in active support of the British, a position which brought them one step closer to complete autonomy. Still, neither the Americans nor the British proved able to produce enough trade goods to meet the needs of Creek hunters and warriors who were, after all, still engaged in a bloody war with the Choctaws. Additionally, most Creeks were convinced that a victory by either side would only lead to increased pressure from both for more land cessions. This belief prevented them from completely throwing their lot in with either combatant in the fall of 1775 or even from acquiescing to the entreaties of both combatants to refuse contact with the other. However, new orders from one of John Stuart's superiors would radically change the course of events involving all Indians in the south.

On September 12, General Thomas Gage, overall commander of British forces in North America, wrote Stuart to inform him that he was altering the British military's plans for Native Americans in the fight against the American rebels. Instead of trying to keep Native Americans loyal but sidelined from the actual fighting, Gage's new orders urged Stuart to encourage the Southern Indians "to take arms against his Majesty's enemies."[33] Gage had been a proponent of employing Indians against the Americans since the earliest days of the conflict, reasoning that if the British did not enlist their aid, the Americans would. By the end of the summer of 1775, he had managed to persuade his superiors, and it finally became the official policy of the British war effort.[34]

Such a change in strategy however was not without its difficulties, particularly for the Southern Department. First, the divisions among groups such as the Cherokees and Creeks would of course have to be overcome. Next, the ongoing war between the Choctaws and Creeks, which the British had fomented in order to keep those two groups from uniting against them, would have to be ended. Finally, Stuart was still not convinced that unleashing Southern Indians on frontier settlements wouldn't simply drive undecided colonists into the revolutionary camp. In light of these concerns, he resolved to encourage Southern Indian warriors to fight only in concert with British and Loyalist troops, as opposed to indiscriminate frontier raiding.[35]

Once again, the success or failure of these efforts depended much more on the way they fit with the specific goals of particular Creek factions than on the individual merits of either the British or American causes. Among the Upper Creeks, who had always been more pro-British in their attitude, Stuart experienced little difficulty in gaining assurances from village leaders that they would send their warriors when called to do so. Despite these assurances, however, the loyalty of the Upper Creeks was not a foregone conclusion. In fact, the Americans had managed to gain some influence among the Upper Creeks through Handsome Fellow of the Okfuskee Creeks, whose loyalty had been swayed by promises from the Americans to pardon a Creek warrior accused of murder, accompanied by a large amount of presents. Meanwhile in the Lower Creek towns, Patriot influence had made even deeper inroads. Despite reassurances by Lower Creek headmen that their people were strongly in favor of the British in the dispute, most leaders among the Lower Creeks still favored neutrality. Yet Stuart, in accordance with Gage's orders and thinking that the Creeks were more fully in his camp than was actually the case, ordered a large cache of ammunition delivered to Pensacola in preparation for a large-scale effort involving Creek warriors; however, in May of 1776 he received orders from Gage to put it all on hold as the general had recently been replaced by Sir William Howe who would issue his own directives.[36] In the end, it probably worked out well for Stuart as the Creeks were already becoming quite hesitant to actively support the British. A few weeks earlier, on March 23, 1776, the headmen of all of the Lower Towns except for two sent a message to Stuart which demonstrates much less willingness on their part to take up arms in the British cause than Stuart had been counting on:

> We are now going to speak to our eldest brothers, the white people; we have heard all your talks to the red people and hope that you will hear ours. We thought that all the English people were as one people but now we hear that they have a difference amongst themselves. It is our desire that they drop their disputes and not spoil one another; as all the red people are living in friendship with one another we desire that the white people will do the same.[37]

Hardly the sentiments of a people steadfastly resolved to march off to war as British allies against the Americans.

This reluctance on the part of the Lower Creek towns to serve as British auxiliaries created ripple effects in other quarters as well. Less than a month later when Governor Patrick Tonyn of East Florida sought to enlist the aid of the Seminoles at Latchaway for a campaign against the Georgians, they refused until they could receive orders from the Lower Creeks as to how to proceed.[38] Earlier that spring no Indians showed up to defend against a rumored American attack on St. Augustine. Additionally, Lower Town representatives held conferences with the Americans at Savannah and at Augusta during this same spring of 1776. At the meeting at Augusta on May 1, American representatives George Galphin, Robert Rae, and other Georgia patriots met with pro-American Handsome Fellow and his followers who had always been anti-British, opposed to Stuart and Emisteseguo, the leader of the Upper Creek pro-British faction. The American commissioners provided them with a considerable amount of rum and delivered speeches blaming the stoppage of trade on the King and his agents. Handsome Fellow and his followers then returned to the Lower Towns fully invested in the belief that neutrality was the best option and even threatened British agents in the area. In the early summer of 1776 all short-term indicators seemed to be pointing to an Americans victory in the battle for the loyalty of the Lower Towns of the Creek Confederacy.[39]

However, over the long-term it was still very unlikely that the Creeks would support the Americans. In the words of historian David Corkran, the Creek Confederacy "was fundamentally hostile to the frontier which Augusta represented." In other words, most Creeks understood that an American victory would likely unleash an all-out assault on their lands by settlers more overwhelming and devastating than any they had previously experienced. It would therefore not take much for the pendulum to swing back in the direction of the British. Any reminder of the American frontiersmen's disregard for

Creek sovereignty, life, and land would likely dissolve all of the goodwill the Americans had built up among the Creeks during the first half of 1776. Such an event occurred when Thomas Fee, a frontiersman involved in various acts of aggression, fraud, and murder in relation to the Creeks in the past, murdered a Coweta warrior near the Ogeechee River. The murder and the failure of the Georgians to provide satisfaction for it drove the Creeks back into the orbit of the British, and by July of 1776 the Latchaways were actively aiding Governor Tonyn in repelling an American raid in East Florida. For their part, the Cowetas took their own satisfaction by killing an American settler in the same area as the murder of their townsman. The Americans would never again threaten to strip away Creek loyalty from the British.[40]

Had it not been for the disastrous Cherokee War of 1776, the Creeks might very well have committed their entire warrior base to defeating the Americans at that early stage of the Revolution; however, the example made of the Cherokees by American forces during that year had the intended effect on the Creeks. American representatives seized upon the outcome of the Cherokee war to warn the Creeks (particularly the Lower Creeks) not to abandon their official policy of neutrality. For example, American general Arthur Lee warned several Lower Creek leaders that if the Creeks went to war they would be destroyed in the same fashion as the Cherokees. While these threats were enough to force many Creek leaders to resist outright war against the Americans, the murder committed by Thomas Fee all but made active Creek support of the Americans an impossibility. The ruthless brutality with which the Americans prosecuted their response to the Cherokees did spill over and catch up many Creeks. Additionally, there was always a considerable amount of trading and military relationships between the Creeks and Cherokees based upon intermarriage and kinship. The disruption to these relationships, the death of many individuals who straddled the line between Cherokee and Creek Confederacies and the threats of Americans such as Lee kindled a desire for revenge against the frontiersmen of Virginia, the Carolinas, and other colonies in the hearts of many Creek warriors. This desire notwithstanding, as a whole the Creeks were not ready to commit themselves as a full-scale partner of either side. However, the fact that the Creeks had at least for now backed off of any thoughts of active support for the American rebels gave British superintendent John Stuart an opportunity to end the Choctaw-Creek war and hopefully bind both the Creeks and Choctaws to the British for the near future at least.[41]

Amid these favorable circumstances Stuart held a conference in October of 1776 at Pensacola for the purposes of both shoring up Southern Indian support for the British and negotiating an end to the

Choctaw-Creek conflict. To varying degrees, all parties (Upper Creeks, Lower Creeks, Latchaways as well as the Choctaws) agreed to support the British and to act in concert with one another; however, as with earlier commitments, the various Creek factions only partially fulfilled them once they returned to their villages. The reasons for this vary, but all stem from the same root cause. Not enough Creek leaders were convinced that their long-term best interests could be served by actively participating in support of one side over the other in the conflict. Some in the Lower Towns, still the least steadfast in their attachment to the British, continued to be susceptible to the machinations of American representatives like George Galphin. Additionally, American general William McIntosh had recently sent a message to the Lower Towns that an American victory was imminent and those who supported the British would be dealt with severely. Fear of frontier retaliation akin to that which was unleashed on the Cherokees kept many Lower Creeks from living up to their promises.[42] In May of 1777, Stuart's deputy David Taitt wrote East Florida governor Patrick Tonyn that until a significant British troop presence arrived in the south, these fears would continue to keep the Creeks largely on the sidelines of the fight. "The fate of the Cherokees has struck the people of this nation with such a panic that, although they have a great aversion to the rebels yet they are afraid to go against them until they hear of his Majesty's troops being at Charlestown or Savannah."[43]

In April of 1777, after months of diplomatic maneuvering had failed to bring the Creeks as a whole into active support of the British, Stuart summed up his frustrations: "The rebel agents have found means to keep up a party there [in Creek country], although not of any weight or consequence, yet sufficient to give much plague and trouble to my officers and by means of emissaries amongst the traders and packhorsemen . . . they disturb and distract the Indians with forgeries and stories calculated to excite their jealousy and give them distrust of all my measures."[44] Stuart's complaints demonstrate the enormous importance trade played in Creek decision making regarding the American Revolution. While the Americans had neither the funding nor the infrastructure to compete with the British Indian agents, as long as the war disrupted British supplies of gifts and trade goods and as long as the Americans could continue to have some trading presence in Creek country, Creek leaders could not afford to ignore them. Once again, securing their people's immediate needs, such as supplies for the winter and ammunition for spring hunting and warfare, had to take precedence over long-term considerations regarding which power, the Americans or the British, they backed. While many contemporary observers characterized the Creeks as inconstant and untrustworthy, they were simply focused on group survival above all else. As always, trade represented an absolute necessity for short-term viability.

The Americans continued to frustrate British plans for Creek involvement in the war throughout the summer of 1777 as well. On June 17, American commissioners George Galphin and Robert Rae, along with representatives of the Georgia revolutionary government, met with a large number of neutralist and openly pro-American Creeks at Ogeechee Old Town. Also in attendance were approximately 500 warriors who held the same sympathies. Over the last few months of that summer, pro-American factions attempted to kill Taitt and British deputy William McIntosh as well as the pro-British leader Emisteseguo and rise up against pro-British Creeks throughout the nation. However, pro-British Creeks uncovered the plot and, under the leadership of a young mixed-race Upper Creek from the powerful Wind clan known as Alexander McGillivray, managed to foil most of these plans despite eventually being forced to flee to Pensacola. While in the short-term the events of the late summer of 1777 seemed to indicate that the neutralist and pro-American factions were winning the day in Creek country, one particular result of the pro-American faction's attacks would prove critical to the future success of the pro-British faction. In the wake of the failed assassination against him, Emisteseguo ceded his leadership of the pro-British Creeks to McGillivray. McGillivray proved himself more than up to the immediate task of restoring the pro-British faction to power and averting an all-out civil war similar to that which the Cherokees had experienced. Over the next 15 years he would rise to become one of the most important leaders in Creek history.[45]

As it turned out, McGillivray didn't necessarily have to work too hard to bring the neutralists back into a coalition with the pro-British faction. The failure of the Americans to live up to their promises did much of the work for him. Though by the winter of 1777 to 1778 it appeared that the neutralists and by extension the Americans had won the day, their victory brought a disaster in terms of trade. They had driven the British traders away to Pensacola, and the Americans were never very reliable as trading partners. Throughout late 1777, the pro-British faction led by McGillivray repeatedly begged Stuart to reestablish British trade, but he refused until the safety of his traders could be assured. At the same time, the neutralist leaders approached Galphin and Rae for both increased trade and to urge them to stop settler encroachment. While Galphin did manage to come up with more trade goods, he did nothing to stem the tide of white settlement. In fact, he even denied that the American settlers were even supporters of the American cause. Instead, he tried to convince Creek representatives that the trespassers were actually undercover agents of John Stuart. This was to prove a critical mistake on Galphin's part. Though his delivery of the promised trade goods in February of 1778 looked like it might tip the scales toward the Americans once and for all, violence, this time perpetrated by Creeks against a group of American rangers in retaliation for illegal settlement, derailed the entire relationship, and trade with the Americans all but dried up.[46]

This most recent American failure to live up to their promises came at a most opportune time for John Stuart, Alexander McGillivray, and the British. Stuart, at the moment flush with fresh goods from England, sent traders back to Creek country and the British once again gained the upper hand in the competition for the loyalty of the Creeks. While the neutralists still retained influence, the pro-American faction was now discredited and pro-British Creeks under the leadership of McGillivray regained overall control. By late summer 1778, Creeks and Seminoles were actively defending British outposts and engaging in British/Loyalist attacks against American settlements and positions. That summer some 800 Creek warriors were operating against the Americans.[47]

Upon those warriors' return in the early fall, the Creek nation nearly devolved into civil war again as many neutralists and pro-American Creeks responded by attacking British positions near Pensacola; however, by late 1778, many American settlers had come to consider any and all Creeks as legitimate targets in retaliation for the attacks of pro-British warriors. Their indiscriminate revenge raids harmed as many pro-American and neutralist factions as they did anglophiles and therefore damaged American credibility among many Creeks who might otherwise have joined the rebels. Additionally, Galphin's inability to consistently supply the neutralist/pro-American factions put him in a tight corner from whence he was unable to adequately support those who might try to rise up against McGillivray and his pro-British warriors. While neutralist Creeks were upset with Galphin for not supplying them, American frontiersmen pressed him to allow them to attack whatever Creek towns they wished. Then in December of 1778, the British captured Savannah, and American hopes for keeping the Creeks neutral were all but dashed. Now that the British had brought the full weight of their military might to the South, the neutralist and pro-American factions had all but lost the fight for the hearts and minds of the Creeks. With Stuart's encouragement, the now ascendant pro-British Creeks began to attack the Americans on the Georgia and Carolina frontier in some of the biggest raids yet seen during the war. Despite rumors of impending joint Spanish-French campaigns against the British in the southeast throughout 1779, the majority of Creeks remained firmly attached to the British.[48]

Ironically, the high-water mark of Creek support for the British war effort may well have been the beginning of the end for the relationship between the two. Creek warriors proved indispensable to the British during the Battle of Augusta in September of 1780. However, in doing so they helped to set in motion a series of events that lessened their importance to British war aims and therefore restricted the flow of British goods to their villages. After taking Augusta, the British moved the center of their operations to Georgia and away from Pensacola as they began to focus on their upcoming, and ultimately unsuccessful, invasion of the Carolinas. With the new campaign too far afield from their territory, the Creeks would not play a role in the upcoming fighting, and with control of Georgia no longer up for grabs, the British no longer felt the need to court them with gifts and trade goods. By the spring of 1781 the Spanish seized upon this opportunity and took Pensacola on May 9. A few months later, the Creeks saw their last action of the war in defense of Savannah when the Americans besieged it during the winter of 1781 to 1782. In the final battle for the city during the summer of 1782, the longtime British ally Emisteseguo was slain while trying to fight through the American lines to the city. By this point, the Creeks found themselves cut off from trade on all sides, and the hold of the pro-British faction on Creek politics withered away with their vanishing trade. American representatives took advantage of this opening and began to make attempts to peel the Creeks away from the British. By the late spring of 1783 rumors swirled that the English planned to abandon the Creeks and leave them to be dealt with by the Americans. On November 1, 1783, Creeks, led largely by pro-American and neutralist leaders, signed a peace treaty with representatives from Georgia. In it, the Creeks agreed to pay all debts to Georgia traders, to allow trade to be regulated by Georgia, and to cede land of more than 800 square miles. However, McGillivray and the pro-British faction refused to acknowledge the agreement thus assuring more division and strife in the postwar era, which of course would only play into the hands of the Americans.[49]

THE CHICKASAW WAR FOR AUTONOMY

The Chickasaws occupied a very important place in British strategy at the outbreak of the Revolution, and the British were quite certain that Chickasaw loyalty would not be an issue. According to John Stuart, the Chickasaws as well as the Choctaws were "absolutely at our disposal." Henry Hamilton, the British commander at Detroit even planned to utilize a combined force of Chickasaws, Cherokees, and Ohio country Indians to raid American frontier settlements up and down the entire length of the

Mississippi River, though his plans never quite came to fruition. Additionally, the Chickasaws, as well as the Choctaws, were to be employed to patrol the Mississippi River to prevent the Spanish from resupplying American frontier settlements and posts in the Illinois and Ohio countries.[50]

Time and again, Stuart's confidence in the willingness of the Chickasaws to do his bidding was disappointed. In 1776, the Chickasaws, citing their oncoming hunting season, refused to patrol the Mississippi, and Spanish boats proceeded up the river unimpeded that fall and winter.[51] In early 1777, John Stuart sent his deputy and cousin Charles Stuart to investigate Chickasaw inaction. Stuart reported back that the Chickasaws were "a spoiled Nation, Proud and Insolent."[52] Stuart interpreted this to mean that the Chickasaws had come under the spell of the rebels, but there is very little evidence to support that conclusion. Instead, this response to the demands of the British was wholly consistent with Chickasaw desires for independence to live according to their long-standing desire as "a people to ourselves."[53] Their claim that to patrol the Mississippi in late 1776 would interfere with their hunting season is certainly a very plausible one. The Chickasaws did not see themselves as British minions, but rather as an independent people who would act in concert with the British only if it served their interests. In this case, hunting very possibly achieved their ends more so than patrolling the river for Spanish boats destined for locales beyond the Chickasaws' borders. To skip the hunt would mean to forego both critical food stores needed to see their people through the coming winter and fewer skins for trade. Given the problems the British were already facing securing adequate trade goods to supply groups closer to them like the Cherokees and Creeks, the Chickasaws would most certainly have known that they could not count on food and supplies sufficient to sustain them from that quarter. Additionally, they may well have experienced the same kinds of factional divisions that were at that time threatening to tear the Cherokees and Creeks apart. While the Chickasaws, unlike the Cherokees and Creeks, had always been their undivided ally, British reaction to the Chickasaws' recent retaliatory killings of some formerly French-allied Indians from the Illinois country just prior to the outbreak of the revolution had seriously damaged the relationship between the two.[54] Given the rather steadfast loyalty they later demonstrated to the British and their relative lack of demonstrated contact with American representatives, it seems more likely that the Chickasaws refused to simply go along with British plans for them due to these internal factors rather than a flirtation with support for the American rebels.

Whatever the case, Stuart decided that bringing the Chickasaws into line would be one of his top priorities for an upcoming conference to be held at Mobile in May and June of 1777. When the time for the Mobile conference arrived, only 40 Chickasaws attended. However, their reason for this poor showing and the actions of the delegation that did attend demonstrate that their own particular survival and welfare were the most important factor in their decision making. Additionally, the Chickasaws' overall inclination was strongly in favor of Great Britain. Most of the Chickasaws had stayed home to defend their territory from a rumored American invasion. The Chickasaws who attended the conference informed Stuart that their leaders "thought it prudent to remain at home to defend their country, which they were determined to do to the last extremity." Those Chickasaws in attendance, however, declared that they would "venture their lives in the cause" of the British, but also cautioned Stuart that unless he was able to ensure regular trade free of fraud and deception, the British could count on little help from them. Once again, the Chickasaws demonstrated both in word and deed that they were not auxiliaries or subjects, but instead independent people seeking what was in their best interests. For their part, Stuart and the British agreed to this stipulation, and true to their word Choctaw and Chickasaw scouting parties began stopping and searching vessels on the Mississippi River during the winter of 1777 to 1778.[55]

Even the Chickasaws' most notable failure to monitor the Mississippi River in February of 1778 proves the point that internal Chickasaw considerations determined their behavior. At that time many of the Chickasaws and Choctaws who were patrolling the river abruptly left their posts and went back to their villages. Not long after, Captain James Willing and a flotilla of frontier militia troops sailed down the river and attacked Loyalist settlements in West Florida.[56] Stuart was incensed. "Had the Chickasaws done what was required of them we might have had earlier intelligence of this invasion," he complained.[57] From their perspective, however, the Chickasaws were perfectly justified in their abandonment of the Mississippi River patrols that February. First, the Choctaws had left because they were expecting to be relieved by another Choctaw party any day. Therefore when the Chickasaws withdrew, they left believing it was safe to do so because the Choctaw relief party would still be monitoring the river. Second, and most important, the Chickasaws would watch the Mississippi as long as it did not conflict with other priorities. They left their posts along the Mississippi River that winter because the Quapaws, their allies, had requested their assistance in a war with the Osages on the western side of the river. So the warriors who had been watching the Mississippi left it to participate in war parties in support of the Quapaws. In their estimation, supporting their allies in the war against the Osages took precedence over protecting white settlers in West Florida, and as we have seen, they thought the Choctaw relief party was on its way. In reality, it did not arrive until after Willing's expedition had already done its damage.[58]

In April of 1778, shortages of trade goods made it nearly impossible for Charles Stuart to rouse the Chickasaws to further action. In a letter to his superiors at Whitehall, John Stuart blamed traders who were attempting to convince the Chickasaws to stay home. According to Stuart, these traders were convinced that if the Chickasaws went to war their (the traders') business would suffer. Though Stuart did mention in his dispatch that Chickasaw towns were vulnerable to attacks by rebels, particularly if the majority of the warriors left to fight for the British, he opted to blame the traders instead. Such an explanation only provides more proof that Stuart's failure to truly understand Chickasaw motivations represented perhaps the biggest obstacle to the Anglo-Chickasaw relationship. Additionally, Stuart also mentioned a conversation he had with the Chickasaw leader Paya Mataha in which Paya Mataha revealed that he could not bring himself to simply declare his neighbors enemies. Those neighbors had lived near the Chickasaws for some time now and traded with them in relative peace. Furthermore, he was also apprehensive of killing Loyalists by mistake. Whether or not this statement was actually representative of Paya Mataha's, and by extension the Chicksaws', feelings was then and is today a matter of debate. Governor Peter Chester of West Florida did not believe it at all and thought it simply a cover for disloyalty. However, Stuart himself remarked that Paya Mataha's reasons for Chickasaw reluctance "could not fail of impressing me with a very high esteem and respect for his character," and personally guaranteed the Chickasaw involvement in combat with Americans would be limited to defending the area against invading American forces.[59]

It is possible that the growing influence of the Spanish, who had not by this point officially entered the conflict but had been operating behind the scenes against the British for quite some time, may represent one possible explanation for Paya Mataha's reluctance to fight the Americans. Stuart himself expressed concern that Spanish agents were actively seeking to win the allegiance of groups such as the Chickasaws. During 1778, he took steps to counteract these efforts by ordering that increased gifts and trade goods be sent to the Chickasaws. His efforts seem to have worked, as later that year the American general George Rogers Clark reported that all of his Indian recruiting efforts had amounted to nothing.[60] In late 1778, the Chickasaws along with their Choctaw allies were still patrolling the Mississippi for the British, and Stuart was justifying the large expenditures in gifts and trade goods it took to keep them doing so. "We have not been able to do without them," he wrote to one of his superiors at the time. Despite Paya Mataha's reticence earlier in the year, the Chickasaws were still firmly in support of the British.[61]

Even John Stuart's death in March of 1779 failed to alter the Chickasaws' belief that their long-term interests were better served by supporting the British over the Americans, the French, or the Spanish. That same month they sent a message to the Spanish in which they upbraided them for, among other things "sending bad Talks to the Chactaws endeavoring to set them against us & our friends the English." The message went on to compare the Spanish to the Chickasaws' former enemy the French and to deliver a rather direct threat to the Spanish should they continue to behave in this manner. "Therefore shou'd We lose any of our People in their hunting grounds by your red people We shall not go to them for redress as We know from what quarter to take Satisfaction in."[62]

Two months later as Chickasaw warriors prepared to head north to join in a campaign with Henry Hamilton's Northern Indian allies, they received a message from Virginia offering them one last chance for peace and threatening their destruction should they not accept. The Chickasaw response is not only entertaining, but also enlightening. In addition to taunting the Virginians, their disappointment in the Americans' decision to ally with the French speaks to a very powerful reason for the Chickasaws' refusal to support the American cause.

> We desire no other friendship of you but only desire you will inform us when you are Comeing and we will save you the trouble of Coming quite here for we will meet you half Way, for we have heard so much of it that it makes our heads Ach, Take care that we don't serve you as we have served the French before with all their Indians, send you back without your heads.[63]

By framing their response to the Virginians in this way, the Chickasaws once again demonstrated that they were interpreting the conflict not necessarily in the way the British wanted them to, but from their own perspective. At that particular juncture their end goals aligned with those of the British. This alignment at this point seems to have stemmed more from hatred of the French than a love for the British or a desire to be subject to the British.

Just as it did for other native communities in the southeast, Spain's declaration of war against Britain in June of 1779 brought new challenges for the Chickasaws. Spanish agents redoubled their efforts to win the allegiance of the Southeastern Indian groups, and many British leaders feared they would lose many of their Indian allies. However, British attitudes regarding their chances of losing the friendship of the Chickasaws are quite revealing. Most British officials considered that possibility highly unlikely, and their reason for believing so only underscores the idea that the Chickasaws had allied themselves with the British because they believed it the surest way of maintaining their independence. The British based their assessment of their high chances of retaining the Chickasaws as an ally on the Chickasaws' long-standing insistence on supporting themselves via their traditional hunts rather than on British trade goods. While they certainly engaged in trade with the British, they had not let it erode their traditional subsistence practices in the same fashion as other Southeastern groups. Therefore, it would take more than trinkets and enticements to bring them to support the Spanish. They would instead have to be convinced that their long-term prospects for living as a free and independent people could be best served by supporting Spain. Despite their best efforts, Spanish envoys failed to make that argument.[64]

If the Chickasaws had been even slightly inclined to ally with the Spanish, the actions of the Americans during this period burned many of the bridges they had attempted to build with the Chickasaws earlier in the war. For example, in January of 1780 Virginia governor Thomas Jefferson entertained the idea of enlisting the Kickapoos, one of the Chickasaws' traditional enemies, against them. During that same year he also ordered the construction of Fort Jefferson on Chickasaw land, five miles below the junction of the Ohio and Mississippi. The Chickasaws responded by launching repeated attacks against the fort, and it was abandoned in June of 1781, a little more than a year after it was built. If the Americans had held out any hopes of drawing the Chickasaws away from the British, Jefferson's actions all but destroyed them. Throughout the rest of the war the Chickasaws remained in the British camp and staunchly resisted efforts by Spain and France to entice them away. In addition, they carried on small-scale warfare against the native peoples allied to Spain and France as well as against Patriot settlements, and chastised groups like the Choctaws who seemed to stray from the British fold.[65]

However, by the spring of 1781 the British war effort in America was crumbling and with it went their ability to convince nations like the Chickasaws that their best interests lay in an alliance with the King. Furthermore, the British case was hindered by General John Campbell's attitude during the defense of Pensacola in February of that year. By treating the Southeastern Indians as subjects and not as allies, he completely alienated them. By May, of the nearly 800 Chickasaws who had defended Pensacola in February, only 6 still remained. Not surprisingly,

Pensacola fell to the Spanish in May of 1781. According to one report, Campbell treated Indians as if "they could be used like slaves or a people devoid of natural sense."[66] In the wake of the surrender at Yorktown, British supplies and trade goods now dried up and the rationale for supporting the British was gone. They could no longer guarantee Chickasaw independence. In the words of historian Colin Calloway, "the Chickasaws had no intention of tamely transferring allegiance to the new masters of West Florida, but it was the beginning of a new era. Chickasaw leaders took stock of the new situation and increasingly shaped their foreign policies in response to Spanish and American, rather than British, initiatives." Very quickly a new struggle over the lower Mississippi developed between Spain and the United States, and the new strategy for the Chickasaws was to play them off against one another. The success of this strategy would determine whether or not the Chickasaws could continue to live as an independent people under the new conditions created by the victory of the American Republic.[67]

CHOCTAW CALCULATIONS

In early 1777, John Stuart sent his deputy and cousin Charles Stuart to investigate why the Choctaws had to that point refused to take action against the American rebels. Charles Stuart reported back to the superintendent that the Choctaws were overcome by drunkenness and refused to do anything until the Chickasaws first acted.[68] Such reluctance to act on the part of the Choctaws must have come as at least a mild surprise to Stuart and other British leaders. Just weeks before they had counted on help from the Choctaws as a given when sizing up the measures to be taken for the coming campaign in the south. General William Howe expressed as much to Superintendent Stuart in a letter dated January 13, 1777:

> The friendly disposition of the Creeks and Choctaws will I hope put it in your power to engage them heartily in the interests of those colonies, and when it is known upon what conditions war or peace with the Indians does depend, I am apt to think the southern colonies, though in rebellion, will not hesitate to determine for the attainment of the latter. [69]

More than likely, the remaining bitterness over the British role in the Choctaw-Creek war, the tension then existing between the Chickasaws and the British, and the relatively brief span of their own relationship with the British account for the hesitancy of the Choctaws in the early phases of the war. Whatever the case, his cousin's report convinced Stuart that he would have to personally engage in diplomacy with the Choctaws and Chickasaws if he was going to use them in the manner that British war planners had initially envisioned. He therefore held a meeting with both groups in May and June of 1777 at Mobile. The meeting paid dividends as both the Choctaws and Chickasaws left it having agreed to patrol the Mississippi River on behalf of the British in return for trade goods.[70] As we know, the Choctaws were partially culpable for allowing James Willing's expedition to slip down the Mississippi and attack West Florida in February of 1778; however, they, like the Chickasaws honestly believed that a relief party was imminent and so felt justified in leaving their position. Additionally, Choctaw actions over the ensuing months left little doubt that at least for the moment, the Choctaws preferred to support the British. Whether this stemmed from an actual affinity for them or simply from a disinclination toward the Americans remains a matter open to debate. According to historian Greg O'Brien, when the Choctaws realized that the Willing expedition had suceeded, the Choctaws ardently threw themselves into the defense of Natchez and were instrumental in convincing the residents there to remain loyal to the British.[71]

Despite this very important and impressive action which may well have saved West Florida from succumbing to the Americans, the British could never completely count on absolute Choctaw loyalty. Throughout 1779, the British held multiple conferences with the Choctaws (more than with any other Southeastern group during this period), at which they distributed thousands of guns as well as other supplies. Clearly, the British saw Choctaw commitment as a questionable proposition at best. However, there exists no evidence of any inclination on the part of the Choctaws to engage in diplomacy, let alone an alliance with the American rebels. This, coupled with the importance of continual gift exchange in maintaining native alliances in colonial America, supports the conclusion that these gifts from the British might not necessarily indicate Choctaw sympathy with the American cause. After all, nearly 250 Choctaws rushed to the defense of Pensacola in late 1779; however, other developments dating back to 1778 and throughout 1779 point to an alternative explanation.[72]

On March 21, 1779, John Stuart died. Given that his personal relationships with many of the most influential Southern Indian leaders had been instrumental in garnering their support for the British against the American rebels, his death placed the entire question of Southern Indian support in a state of uncertainty. While no Southern Indian group seemed likely to run out and ally with the Americans simply due to Stuart's passing, his absence and more importantly the success or failure of his replacement, could at best make maintaining their active support more difficult. Failure on the part of his replacement could drive many Southern groups to choose neutrality. For the Choctaws, however, Stuart's death, now compounded by the official entry of the Spanish into the war almost exactly three weeks later, held the potential to seriously alter the equation. The Choctaws had always been a very factionalized polity with certain towns favoring the Spanish, others the British, and still others the French. Now that the French and Spanish had officially allied with one another via the April 1779 signing of the Treaty of Aranjuez, the Francophile, and Hispanophile factions among the Choctaws, if they so desired, could now overwhelm those who favored continued alliance with the British.[73]

Once again, according to O'Brien, this development reignited factionalist division among the Choctaws. "Choctaw people had always constructed relationships with as many European entities as possible to get access to trade and enhance their status." Furthermore, "Choctaws never allowed themselves to become so devoted to either the cause of Britain or Spain that they would spill the blood of other Choctaws." The unique placement of the Choctaws at a strategic location between the French, the Spanish, and other native groups such as the Chickasaws lent itself to a strategy of playing the various European powers off against one another to achieve their ends, just as had the Iroquois and the Creeks. Additionally, like the Iroquois and Creeks, Choctaw political authority was decentralized, with decision-making power located among three divisions, one in the east, another in the west, and another known as the Six Towns division located in the southern portion of their territory. Political authority was further dispersed among the individual towns of those divisions. Therefore, decisions about whom to support were made at the town level. So it was entirely possible for one town to support one side in the conflict and another town to support the other. Thus, even before the Spanish entry into the war, Choctaws could be found aiding all sides, but in general the Western and Eastern division leaders and warriors tended to support the British while the Six Towns tended to side with the Spanish.[74]

By June of 1780, such volatility in the level of Choctaw support for the British war effort led one British official to characterize them as "the most mercenary of Indians," but in this respect, the Choctaws were no different than the Chickasaws or any other Native American community caught in the crossfire between the British and their rebellious colonists. The Choctaws' calculations about what was best for their own people led them to a different conclusion than the Chickasaws, but the motivation was the same.[75]

The entry of the Spanish into the war exposed the disastrous inability of the British to grasp the fundamental reasoning that motivated the participation of Southeastern Indian groups in the American Revolution. Officials such as the author of the "mercenary" quote cited above and Major

General John Campbell, overall commander of British forces in West Florida, and even the late John Stuart often responded in the worst possible way to the ebbs and flows of Choctaw participation in the war. What they never understood was that "the American Revolution was not a Choctaw fight . . . as a group they harbored no blind allegiance or ideological commitment to either side."[76] Instead as a group of Choctaw leaders informed one British Indian agent November of 1779, "two people loves us whoever gives us the most will be the most regarded So I would advise you to give presents superior to the Spaniards."[77] In short, the Choctaws would decide for themselves which side could offer them the best opportunity to increase their own trade and prestige and provide them the best chance of securing their future as a people.

The fall of Mobile to the Spanish in March of 1780 was the beginning of the end for the British-Choctaw alliance. The Six Towns division, located near Mobile and already leaning toward open alliance with the Spanish, could now openly throw their support behind them. British officials met with little success when sent there in August 1780 to try and ensure the loyalty of the Six Towns division. The Spanish now represented the most reliable source of European goods. Additionally, the Spanish often treated the Choctaws with much more respect and accorded Choctaw leaders the status they felt they deserved as allies. These two elements meant the British would never be able to count on a united Choctaw ally. With Stuart dead and Campbell now in overall command, the British suddenly lost the ability to compete due to the shortages caused by their declining fortunes in the war. In fact, not long after the fall of Mobile, Six Towns Choctaws were being dispatched by the Spanish to assassinate British officials in the area. Choctaws from the Western and Eastern divisions who were still loyal to the British had neither the arms nor the ammunition to oppose the Spanish and their Six Towns allies. Even if they had the materiel on hand, many Western and Eastern division Choctaws were unwilling to do so. Being a people among whom regular gift exchange served as a barometer of the esteem in which one's trading partners held one, the Choctaws were quite disturbed at the inability of the British to supply them in the fashion to which they had become accustomed.[78]

Then in August of 1780 a group of British-allied Choctaws from the Eastern division killed and scalped several Spanish soldiers, who had been awaiting escort under a flag of truce to deliver messages from Spanish officials to the British at Pensacola. In doing so, the Choctaws had violated the European rules of warfare. Of course, the Choctaws in question were not aware of these conventions regarding the conduct of war. Had they been, they still would not have felt bound by them. Campbell was incensed by the incident because of the difficulties it created with the Spanish. Needing to distance himself from these acts in order to avoid reprisals by the Spanish and their allies, Campbell and Indian agent Alexander Cameron upbraided the Choctaw leader of the party, Mingo Pouscouche. The Choctaw leader reacted angrily and defended his actions, saying that he had been trying to take the Spaniards captive in accordance with British directives and only killed them when they wounded some of his men.[79]

In the end, the incident eventually blew over, but as a result Campbell became even more distrustful of Native Americans and stated as much in September of 1780: "I sincerely regret the Necessity of ever employing Savages, or being obliged to court them to War." For their part, British-allied Choctaws become even more zealous to prove their loyalty and therefore stepped up their patrols, which only led to further incidents. In October of 1780, another Choctaw party raided a French plantation near Mobile Bay, killing 3 and capturing 14 others. As all of the casualties were noncombatants, Campbell and the other British leaders were once again unhappy with their Choctaw allies. In the meantime, Cameron and Campbell had begun to argue often about Campbell's unwillingness to even recognize, much less abide by, Indian customs. For his part, Cameron argued for the necessity of constant gifts for the Choctaws as a way to ensure their loyalty, but by November, Campbell had cut off gift exchanges with Native Americans completely. He refused even to provide arms and ammunition to those Choctaw raiding parties still out fighting the Spanish and their allies. Campbell only restored gift giving a few weeks later when it became obvious that the Spanish were moving against Pensacola, and he reluctantly acknowledged the need for Choctaw allies in defending it.[80]

Spanish forces finally besieged Pensacola in March of 1781. When the Spanish arrived nearly 1,000 Indians defended Pensacola, as much as 800 of which were Eastern and Western division Choctaws. Despite this, Campbell still refused to adequately provision or supply them. By the end of March, Choctaw leader Franchimastabe had reached the end of his rope. In a speech to Cameron, he complained of a lack of support from the British military and demanded to be shown the proper respect as an ally in terms of gift exchange. Without such gifts and the respect they brought, a chief such as he could not hope to convince his young warriors to follow him to battle. When it became clear that the British would not be able to produce the gifts, Franchimastabe left on April 1. Despite the presence of some remaining Choctaws throughout the rest of April and early May, Pensacola surrendered to the Spanish on May 10, 1781. British control of West Florida was now finished, and the Choctaws moved on to establish relationships with the Spanish and later the Americans.[81]

CATAWBA ALLIES

Unlike many other Southern Indian peoples, the Catawbas of North and South Carolina had very little choice regarding with whom to ally themselves during the American Revolution. Perceiving that their best chance for continued existence after the Seven Years' War lay in allying themselves closely to the nearest and most immediate power, in this case the Carolinas, the Catawbas were one of the few groups whose loyalty was for the most part unwavering during the chaotic early phases of the American Revolution. Southern Indian superintendent John Stuart realized this very early on in the conflict. "They are domiciliated and dispersed thro' the Settlements of north and South Carolina," he wrote in September of 1775. Therefore, it was "no wonder that they should be practised upon and seduced by the Inhabitants with whom they live," he concluded.[82] Stuart's explanation that Catawba adherence to the American cause stemmed simply from their susceptibility to the machinations of Carolina rebel emissaries fails to acknowledge the agency of the Catawbas themselves. While, in the grand scheme of things, the Catawbas contributed little to the overall American victory, their willingness to make great sacrifices for the American cause brought them tangible rewards in the immediate aftermath of the conflict and an enduring place in the commemoration of the Revolution in the Carolinas. They became an integral part of the myth of the Revolution in the Carolinas and in so doing gained an opportunity to influence not only the postwar state, but also the memory of the creation of that state.

In July of 1775, the Catawbas sent two emissaries to Charleston to learn firsthand about the dispute between the colonists and the British. The local Charleston Committee of Safety received them and presented them their version of events. When the Catawba diplomats left Charleston, the Committee of Safety also provided them letters to spread throughout the rest of the nation. According to historian James Merrell, "The talk summarized the colonists' grievances, [and] reminded [the] Catawbas of their long friendship with South Carolina." The Carolinians pledged that the Catawbas would enjoy a lucrative trade with the Americans and that individual Indians who fought would be paid for such service. The talk contained a warning in case the Catawbas refused to go along: "If you do not mind what we say, you will be sorry for it by and by." It did not take long for the Catawbas to send word to Charleston of their intention to support the rebellion.[83]

By the fall of 1775, a force of 40 Catawbas was regularly patrolling for loyalists and runaway slaves. The following spring, Catawba warriors joined Carolina troops in the war against the Cherokees. By war's end they had served in various engagements throughout the state as well as in engagements against British general Charles Cornwallis's southern invasion in Georgia and North Carolina including service under American commander Nathanael Greene at Guilford Courthouse.[84]

When the British captured Charleston in May of 1780, scattered South Carolina rebel forces under the command of Thomas Sumter selected the principal Catawba settlement of Catawba Old Town, in what is today southern North Carolina, as their July rendezvous point. Upon arriving there, they were provided food, corn, and cattle by the Catawbas, despite the fact that only one month previously British forces under Francis Rawdon had destroyed a large portion of the Catawbas villages, fields, and livestock, forcing many Catawbas to seek refuge in Virginia. Upon their return after the British surrender in 1781, they were faced with the monumental task of rebuilding their nation. They would not do so alone. In return for the Catawbas' willingness to fight alongside the Americans, South Carolina provided both funds and desperately needed corn to aid the rebuilding effort. Catawba participation in the Revolutionary War had earned for them, at least in the short-term, a place of honor in the remembrances of the struggle. Once again, according to James Merrell, "The Catawba warriors' travels all over the South and Sumter's decision to make the reservation his headquarters acquainted hundreds, even thousands, of settlers and solders with the Indians' devotion to the United States."[85] Much like other large and more well-known Southern Indian groups, the Catawbas seized upon the upheaval wrought by the American Revolution to advance their own particular goals, and it was the attainment of those desires unique to their particular place and time that determined their decisions as to when, how, and with whom to engage in the conflict.

6

The Revolutionary War in the North

On January 19, 1777, an Oneida messenger arrived at Fort Schuyler (formerly known as Fort Stanwix, but renamed in honor of the New York Patriot leader in 1776) near present-day Rome, New York, bearing distressing news. The message he carried to the fort's commander from a group of Oneida chiefs recounted the results of a recent epidemic at the Iroquois capital of Onondaga. Ninety Onondaga villagers had succumbed to the epidemic, including three sachems. Beyond the multiple deaths, the disease outbreak claimed one other symbolic victim: the Great Council Fire, which served as the symbolic representation of the unity of the Six Nations of the Iroquois. While this was not the first time the Great Council Fire had been extinguished, the impact of this news must have been taken as an ominous sign. Unlike previous occasions upon which the fire was raked out, this instance occurred against the backdrop of the actual disintegration of the confederacy.[1] The coming summer of 1777 would see Oneida and Tuscarora warriors engage in a bloody battle with their Mohawk and Seneca cousins, thus confirming the worst fears of those who interpreted the extinguishing of the Great Council Fire at Onondaga as an evil omen.

The experience of the Iroquois as well as other Northern Indian peoples epitomizes the very perilous situation the American Revolution created for many native communities. In the cases of the Western Abenakis, the praying Indians of Stockbridge, and the Six Nations of the Iroquois Confederacy, all of the options available to them led to disastrous consequences. Regardless of the eventual outcome, however, each and every native community in the northern colonies made its decisions regarding the Revolutionary War for reasons specific to its own situation and for the purpose of ensuring its own survival.

WESTERN ABENAKI SURVIVAL

To the outside observer the actions of the Western Abenakis of Vermont during the American Revolution appear contradictory and rather inconstant; however, a closer examination reveals the cultural foundation that underlay their seemingly contradictory response. While they would have preferred neutrality, the very early emergence of their homeland as a major theater of operations precluded that possibility. Instead, various groups of Abenakis could be found fighting on both sides of the conflict, and in some cases particular individuals found themselves traversing back and forth between the Americans the British as circumstances dictated.[2] As early as August of 1775 an Abenaki chief named Swashan arrived at American commander in chief George Washington's headquarters in Cambridge, Massachusetts, pledging "half his tribe if they were wanted" for the American cause. Later that year, Abenakis from the village of St. Francis in Southern Quebec served as guides for Benedict Arnold in his invasion of Canada. At the same time however, Sir Guy Carleton included many Abenakis among the defenders he dispatched to both St. Johns and Quebec.[3] What accounts for this seemingly schizophrenic response to the conflict among the Abenakis? To many on both sides this must have been taken as proof that Indians could not be counted on to honor their pledges of support; however, as we have seen earlier, the Western Abenaki were an extremely decentralized polity. Therefore, individual family bands and villages were free to chart their own course through the turbulent years of the Revolutionary War. Given what we now understand regarding their political structure, it is no surprise that they could be found aiding all sides in the conflict.

Ultimately, Arnold's invasion of Canada faltered at Quebec, and with that failure, settlers along New England's northern borderland expected any day to suffer "the ravages of the Canadians and Indians."[4] The refusal of Western Abenakis to exploit this seemingly golden opportunity to rid themselves of encroaching settlers speaks volumes about the Abenaki approach to the conflict. In short, it was not their fight. Their most important goal was survival, and the safest way to ensure it was to avoid conflict if at all possible and only to serve the war effort of either side if left with absolutely no other choice. Regardless of Abenaki motivations for showing restraint, their refusal to attack now undefended American settlements in New England led many rebels to see them as useful in that they could serve as a buffer zone between the border settlements and the more openly British-allied Indians operating out of Canada. In fact, the combination of invitations by New England settlers to draw closer and intense British pressure to fight drove many Abenakis to leave southern Quebec and relocate closer to the American settlements of New England. By the winter of 1776 to 1777 it looked as if the Western Abenakis may have found a way to avoid fighting for either side without engendering the ire of either the Americans or the British. From the American perspective, the Abenakis living between their villages and the Canada border were providing a useful barrier, thus eliminating the need to evacuate the entire Northern New England frontier during the war. From the British perspective, while they might not be happy that the Abenakis had refused their demands that they place their warriors at the disposal of the British army, at least they weren't actively serving as auxiliaries for the Americans either. But 1777 brought a new British campaign, and with it came new challenges for the Abenakis from both sides of the conflict.

During the spring and summer of 1777, the British used coercion as well as gift exchange to enlist hundreds of Abenakis in support of General John Burgoyne's campaign in western New York. One Abenaki family who had fled Canada rather than be forced to fight complained that the British were withholding basic supplies such as blankets and powder if Indians did not first agree to serve Burgoyne's army.[6] According to historian Colin Calloway, despite knowledge of these coercive practices, Americans began to view even the friendly Abenakis whom they had invited to settle in their midst with suspicion, especially after Burgoyne's defeat at Saratoga and the murder of American settler Jane McCrea in New York:

> Burgoyne's employment of Indian allies as a psychological weapon, and the Patriots' propagandizing of the Indian murder of Jane McCrea, hardly encouraged the Americans to look favorably on the Abenakis in and around the Champlain Valley, especially since Abenakis from St. Francis had joined Burgoyne's army.[7]

In the end, anger over what they considered poor treatment by Quebec governor Guy Carleton, who had reportedly threatened them during the Saratoga campaign, outweighed Abenaki concerns about the suspicions with which New Englanders viewed them. Many more Abenakis now came to live near the upper Connecticut River settlements. The decentralized nature of Abenaki decision making, as well as British mistreatment and the American policy of bringing the Abenakis closer while still questioning their loyalty makes it very difficult to determine just whose side the Western Abenakis were on in 1777 and 1778. The key to understanding Abenaki loyalty during this period was the same as ever. Whichever option provided the best hope for both the short- and long-term security of their people would more often than not represent the option chosen.[8]

One particular Abenaki leader exemplified the way in which Abenakis attempted to navigate this tangled web of shifting loyalties and ever-changing alliances. Joseph Louis Gill, a principal chief of the village of St. Francis, had harbored an intense hatred for the British ever since Robert Rogers and his rangers had destroyed St. Francis in the waning days of the Seven Years' War as punishment for the Abenakis' support for the French. Gill had lost his wife and children in Rogers' raid, and so therefore was already inclined toward the Patriots when the American Revolution broke out. But as the war dragged on, Gill did not allow his anger to shut him off from possibilities to further his village and his people's interests by lending support to the British. In the early spring of 1780, Gill was rewarded by the Americans with a major's commission for his service to the revolutionary effort.[9] Six months later, when presented with the promise of a full pardon by the King for his activities, Gill took an oath of loyalty to the British, even while he still continued his dalliance with the Americans. Later, when he felt the British were starting to lose faith in him, he led a daring raid that captured American major Benjamin Whitcomb. But once Gill reportedly extracted a promise from Whitcomb that St. Francis would be spared in any upcoming American operations, Gill conveniently let his prisoner escape.[10] Gill's behavior perfectly demonstrates the shifting loyalties so prevalent in this region, but it also provides an excellent reminder of what Indians were fighting for: simple survival.

As if Gill's own divided loyalties and ulterior motives did not inject enough confusion into the situation among the Abenakis, the British decision to permanently station an officer at St. Francis created even more uncertainty. In 1778, British lieutenant Wills Crofts of the 34th Regiment was sent to live among the Abenakis at St. Francis with orders to organize them into scouting parties. His presence there over the next two years would serve to divide the village even further.[11]

Beyond those Abenakis who did choose a side in the war, those who attempted to remain neutral also suffered. Because they were viewed with suspicion by both sides, they often found themselves welcome nowhere.

What's more, no matter what decision Abenakis made, the war seriously disrupted their subsistence cycle, with planting and hunting often neglected and trade from both the Americans and the British erratic at best. The last two years of the war brought even more confusion. In 1780, Crofts was accused of involvement in the death of a chief at St. Francis, and the British were forced to recall him in order to quell the disturbance. Meanwhile, St. Francis Abenakis continued to raid American settlements at the behest of the British, while at the same time feeding the Americans some of their best intelligence regarding the movement and troop strength of the British. Once again, from their point of view, the Abenakis did not see this behavior as duplicitous. Different Abenakis engaged in these activities for their own reasons based on their own personal calculations regarding what was best for them and their people. Needless to say, the eventual victors of the war did not see it that way. Unlike other groups who had aided the Americans, the Western Abenakis received no rewards for their service to the Patriots' cause. Worse yet, the Peace of Paris cut the Western Abenaki homeland in two: St. Francis was included as part of the new United States, while the other principal Abenaki village, Misisquoi, was ceded to the British in Canada. According to Calloway, despite the Abenakis' best intentions to preserve their land base and their autonomy, the American Revolution instead brought them to the brink of collapse.

PRAYING INDIANS AS PATRIOT SOLDIERS: THE CASE OF THE STOCKBRIDGE

Even before the actual outbreak of hostilities, Stockbridge Indians were serving not only as enlisted men, but also as officers in area militia companies. In February of 1775, the Massachusetts Provincial Congress offered gifts to area indians as an inducement to enlistment. One month later, the Continental Congress itself officially welcomed the services of the Stockbridge Indians, 17 of whom joined Washington's army at Cambridge later that spring. It was the employment of these very Stockbridge Indians that triggered British commander Thomas Gage to issue the letter to Southern Indian superintendent John Stuart (excerpted earlier in this volume), which authorized the unlimited use of Indian allies in the conflict.[12]

Early on, the Stockbridge made their greatest contributions in the area of diplomacy with other Indian peoples. Various Stockbridge emissaries took the Americans' message to the member groups of the Six Nations as well as to the Indian communities of Canada, the Shawnees, and the Delawares. At the Treaty of Albany in 1775, Stockbridge representatives went so far as to disobey the Mohawks, whom they had to that point regarded as their elder brothers in the Covenant Chain, and pledge their unwavering support to the American rebels. In the words of Captain Solomon, one of the Stockbridge representatives at the meeting, "wherever you go we will be by your Side our Bones shall lay with yours." By August of 1776, Congress had authorized General Washington to organize whole companies of Stockbridge Indians who would wear red and blue caps to distinguish them from enemy Indians.[13]

Given that Stockbridge, which had come into existence as a community for praying Indians and the clergy attending them, was increasingly being taken over by white land speculators and residents moving in from other New England locales, it seems quite surprising that the Stockbridge Indians would so fully commit themselves to supporting the Americans. While there seems to be no definitive answer to this question, the combination of their religious connection to New England Congregationalists, their lack of a direct and regular relationship with the English government, and the fact that the New England rebels represented the friends, neighbors, and colleagues with whom they interacted on a daily basis all seem to have played a role. Whatever the case, Stockbridge companies saw combat in New York, New Jersey, and Canada during the early phases of the war, including service with Benedict Arnold at Valcour Bay, during which many were actually taken prisoner, but released shortly thereafter. Their brief captivity and, more important, their hasty release speak volumes about the goals of Native American groups who participated in the conflict on both sides. It seems that the Canadian Indians to whom the Stockbridge captives were turned over released them as part of a deal struck between them. According to Calloway, "it was reported that they made a private agreement to return to Canada if the Stockbridges would also return home, so that Indians could avoid killing Indians in a white man's war."[14]

It is not clear whether these same former Stockbridge prisoners discussed above reneged on their promise and returned to service, but a group of Stockbridge men served under Horatio Gates against John Burgoyne's Saratoga campaign in 1777. From this point forward, Stockbridge warriors insisted on serving together in exclusively Indian units. For a people descended from refugee Indian communities and who daily faced the disruption of ever-encroaching white land speculators and settlers, the opportunity to serve in war might possibly have represented a way to reconnect with a lost sense of identity as warriors. In much the same way, more than 150 years later for Indian people of the plains and southwest service in the U.S. Armed Forces during World War II would provide an opportunity to reconnect to a long lost warrior past. In any event, their service together was short-lived. In a skirmish near New York City on August 31, 1778, the Stockbridge units were trapped between elements of the British army and were almost completely slaughtered.[15] According to one eyewitness, "No Indians, especially, received quarter, including their chief called Nimham and his son, save for a few."[16]

At the same time, those Indians remaining in Stockbridge (mostly women, children, invalids, and the elderly) were experiencing extreme privation. The warriors that had survived military service and returned home soon asked the Massachusetts government for blankets, coats, and funds, as well as assistance for the families of the men who had died. One year later, the Stockbridge Indians were still in dire straits, lacking basic needs such as adequate clothing. These difficulties notwithstanding, more than 30 Stockbridge warriors served with John Sullivan in his campaign against the Six Nations Iroquois in 1779. In September of 1780, Washington reported that the 20 Stockbridge warriors still with his command at that time had requested leave to return home as the main action of the war had then moved to the south. Washington reported he was more than happy to accommodate the request, as he was completely unable to supply them. In fact, the Americans' general inability to adequately support their Stockbridge allies created diplomatic problems for them as it cost them their ability to employ the Stockbridge as envoys to many neutral and British-allied Indians. These British allies were beginning to waiver as the Stockbridge emissaries were therefore unable to provide the gifts required for effective diplomacy. By the end of the war Washington was actually refusing Stockbridge offers of service due to both his inability to pay them and his belief that the return on the investment had decreased so far that it was no longer worth it; however, this may have resulted as much from the fact that the Americans no longer needed the services of the Stockbridge to the extent that they had earlier in the war when New England and New York constituted the main theater of action. Either way, by 1782 the relationship between the Americans and the Stockbridge Indians had disintegrated so much that British officials were convinced that Stockbridge loyalty to the Americans had waned to the point that they could possibly be convinced to drop out of the war altogether and at the very least declare neutrality. The British had good reason for believing this as well. Additionally, the Stockbridge community that those Indians returned home to must have clearly demonstrated the negative consequences of their support for the Americans.[17]

THE SPLINTERING OF THE SIX NATIONS

Predictably, the 1768 Treaty of Fort Stanwix, in which the Iroquois signed away the lands of their "younger brothers" west of the Appalachians in an effort to save their own, created a firestorm in the Ohio Valley. As discussed in chapter 4, the influx of white settlers to the Ohio Valley eventually touched off the conflict known as Dunmore's War, which in turn, generated potentially dangerous complications for the Six Nations. In the preliminary phases of Lord Dunmore's War, the Shawnees, Delawares, and Mingos invoked the protocols of the Covenant Chain relationship and formally requested the aid of their Iroquois brethren from the Six Nations; however, such a request placed the Six Nations in an extremely difficult position. Northern Indian superintendent Sir William Johnson was decidedly against such a move due to its potential to create another general Indian war similar to the Pontiac War. Financially, such an outcome would be catastrophic for the British. While most of the leadership of the Six Nations expressed little or no interest in intervening in the Ohio Valley conflict, the Senecas, upset at the seeming indifference of British officials to a series of murders perpetrated by western Pennsylvanians, threatened to derail the consensus. The crisis exposed the sorry state into which the Covenant Chain had fallen. In the end Johnson and the Iroquois were powerless to convince the Ohio Valley groups to desist from their confrontation with the Virginians. Likewise, the Covenant Chain relationship brought very little in the way of support for that effort from the majority of the Six Nations. According to historian Alan Taylor, "Neither Johnson nor the chiefs seemed to recognize how hollow their mutual words had become pressing each other to revive pretensions to fictional powers."[18]

Of course, Sir William's death in July of 1774 complicated this situation. By the time of his funeral the entire confederacy had been thrown into extreme confusion. Johnson's death made British commander in chief Thomas Gage's task all the more complicated. "I should at all times consider this event as a Publick Loss," he wrote, "I look upon it as a heavy one at this Juncture."[19] Sensing that the end of his life was near, Sir William had requested that his nephew Sir Guy Johnson, who was also his son-in-law by virtue of his marriage to Johnson's daughter Mary, be designated as his successor. Although Sir Guy had yet to be confirmed in that position at the time of his uncle's death, the Six Nations immediately looked to him as their de facto superintendent. Two days after Sir William's death, the Iroquois performed the condolence ceremony, and from that moment on Guy Johnson took the lead in British–Six Nations diplomacy.[20]

Guy Johnson had not been the only candidate to succeed his uncle, however. Sir William's own son, Sir John Johnson, and his trusted deputy and son-in-law Daniel Claus also received consideration. While none of the three possessed the singular abilities of the late superintendent, Guy Johnson eventually gained Sir William's approval. Despite his obvious deficiencies in many of the areas critical to success in the position, Guy Johnson began his tenure as superintendent of Indian Affairs rather capably. His first official act was to take steps to dissuade Iroquois dependents in the Ohio country from joining the Shawnees in their war against the Virginians. He pursued this goal so vigorously at first that he was even willing to put aside the differences that had existed between Sir William and the missionary Samuel Kirkland due to their mutual agreement that Six Nations participation in Lord Dunmore's War would spawn disastrous consequences for all involved. Thanks in part to Guy Johnson's steady handling of the days immediately after Sir William's death, but more so to the crisis then brewing between the colonies and Great Britain, word arrived in late 1774 that he had been appointed as the official interim superintendent of Indian Affairs for the Northern Department.[21]

In the Iroquois condolence ceremonies which followed Sir William's death the Six Nations representatives present had affirmed that only unanimous agreement of the Council at Onondaga would stir them to act on the Shawnees' request for assistance. Therefore, a congress was called to meet at Onondaga to discuss the matter in September. In the weeks leading up to the Onondaga Congress, Guy Johnson came to rely heavily on a younger brother of Molly Brant, Sir William's common-law wife at the time of his death. Joseph Brant, or Thayendanegea in the Mohawk tongue, was born sometime in the early 1740s. He was more than likely born among the refugee Iroquois settlements in the Ohio Valley. His early years, which included schooling at the Anglican Mohawk Mission as well as Eleazar Wheelock's School for Indians, prepared him for a life as a person equally adept at operating in both English and Iroquois culture. By the time of Sir William Johnson's death, Brant was in his early thirties. He had been married twice, fathered two children, and buried one of them along with his first wife. He was also both a Freemason and a devout Anglican who had translated the Book of Common Prayer into his native language. In addition to Mohawk and English, he spoke most if not all of the other languages of the Six Nations and had experience as an interpreter, secretary, farmer, and warrior. Through both of his wives he had gained kinship connections to powerful Oneida leaders. Likewise, through his sister's relationship with Sir William Johnson, Brant made himself a trusted friend of the family as well as an indispensable deputy of both the late Indian superintendent and his successor, Sir Guy. According to historian Barbara Graymont, Brant's connections to prominent leaders of both the Six Nations and the British proved instrumental in determining his loyalties during the American Revolution. "His attachment to the Johnsons and his devotion to what he considered to be the best interests of his Indian people were factors that would make him a valuable ally for the British in the years ahead."[22] Guy Johnson's agenda for the upcoming council at Onondaga largely represented the work of both the new Indian superintendent and Brant, who was fast becoming his most trusted deputy.

Though originally scheduled for September, the Onondaga Congress did not actually commence until late October. By the time it ended on November 11, Guy Johnson and Joseph Brant had received a significant vote of confidence in their leadership. The council, despite spirited rhetoric on all sides, not only rebuffed the Shawnee request for aid from the Six Nations, but also reprimanded the Cayugas for allowing war parties to join the Shawnees in their war against the Virginians before learning the mind of the council.[23]

It was the last major decision upon which the Grand Council of the Six Nations would stand unified. Despite dealing with the immediate issue of what to do about Lord Dunmore's War, the Iroquois Confederacy was facing long-term structural weaknesses that the American Revolution would ultimately exacerbate to the point of disintegration. According to anthropologist William Fenton, the Iroquois Confederacy had been in decline since 1768 when "the center of political gravity had shifted from Onondaga to the forks of the Ohio." Because of this shift, "the western door to the confederacy had sprung its hinges; the Longhouse was being pulled apart."* To compound this development, the continual erosion of the Mohawks' land base due to their close proximity to English settlement in New York had severely weakened the ability of the Mohawks to fulfill their traditional role as leaders of the confederacy. Finally, the Cayugas and Oneidas, who had traditionally operated in tandem, had now increasingly begun to disagree over issues ranging from Lord Dunmore's War to the growing rift between the British government and the American colonies.[24]

The growing relationship between the American revolutionaries and Samuel Kirkland, posed a serious threat to the unity of the Six Nations as well. Kirkland provoked Guy Johnson's ire for two reasons. The first of

---

* The Six Nations often used a metaphor to describe their confederacy that compared it to a Longhouse, their traditional dwelling. In the metaphor, the Mohawks, the easternmost nation, represented the Eastern door of this proverbial Longhouse while the Senecas represented the Western door.

which is that his growing influence among the Oneidas had always been viewed by the Johnson family as a threat to their control of diplomatic affairs with the Six Nations. Additionally, as a faithful servant of the crown he viewed the activities of the Patriots as nothing short of treason.[25]

Despite Kirkland's protestations to Johnson that he had only read the proceedings of the Continental Congress to the Oneidas when requested to by his parishioners and did so with no desire to influence them, his other writings paint a different picture. In June of 1775, he wrote Patriot leaders in Albany that his interpreting the conflict in terms favorable to the revolutionaries had "done more real service to the cause of the Country, or the cause of truth and justice, than five hundred pounds in presents would have effected." Hardly the words of an impartial observer let alone a loyal servant of the British Indian service.[26]

In addition to Kirkland's own activities, which were problematic for Johnson in and of themselves, Kirkland also reported to him that Patriot opposition to the Stamp Act, Townshend Duties, and of course the recent dumping of the tea in Boston, had severely limited the supply of goods available to the Indian superintendent for trade with the Six Nations. Despite Guy Johnson's outward expressions that Kirkland's interpretation was unduly influenced by his obvious sympathy for the Patriot cause, deep down he was worried. According to William Fenton, "both Johnson and his sachems surely knew that hope without gunpowder would not put meat in their corn soup."[27]

Beyond these issues there were other signs that the unity of the Six Nations confederacy was in danger. The Senecas, who boasted the majority of the warriors in the Confederacy, were experiencing difficulties in keeping their men from disobeying the council and aiding the Shawnees in the Ohio country. All of these developments occurred at exactly the same time that the administrative and personal disagreements between Kirkland and Johnson reached their boiling point and against the backdrop of t he ever-widening rift between Britain and its colonies. As the unity of the confederacy was above all else the most important goal for many of the sachems, the leadership of the confederacy endeavored to steer the Six Nations clear of the conflict. Oneida leaders gave voice to these sentiments regarding the civil war taking shape within the British Empire. "We are unwilling to join on either side of this context for we love you both—old England and new," they informed Governor Trumbull of Connecticut. They continued, "Should the great King of England apply to us for our aid—we shall deny him—and should the Colonies apply—we shall refuse."[28]

In reality though, neutrality was more realistic for some confederacy members than for others. As early as March of 1775 (a few weeks before

Lexington and Concord) cracks were already appearing in the neutrality policy. Given their long relationship with both Eleazar Wheelock and Kirkland, many Oneidas were simply too entangled with the Americans to consistently resist their entreaties. Likewise, the Mohawks had enjoyed the benefits of their close connection to Sir William and now Colonel Guy Johnson for too long to give it up at the request of people who had until recently, openly thirsted for their lands. In the case of the Mohawks, the British were keenly aware of all of these factors. Early on in the war, General Gage instructed Guy Johnson to remove Kirkland and other non-Anglican missionaries and replace them with Loyalist Anglicans from Albany. Gage was also betting that the King's support for the Iroquois in their ongoing land disputes with the colonies would keep them loyal to the crown.[29]

By the spring of 1775, Johnson decided he could wait no longer. He took steps to oust Kirkland and invited John Stuart, the Anglican missionary to the Mohawks, to challenge him among the Oneida. A long-distance war of words then ensued between the superintendent and Kirkland, who in the end removed to Boston in protest. While there he further solidified his break with the British as he set about advising the Continental Congress on how best to keep Indians out of the fight and thus deprive the British of key allies. When dissent turned to open rebellion at Lexington and Concord on April 19th, Johnson resolved to take more definite action regarding Kirkland. In May of 1775, as Kirkland was returning home from his trip to Boston, Johnson had the missionary detained and kept him under house arrest at his estate of Guy Park.[30]

Johnson's actions however, only created more division. Rumors abounded during the early summer of 1775 that the "Bostonians," as many of the Iroquois had taken to calling the revolutionaries, were coming to apprehend the superintendent any day. Such rumors prompted the Mohawks to inform Johnson that they would defend him from any such attempts should they occur and would support him in the conflict. But this assurance did not come from individuals authorized to speak on behalf of the Mohawk nation, and its wording stopped short of stating that the Mohawks would ally with the British. Nevertheless, it made clear the direction in which the largest portion of Mohawk sympathies lay.[31] Conversely, on June 2, 1775, 12 Oneida leaders gave the Americans exactly what they had been working for when they signed a declaration of neutrality presented to them by one of Kirkland's deputies. This pledge not only committed the Oneidas to neutrality, but also the rest of the confederacy despite the fact that no sachems from the other member nations were even present.[32]

Also in June, the Continental Congress created an Indian Committee and three Indian departments. At that time, Kirkland, having been released from his detainment at Johnson's estate, spent a week teaching the newly appointed American Indian superintendents how to communicate effectively with native people in general and how to invoke Covenant Chain language to their own advantage specifically. It was the beginning of Kirkland's service as an official agent of the American Revolutionary cause. Even with the help of someone like Kirkland, the Continental Congress harbored no illusions about enlisting large numbers of Native Americans as military allies. In fact, given the fact that most members of the body saw in the Revolution an opportunity to possibly rid themselves of Indians altogether and acquire their land, the idea of creating long-standing relationships with Indian communities was hardly their goal. Instead, the American revolutionaries hoped simply to keep the majority of Indians from actively supporting the English and they were well aware that to do so required they start with the Six Nations.[33]

Meanwhile, Colonel Guy Johnson, increasingly concerned that local Patriot sympathizers were planning to apprehend him, fled to Fort Ontario with several Mohawks and deputies. Before leaving, he held a hastily arranged meeting with Oneida, Tuscarora, and Seneca representatives in which he offered gifts and other inducements in an effort to convince them to stay loyal to the King and accompany him to Fort Ontario. His enticements failed to convince his audience. Unlike his uncle before him, Johnson lacked the necessary powers of persuasion, and once he arrived at Fort Ontario and convened a conference the Indian representatives who attended formed less than a quorum. That summer, the Grand Council of the Six Nations meeting at Onondaga also struggled to maintain both unity and the policy of neutrality. Clearly, the Six Nations Confederacy was irreparably damaged, if not completely broken.[34]

The Continental Congress in the meanwhile seized on Johnson's absence and sent commissioners to address the Six Nations while also attempting to arrest Sir John Johnson and occupy Johnson Hall. Out of this came a proposed meeting between the Six Nations and American representatives to occur at Albany in August of 1775. Colonel Guy Johnson, Joseph Brant, and other Mohawk representatives reacted angrily in response to the Albany conference and vehemently urged the other members of the Six Nations to boycott it. Brant in particular spent a tremendous amount of energy railing against the Americans in an effort to convince his fellow Iroquois brethren to forget their flirtation with the Patriots. Brant reminded his fellow Iroquois of the inherent racism and lust for Indian land that motivated many of the men with whom the Six Nations would be negotiating at Albany, asserting that the Americans "began this Rebellion to be sole Masters of the Continent." As such, they would conveniently forget any promises made to the Six Nations once the British were vanquished and they were no longer useful to American aims.[35]

Despite Brant's admonishments as well as those of Guy Johnson, the Oneidas and Cayugas, two of the groups closest to the Americans, reacted angrily. Even the leadership of the Senecas and Onondagas, who were no great friends to the revolutionaries, objected to what they viewed as threats by Johnson against Kirkland. While representatives of all of the Six Nations attended the Albany meeting with the Americans, only the Oneida and Tuscarora sent leaders of sufficient stature to be able to speak on their respective group's behalf.[36]

After a few days taken up with preliminary ceremonies, the meeting formally commenced on August 25, 1775. The American representatives wasted little time in demonstrating that they had taken Samuel Kirkland's advice to heart. From their very opening statements they sought to lay claim as the rightful partners of the Six Nations in the Covenant Chain by presenting the Six Nations representatives with a belt of wampum and the following address:

> Brothers,
> We are now Twelve Colonies united as one man. We have but one heart and one hand. Brothers, this is our Union Belt. By this belt, we the Twelve United Colonies, renew the old covenant chain by which our forefathers, in their great wisdom, thought proper to bind us and you, our brothers of the Six Nations, together, when they first landed at this place; and if any of the links of this great chain should have received any rust, we now brighten it, and make it shine like silver. As God has put it into our hearts to love the Six Nations and their allies, we now make the chain of friendship so strong, that nothing but an evil spirit can or will attempt to break it. But we hope, through the favor and mercy of the good Spirit, that it will remain strong and bright while the sun shines and the water runs.[37]

According to Alan Taylor, covering themselves in the mantle of the Covenant Chain was a concerted strategy on the part of the American revolutionaries in which they actively sought to remove the Six Nations from the Johnsons' orbit.[38]

By the time the congress adjourned in early September, the Americans must have considered it a rousing success. Their strategy had managed to elicit a promise from the representatives present that the Six Nations would take no part in what they considered a family quarrel. In return for this, the Americans only had to promise to address Iroquois complaints regarding rampant American settlement in their country at a later date. Of course, this meeting did not in fact represent the entire Six Nations Confederacy. It was largely a meeting between the Americans and the components of the Six Nations that were already friendly to the Americans and their cause, mainly Oneidas and Tuscaroras. But why would even the Oneidas and Tuscaroras accede to American demands while receiving very little in return? After all, they too were experiencing similar encroachment on the part of American colonists. The answer lies in internal Iroquois politics. The Oneidas had long felt disregarded by the British and had even begun to feel (and rightly so) that Sir William Johnson had often abused his relationship with the Iroquois for his own benefit. Given these feelings, the Oneida relationship with the Mohawks, the favored nation of the Johnsons, had become an uneasy one at best. When the Americans presented the Oneidas and the Tuscarora with an opportunity to get themselves out from under the shadow of their Mohawk brethren, they took it. In fact, they began this process long before the Albany Congress by entering into a close relationship with Samuel Kirkland. Just as so many other native communities examined here, the Oneidas and Tuscaroras entered into their relationship with Kirkland and the Americans for their own reasons, which may or may not have been the same as those of the Patriots. Regardless, not long after the Albany Congress, the Mohawk, Cayuga, and Seneca contingents that had gone to Canada with Colonel Guy Johnson returned and informed their brethren that they were going to war against the Americans. Additionally, Colonel John Butler, one of Sir William Johnson's former deputies, arrived at Fort Niagara in the fall of 1775 and immediately began distributing a large number of supplies and presents to the Cayugas, Onondagas, and Senecas who had gathered there. Employing extremely effective rhetoric as well as wielding a considerable amount of trade goods, Butler soon won large numbers of the Iroquois warriors (to the mortification of their own elders) over to active support of the British alongside their Mohawk brethren. Six Nations unity was irrevocably shattered.[39]

This disintegration only picked up pace throughout the winter of 1775 to 1776. By the spring of 1776, Seneca, Cayuga, and Onondaga leaders were desperately trying to maintain neutrality as official policy, but the rest of the confederacy had already begun to take up sides, with the Oneida and Tuscarora exhibiting even more openly their support of the Americans and the Mohawks remaining staunchly connected to Guy Johnson and the British. At a grand council in March of 1776, American general Philip Schuyler's account of the British evacuation of Boston engendered divergent responses indicative of the extent to which Six Nations unity had fractured.

According to interpreter James Dean, who was present at the reading of Schuyler's account, "a variety of passions appeared in the faces of the assembly on the recital. Some seemed elated with joy, and others as much depressed with vexation and disappointment."[40]

By May of 1776, neutrality formally ended as the Oneidas and Tuscaroras threw off all pretense and came out openly in support of the Americans; however, British control of the Atlantic Ocean complicated matters. The Americans were barely able to live up to their obligations due to their inability to secure enough goods to supply the Tuscaroras and Oneidas, let alone cultivate the rest of the Six Nations. In the words of Alan Taylor, "needy Indians could not afford a neutrality that would deprive them of access to essential trade goods." Thus, the internal politics of the Six Nations themselves and the inability of the Americans to effectively compete with the British in terms of trade goods created a situation which fatally divided the Iroquois Confederacy and created similar divisions among their client states.[41]

Turf battles between the British military and Indian service only added to the chaos in Iroquois country in the short-term, but they also helped to produce critical leadership that would guide many of the Iroquois for years to come. As early as July of 1775, Guy Johnson, Daniel Claus, and Joseph Brant had tried to convince Sir Guy Carleton, the British governor of Quebec, to authorize raids against Patriots in the Mohawk Valley, but to no avail. Carleton distrusted Indians and worried that raids would only serve to drive many would-be Loyalists into the revolutionary camp. This decision was also motivated by a long-standing bureaucratic and personal struggle between Carleton and the Johnsons for control of Indian affairs. Furthermore, Carleton felt threatened by Guy Johnson's assertion that as superintendent of Indian Affairs his authority extended to the Indian communities of Canada, whom Johnson intended to use in the proposed raids. When Carleton not only vetoed the raids, but also informed Johnson that he possessed no authority over any Indians in Canada, Johnson and Claus set sail on a fateful voyage to England to protest.[42]

Along with the two Indian agents went Joseph Brant and one other Mohawk. Ostensibly included to provide proof that the Mohawks preferred the leadership of the Johnson faction to that of Carleton, the two Mohawks undertook the journey for their own reasons. According to Alan Taylor, Brant was "no mere pawn of the British," but instead he "embraced Loyalism to serve Mohawk interests."[43] Specifically, he and his Mohawk companion intended to seek pledges from the King and other British officials that Mohawk title to their lands would forever be respected. For Johnson and Claus's sake, it was indeed fortunate that Brant accompanied them. Most accounts of the trip agree that it was largely due to Brant's abilities that they were successful in achieving at least some of their goals.[44] They returned to America in July of 1776 bearing dispatches that confirmed Colonel Guy Johnson's position as permanent superintendent of Indian Affairs, as well as a deputy post for Claus and promises to Brant that once the rebellion was put down, the Mohawks would be granted redress of their grievances. While they failed to extend Johnson's authority to the Indians of Canada and the promise to Brant was quite vague, the trip did much to cement Brant's reputation as a favorite of the British government, aristocracy, and military leadership.[45]

The trio arrived in New York just in time for Brant to participate in Howe's campaign against Washington's forces in and around that city. By the late fall and early winter, his service to Howe's army complete, Joseph Brant had returned to Niagara on a mission to finally put into motion the plans that he and Guy Johnson had devised to reclaim the Mohawk Valley; however, he ran into a series of unexpected obstacles. Many of his own Iroquois brethren, particularly among the elders and political leaders of each of the Six Nations, still clung to the myth of neutrality. What's more, Brant was only a minor war leader and not a traditional sachem or, for that matter, a person of great importance. Therefore, many leaders such as the Oneida sachem Skenandon, as well as Cornplanter and Red Jacket of the Senecas, were reluctant to listen to him. Finally, the ease with which Brant operated among whites also troubled many of the decision makers he attempted to win to his support.[46]

Unable to recruit more than a handful of warriors to join him, Brant turned to the Loyalists, among whom he found many willing recruits. He raised an irregular unit of over 100 men, only 20 of which were Mohawks, with the balance of his force consisting of white loyalists. After he forced the Patriot-sympathizing residents of Unadilla to provide him and his men supplies in early June of 1777, the local Committee of Safety dispatched militia general Nicholas Herkimer, a man whom Brant addressed as his former neighbor, to confront Brant at Unadilla about his intentions. At the meeting that occurred in July, Brant (though Herkimer outnumbered him two to one) rejected neutrality. He promised Herkimer that the King intended to put the Bostonians in their rightful place of subjection and ordered his men to fire their guns in a spirited display of defiance. If there were any doubts remaining regarding which side of the conflict Brant supported and what his intentions were, the meeting dispelled them.[47]

Later that same month, Brant and his men joined Colonel Barry St. Leger's combined force of Indians and British regulars at Oswego. This combined force represented one prong of General John Burgoyne's intended invasion of western New York. Not long after, at a conference held at Oswego,

St. Leger and Sir John Johnson, among others, convinced several hundred Iroquois, mostly Senecas and Mohawks, to join Caughnawaga Mohawks and other non-Iroquoian Indians from Canada who were already part of the expedition.[48]

Since the beginning of hostilities though, the Americans had also stepped up their diplomatic endeavors among the Iroquois. In August of 1776, General Philip Schuyler met with Iroquois representatives and promised protection of the lands of those who would swear loyalty to the Revolution. This was quite a step both for Schuyler and the Americans. Schuyler was himself one of the more forthright advocates for the dispossession of Indian land in New York, and the leaders of the revolutionary movement had hitherto been extremely reluctant to actively recruit Indians as allies, let alone promise them protection of their lands in return. But now their situation was growing desperate. At the time the promise was made, General William Howe was in the process of cutting Washington's army to pieces in and around New York City. Additionally, the massive advantage the British enjoyed in terms of supplies meant that promises to respect Indian title to their lands (however hollow they might be) represented just about the only bargaining chip the Americans possessed.[49]

The diplomatic maneuvering and the slow disintegration of Iroquois unity all came to a deadly climax on August 6, 1777, at the Battle of Oriskany near present-day Rome, New York. St. Leger's force, combining 700 British and Loyalist troops with another 800 Indian warriors— Senecas, Cayugas, Onondagas, Mohawks, Hurons, and Canadian Indians—smashed into a Patriot defense, which included Oneida and Tuscarora warriors. Technically, the ensuing day long battle resulted in a British victory, but the particularly bloody and costly nature of the affair disheartened many of St. Leger's Indian allies, who subsequently deserted him and forced St. Leger to retreat. For the Iroquois warriors who participated in the battle against one another, particularly the Oneidas and Mohawks, Oriskany unleashed a torrent of retaliatory raids against each other's crops and villages. Civil War had come to the Six Nations.[50]

Also in retaliation against those Iroquois who had violated their pledges of neutrality and fought for the British at Oriskany, Patriot sympathizers and militias increased their prosecution of Loyalists in the Mohawk Valley. The combination of their activities and Oneida raids against Mohawk villages only served to drive hundreds of Mohawk Valley residents who heretofore had attempted to stay out of the conflict into the arms of the British in Canada and bolster the forces with which British Loyalists, and most of all, their Mohawk allies, would terrorize the valley. Joseph Brant's force of irregulars benefited considerably from this situation and it was not long after Oriskany that he made a name for himself as an extremely effective leader in the partisan warfare that would wrack the Mohawk Valley for the duration of the war.[51]

On May 30, 1778, Brant and his men were discovered near Cobleskill, New York, by a combined detachment of about 50 American regulars and militia troops. In the ensuing fight, Brant and his men killed most of the American officers and set fire to a house in an effort to drive out the American troops who were firing upon them from within. All five of the Americans who had taken up positions in the house died in the flames. By the time the fighting ended, Brant had won a victory, but at a significant cost. He reportedly lost nearly 30 men as a result of the skirmish while the Americans suffered somewhere around 29 casualties. Brant's men mutilated the corpses of the officers (in a way consistent with Mohawk cultural norms that required proof of one's military exploits in the form of scalps or other trophies as well as the possessions of the vanquished foes) and plundered the remains of the village for supplies. The incident would serve as the beginning of a larger-than-life reputation for savagery, mutilation, and depredation ascribed to Brant and his men by Americans eager to motivate the citizens of the Mohawk Valley both to support the American war effort and to aid them in capturing Brant.[52] In reality, Brant and his men were certainly no more and in Brant's case possibly less violent or brutal in their tactics than both other British irregular units and their Patriot counterparts. Nine months earlier in the aftermath of Oriskany, American and Oneida parties raided Mohawk towns such as Canajoharie (where they looted and destroyed the home of Brant's sister and Sir William's Johnson's widow, Molly) and Fort Hunter. No doubt the destruction of his sister's home and the destruction of a Mohawk town as important as Canajoharie occupied an important place in Brant's mind during the early summer of 1778.[53] Just a few weeks before Brant's victory at Cobleskill, Patriot general Philip Schuyler had written the Continental Congress requesting a "Body of Troops to destroy [Indian] Towns," as he considered such a force "necessary to protect the Frontier Inhabitants."[54] The idea of visiting total warfare upon whole towns, noncombatants and combatants alike, was neither a new one nor was it the exclusive strategy of Indians. American forces proved themselves quite adept at it as well in the Mohawk Valley.

In July of 1778, Colonel John Butler's force of Loyalists and allied Mohawks laid waste to the Patriot settlement of Wyoming on the Susquehanna River in Pennsylvania. Despite the fact that Joseph Brant was not part of the raid, American propaganda painted Brant as the culprit rather than Butler. The picture of savage Indian chieftains destroying whole villages was much more effective in firing up the ire of colonists already predisposed to hate Indians than laying the blame for Wyoming's destruction at the feet of one of their own who had once been considered a hero because of his service during the Seven Years' War. According to one scholar, Brant's "notoriety led alarmed Patriots to see his hand in every frontier atrocity, although most were committed by other raiders." In fact, Brant and his men exercised more restraint than his Patriot counterparts demonstrated when they attacked Iroquois villages.[55] For example, in October of 1778, Patriot militia from Cherry Valley aided by Continental soldiers destroyed Brant's home village of Onoquaga while the Mohawk leader was away. Lieutenant Colonel William Butler, the overall commander of the expedition, described Onoquaga as "the finest Indian town I ever saw." Nonetheless, on October 9 he burned it to the ground and with it over 2,000 bushels of corn, the apple orchard, and most of the livestock. When they discovered some of the village children hiding in a nearby cornfield, the Americans put them to death as well.[56]

Less than one month later, Loyalists and Iroquois warriors led by John Butler's son Walter exacted revenge on Cherry Valley, but this time, unlike at Wyoming, Butler was unable to stop his Seneca allies from killing 32 noncombatants; however, Brant himself managed to save many of the settlement's civilian population from such a fate. It did not matter in the end. Patriot chroniclers of the event still painted him as the bloodthirsty, savage brute responsible for the killings.[57]

By early 1779, Sir Frederick Haldimand had replaced Guy Carleton as the officer in charge of operations in the Mohawk Valley. Not long after, he provided Brant both a captain's commission and promises that, were the British to succeed in defeating the Americans, all Mohawk lands taken during the conflict would be restored to them. With his captain's pay as well as his share of the plunder taken over the past year, Brant set himself up on a large farmstead along the Niagara River in a style strikingly similar to his former benefactor Sir William Johnson. He also married a woman who enhanced his standing in both white and native circles. His third wife, Catherine Croghan, was both the daughter of Sir William Johnson's former deputy George Croghan and the niece of a powerful Mohawk chief. These kinship connections along with his success in war and his growing reputation among his American adversaries propelled Brant to a level of power and standing among both the Loyalist and Mohawk communities that he would not relinquish until late in his life.[58]

Of course as the Mohawks, Senecas, Onondagas, and Cayugas became important British allies, so too did the Oneidas and Tuscaroras provide critical assistance to the Americans. Once the initial anger over Oriskany subsided, both the Oneidas and Tuscaroras managed to avoid combat with their former Iroquois brethren who reciprocated the practice. Oneida and Tuscarora military contributions as well as their service as spies and disseminators of American propaganda won for them a place of trust and admiration among the Patriots. Even so staunch an Indian hater as Philip Schuyler referred to them as "good friends."[59] In January of 1779, the Oneidas and Tuscaroras were joined by a faction of Onondagas who had decided to break with the rest of their Onondaga kinsmen and relocate to Oneida villages, thus transferring their support to the Americans. They did so just in time to avoid the entire destruction of their former village a few months later at the hands of an American invasion force determined to silence resistance in the Mohawk Valley once and for all.[60]

Throughout 1777 and 1778, the operations of Brant, the Butlers, and other British and Iroquois partisans had not only damaged the local American war effort, but also jeopardized valuable grain supplies intended for the Continental Army. Therefore, sometime in early 1779, General George Washington decided upon an expedition to western New York and Pennsylvania designed to punish those they deemed responsible for these disruptions so severely that they would no longer have either the capacity or the will to resist the American war effort. The campaign, led by General John Sullivan during the late summer and early fall of 1779, fought only one pitched battle against their Iroquois and Loyalist opponents, a victory for the Americans at Newtown on August 29th. After that, Sullivan and his men rarely encountered Iroquois warriors and almost always arrived at abandoned Iroquois villages; however, the scorched earth policy Sullivan employed during September represents the most devastating aspect of the expedition. By the time Sullivan and his army returned to winter quarters at Morristown, New Jersey, in early October, over 40 Iroquois villages along with their cornfields and orchards lay smoldering. A particularly harsh winter in 1779 to 1780 combined with the deprivations caused by Sullivan's campaign visited untold misery and countless deaths on the British-allied Iroquois, yet despite Washington and Sullivan's destructive campaign of 1779, the determination of those Iroquois who chose to cast their lot with the British was not broken. If anything, the Sullivan expedition only hardened the resolve of Mohawk Valley Loyalists and Iroquois.[61]

Almost as soon as Sullivan's forces left the area, British-allied Iroquois and Loyalists began to plan their response. Retaliatory raids by Brant, Walter Butler, Sir John Johnson, and the Seneca leader Cornplanter, who had now abandoned his earlier stance for neutrality, nearly overwhelmed both Patriot sympathizing whites and Indians alike during the spring of 1780. By early summer, they had succeeded in forcing many of the Tuscaroras to abandon the Americans altogether. This in turn left key

Oneida villages open to attack, which resulted in considerable defections from that quarter as well.[62]

In July, Brant and his force laid waste to the Oneida village of Kanonwalohale, which had been the principal site of Samuel Kirkland's mission. Reportedly, Brant exercised little of the restraint that had characterized his previous raids on his enemies' settlements. No doubt the central role played by Oneida warriors from Kanonwalohale in the destruction of his own house and that of his sister Molly at Canajoharie in 1777 motivated his obliteration of the Oneida village and mission. Whatever the case, his tactics were effective. Both Kirkland and Philip Schuyler remarked on how difficult it became after the destruction of Kanonwalohale to recruit Oneidas to fight for the American war effort.[63]

With the Oneida now effectively on the sidelines, Patriot settlements in the Mohawk Valley were left dangerously unprotected. By the spring of 1781, Iroquois and Loyalists were raiding at will to the point that Fort Schuyler (formerly Fort Herkimer) had to be abandoned. According to Alan Taylor, nearly two-thirds of Patriot residents in the Mohawk Valley had become refugees by that spring. But this increased raiding activity was ultimately unsustainable. In order to achieve it, British Indian agents and military officers in America had to increase their distribution of presents to the Iroquois to such a large amount that government officials back in London became alarmed at the massive amounts of money spent in these efforts. Eventually, their displeasure landed squarely on Guy Johnson. Facing charges of malfeasance, he was replaced as Indian superintendent by Sir John Johnson in the opening weeks of 1782. Never as energetic as his cousin, Sir John stayed at Montreal and delegated his duties to others, most of whom had very little experience in the area. Of course, it mattered little in the end, as a few months earlier in October of 1781 Lord Charles Cornwallis had surrendered his entire command to Washington at Yorktown, Virginia. The war was effectively over. The news of the defeat sapped the last drop of patience the British public had for the conflict and the government of Lord North fell shortly thereafter. The new government of Lord Cavendish agreed to come to the negotiating table.[64]

Upon receiving orders to act only defensively for now, Joseph Brant was incensed and accused the British of intending to betray their Iroquois and Loyalist allies. Frederick Haldimand's secretary, Captain Robert Mathews, sought to reassure Brant and his fellow Iroquois that "they will never be forgotten. The King will always consider and reward them as his faithful children, who have manfully supported his and their own rights." Brant was not convinced, and rightly so as it turned out. In the end, his worst fears came true.

7

The Revolutionary War in the West

During the winter of 1779, the Virginian George Rogers Clark led a campaign to recapture Fort Vincennes in the Illinois country from the British forces of General Henry Hamilton. During Clark's siege of the post an incident occurred that provides a telling glimpse into the nature of the American Revolution west of the Appalachian Mountains. Sometime during the afternoon of February 24, a party of approximately 20 Indians, mostly Ottawas returning from a raid near the falls of the Ohio River, came in sight of Vincennes. According to Clark's later account of the expedition, one of Clark's subordinates sent a party out to capture them. Since the Indians approaching the town could not see the fort, they did not detect anything out of the ordinary. When the American detachment came out to meet them, they at first thought it was a party sent by Hamilton to greet them. Before the Indians realized their mistake, the Americans fired upon them. In a matter of seconds, the Americans killed several in the party and captured the rest.[1]

In his journal, Hamilton claimed that the Americans captured the party at nearly the same moment he made up his mind to seek terms from Clark. He went on to claim that as he ordered his officers to display a flag of truce,

Clark himself ordered his men to line the prisoners up in front of the stockade. Hamilton's own words best describe the ghastly scene that followed:

> One of the others was tomahawked either by Clarke or one of his Officers, the other three foreseeing their fate, began to sing their Death song, and were butcherd in succession, tho at the very time a flag of Truce was hanging out at the fort and the firing had ceased on both sides—A young chief of the Ottawa nation called *Macutte' Mong* one of these last, having received the fatal stroke of a Tomahawk in the head, took it out and gave it again into the hands of his executioner who repeated the Stroke a second and third time, after which the miserable being, not entirely deprived of life was dragged to the river, and thrown in with the rope about his neck where he ended his life and tortures—This horrid scene was transacted in the open Street, and before the door of a house where I afterward was quartered, the master of which related to me the above particulars—The Blood of the victims was still visible for days afterwards, a testimony of the courage and Humanity of Colonel Clarke.[2]

According to the Englishman's journal, Clark washed the blood and stench from his hands and face in front of Hamilton, and then began the parley. Hamilton claimed that Clark boasted of his part in the massacre and then proceeded to tell Hamilton that to defend the fort was useless, as he would soon have his cannon in position. He declared that if Hamilton forced him to assault the fort, he would spare no one. If Hamilton surrendered the fort and all its stores at ten o'clock the next morning, Clark proposed to allow Hamilton and his men to retain their baggage and personal belongings. After deliberating with his officers for a short time, Hamilton agreed and signed the articles of capitulation.[3] This incident and countless others like it demonstrate that the Revolutionary War in the Ohio Valley and Illinois country constituted nothing less than a blood feud between Indians (sometimes aided by the British) determined to keep their land and whites determined to take it.

As the American Revolution began, the attention of both colonists and Indians in the Ohio country was focused much less on issues of taxation, representation, and Parliamentary versus local control than on the results and repercussions of the recently concluded Dunmore's War. Despite their growing disagreement regarding the power of the legislature versus that of the Royal governor, Virginians of all ranks concurred with Dunmore that the purpose of the conflict with the Ohio Valley Indian groups had been to establish once and for all, "an idea of the power of the White People upon the minds of the Indians."[4]

The Revolution obliterated the last obstacle holding the torrent of settlers and land speculators back from completely flooding the Ohio Valley and the Illinois country beyond. However, the native people of the Ohio Valley, while certainly defeated in Dunmore's War, were not ready to concede the overall struggle. They realized early on that whites would use the conflict as an excuse to extend their settlement activities.

INITIAL OHIO INDIAN NEUTRALITY

Many of the Shawnee villages in the Ohio Valley were determined to prevent any further extension of American settlements beyond the limits agreed to as a result of Lord Dunmore's War. In July of 1775, Cornstalk and several other Shawnee leaders expressed their belief that the continuing influx of American settlers had left them no choice but to resort to violence. "We are often inclined to believe," the Shawnees told a delegation of Virginians, "there is no resting place for us and that your Intentions were to deprive us entirely of our whole Country."[5] They and their Delaware, Mingo, and Miami allies, among others, viewed the outbreak of the American Revolution as an opportunity not only to arrest American settlement of their lands, but also to roll it back.[6] After conferring with native leaders at Fort Pitt the month before, British agent John Connolly expressed his certainty to General Thomas Gage that the Ohio Indians to a man would rise to support the British.[7]

Despite Connolly's confidence and the overwhelming case in favor of an alliance with the British none of the Ohio Indian groups was completely in favor of making war on the Americans. Even the Shawnees, the most militant of them all, were sharply divided over which belligerent to support in the conflict. In fact early on in the war, moderate and cautious older chiefs held the line for neutrality. According to Colin Calloway, while the popular notion of the Shawnees remains one of defiance and unrelenting resistance, their experience in the American Revolution exemplifies "the inadequacy of standard portrayals" of native people, and Shawnee "participation was never total."[8]

To understand the initial reluctance of the Shawnees to participate in the war, one must understand the nature of Shawnee political organization. The Shawnee polity was traditionally subdivided into five separate components: the Chillicothe, Thawekila, Piqua, Maquachake, and Kispoki divisions. Traditionally, each division had its own areas of responsibility. For example, the Kispoki division usually exercised jurisdiction over matters of war, while the Piquas took the lead in religious issues and so forth.[9] However, as the imperial wars between France and England roiled throughout the colonies during the 18th century, these spheres of responsibility began to break down, and the individual Shawnee divisions increasingly took control of all aspects of their society rather than deferring to their brethren in the other divisions. Thus, when the American Revolution broke out, individual Shawnee communities now felt free to make their own decisions as to how to respond. The Shawnee response to the Revolution was anything but monolithic. No Shawnee divisions seriously considered supporting the Americans, but the Maquachakes, led by Cornstalk, at first sought to stake out a position of neutrality and attempted to convince their fellow Shawnees to do likewise.[10]

However, American settlers just kept coming. In the spring of 1775, settlers reoccupied the previously abandoned Kentucky settlement of Harrods Town southwest of present-day Lexington. News of the so-called shot heard round the world, as the first shots of the war fired at Lexington and Concord have come to be called, finally reached the frontier nearly three weeks after the battle. The citizens of Kentucky now saw in this conflict an opportunity to legitimize their illegal settlements.[11]

At a June 6 meeting of delegates appointed by the Kentucky settlements, it was decided to appeal to Virginia for rights as a recognized county of that state. The delegates also drew up two petitions now known as the West Fincastle Petitions. One dated June 15, 1776, spells out the reasons why the Kentuckians felt the Virginia legislature should include Kentucky under its protection. In addition to the obvious increase in Virginia's population the petitions argued that, by annexing Kentucky "a new source of wealth would then be opened, as Trade and Navigation under the Auspices of Virginia would Flourish in this Western world."[12] In addition to asking for county status, the Kentuckians at Harrods Town decided to send two representatives along with the petitions to try to force the issue by demanding seats in the legislature. When the question of who to send came to a vote, the delegates chose John Gabriel Jones and George Rogers Clark.[13]

After a long journey, Clark and Jones arrived in Williamsburg in August of 1776, only to find that the Virginia legislature had adjourned for the summer. They decided to wait until the beginning of the fall session to present their case and to attempt to take their seats. When the legislature finally convened for the autumn session, they denied the Kentuckians seats; however, later in the session the Virginia Assembly did recognize Kentucky as a separate county of the state of Virginia and ordered ammunition and supplies sent there under the guard of Jones and Clark. These actions on the part of Virginia and by extension the united colonies, sent a very powerful signal to the native people of the west that the Americans viewed the conflict as an opportunity to wrest even more land from them.[14]

This was not lost on the Shawnees. In November of that year, in an address to the Second Continental Congress, now acting as the provisional government of the United States, Cornstalk summed up Shawnee outrage over the authorization of further settlement, which the annexation of Kentucky had created:

> Our Lands are covered by the white people, & we are jealous that you still intend to make larger strides. We never sold you our Lands which you now possess on the Ohio between the Great Kanawha & the Cherokee, & which you are settling without ever asking our leave, or obtaining our consent. . . . Now I stretch my Arm to you my wise Brethren of the United States met in Council at Philadelphia. I open my hand & pour into your heart the cause of our discontent in hopes that you will . . . send us a favorable Answer, that we may be convinced of the sincerity of your profession.[15]

Despite the anger of Indians such as Cornstalk and the obvious intentions of colonies such as Virginia, Pennsylvania, and North Carolina, the American Revolution created a generational divide among Ohio Valley Indians quite similar to that among the Cherokees. As Virginia, in particular, increasingly supplied and supported illegal Kentucky settlements, young militants in the Indian communities of the Ohio Valley gradually won the argument between a violent response on one hand and neutrality on the other. In February of 1777, warriors from Pluggy's Town, a refugee community of Mingos, Shawnees, Delawares, and Wyandots, raided multiple settlements in Kentucky. Fearing an all-out Indian war and hoping that neutralist factions might ultimately win the day, Virginia Governor Patrick Henry eschewed retaliation, but his hopes were ultimately dashed.[16]

THE DEATH OF CORNSTALK AND THE END OF SHAWNEE NEUTRALITY

In June of 1777, the Moravian missionary David Zeisberger noted that a party of young Shawnee warriors had recently visited his mission among the Delawares carrying the trophies and spoils of raids against American settlements. According to Zeisberger, "the warriors are no longer listening to the chiefs who want peace; they want to have war."[17] Earlier that same year, Cornstalk and other traditional leaders who had led the push for neutrality, signaled to the Americans that they were no longer able to stop their young warriors from heeding the British call to bring the war to American colonists living west of the Appalachians. In a message to American Indian agent George Morgan, Cornstalk expressed his deep frustration with the situation. "They will not listen to me," he wrote. "When I speak to them they will attend me for a Moment & sit still whilst they are within my Sight.—at night they steal their Blankets & run off to where the Evil spirit leads them." Later that year, a majority of Shawnee warriors accepted a war belt offered them from British general Henry Hamilton at Detroit.[18]

In October of 1777, Cornstalk and two other neutralist Shawnee leaders traveled to Fort Randolph near the site of his people's defeat in the Battle of Point Pleasant in 1774. Having resigned himself to the fact that they had lost the argument to the young warriors who itched for war against the Virginians, Cornstalk and his companions felt that they should notify the Americans of their failure. What happened next demonstrates the ultimate failure of neutrality as a response to the American Revolution for native people. Eventually, the British, the Americans, or both would employ the maxim "if you're not with us, you're against us," and death and destruction would likely follow.[19]

According to one account, Cornstalk "made no secret of the disposition of the Indians declaring that he was opposed to joining the war on the side of the British, but that all the rest of the nation but himself and his wife were determined to engaged in it."[20] Upon hearing this news, the Fort's commander, Captain Matthew Arbuckle, decided to detain Cornstalk and his fellow Shawnee leaders. On November 7th he informed General Edward Hand, American commander at Fort Pitt of his decision. He requested that Hand "give particular directions relative to Cornstalk as I am well satisfied the Shawanese are all our enemies."[21] Not long after this, Cornstalk's son arrived to protest his father's detainment. Shortly after his arrival, a party of British-allied Indians attacked a patrol near the fort. When the body of one of the victims was brought inside the stockade, many of the militiamen stationed there went looking for an Indian, any Indian, upon whom to exact their vengeance.[22] A Captain Stuart, one of the officers attached to the fort, recounted what happened next: "The men advanced to the door, the Corn Stalk arose and met them, seven or eight bullets were fired into him, and his son was shot dead as he sat upon a stool." Cornstalk's other companions were also killed. Stuart went on to lament, "thus died the great Cornstalk . . . I have no doubt if he had been spared but he would have been friendly to the Americans."[23] The hatred of Indians so common among the frontier settlers who made up the majority of the militia stationed at Fort Randolph had cost the Americans what little hope they had of keeping the Shawnees out of the war. Writing a few weeks later, General Edward Hand concluded as much: "if we had anything to expect from that Nation it is now Vanished."[24]

Cornstalk's murder played into the hands of militants on both sides. In February of 1778, Virginia governor Patrick Henry warned western settlers to prepare for Shawnee reprisals: "the Murder of the Shawanese Indians will no doubt bring on Hostilities with that People. In order to ward off the Stroke which may be expected it is necessary to have every Gun in your County put into good order and got ready for Action."[25] His official orders, though stopping short of sanctioning pre-emptive strikes on western Indians, no doubt encouraged westerners already bent on driving all native people from the area. Additionally, many of Governor Henry's following actions during this period seem to indicate that his true intentions were in reality much more offensive than he let on.

GEORGE ROGERS CLARK'S EXPEDITION TO THE ILLINOIS COUNTRY

The Illinois country occupied what is now present-day Illinois, Indiana, and parts of Kentucky and Ohio. As such, it was an essential staging area for Indian raids into Kentucky and Ohio. From their stronghold at Detroit, the British supported the outposts of Cahokia and Kaskaskia in what is now Illinois, and Vincennes or St. Vincents in present-day Indiana. From these outposts, British regulars aided and supplied the various Native American groups hostile to white encroachment. George Rogers Clark knew that taking these posts and then ultimately Detroit would deliver a serious blow to the British and their Indian allies' ability to raid into the American settlements.

Upon his arrival in Williamsburg, Clark wasted no time in presenting his plan to the proper authorities. "I proposed the plan to a few Gentlemen, they communicated it to the Governour, it was immediately determined on, to put in Execution as soon as a Bill could be passed to enable the Governour to order it. . . ." Governor Patrick Henry, however, recognized that the plan had one serious flaw. Most of the areas Clark wanted to attack with Virginia militia were far beyond even the most liberal interpretations of the state's borders. The government of Virginia did not technically have the power to order such an expedition. In addition, few Virginians were willing to serve in a militia action hundreds of miles away from their homes. Therefore, Governor Henry ordered one of the first, but certainly not the last, covert operations in the history of the United States. According to Clark, "it [the bill] accordingly passed, though but a few in the House knew the real intent of it."[26]

Henry's plan called for two sets of instructions regarding the expedition. The first, barely a paragraph in length and distributed in public, mentioned only that the object of the men under Clark's command was to defend Kentucky:

> You are to proceed without Loss of Time to inlist Seven Companies of Men officered in the usual Manner to act as Militia under your Orders They are to proceed to Kentucky & there to obey such orders and Directions as you shall give them for three months after their arrival at that place, but to receive pay &c. in case they remain on Duty a longer Time.[27]

The second set of instructions, written on the same day as the first, contained much more detail. In them, Henry sanctioned Clark to "attack the British post at Kaskasky" and to "keep the true Destination of your Force secret."[28] According to historian Kathrine Wagner Seineke, the authorization for Henry's behavior rested in an act passed by the assembly that same October that allowed the governor to "provide for the farther protection and defence of the frontiers . . . against any of our western enemies."[29] To Henry, the complete secrecy of Clark's mission was a critical factor in implementing the act. Therefore, he felt justified in hiding the true aim of the Clark expedition from the legislature.

It was with this carte blanche authorization that George Rogers Clark, now a lieutenant colonel in the Virginia militia, set out from Williamsburg in January of 1778. From the very beginning, Governor Henry saw the expedition to the Illinois as more than just a military exercise. Long before Clark presented the Virginia legislature with the West Fincastle Petitions containing Kentucky's reasons for its incorporation as a Virginia county, many Virginia statesmen looked covetously upon the Illinois country and dreamed of the riches such a fertile area could bring to the coffers of the newly formed state. Apparently some of the Virginia Assembly were indeed privy to Henry's secret instructions for Clark. On January 3, 1778, just over two weeks before his departure from Williamsburg, Clark received a letter signed by prominent statesmen George Wythe, George Mason, and Thomas Jefferson.

> As some Indian Tribes . . . without any provocation, massacred many of the inhabitants upon the Frontiers of this Commonwealth, in the most cruel and barbarous Manner, and it is intended to . . . punish the Aggressors by carrying the War into their own Country.

We congratulate You upon your Appointment to conduct so important an Enterprize in which We most heartily wish you Success; and we have no Doubt but some further Reward in Lands, in that Country, will be given to the Volunteers who shall engage in this Service.[30]

Judging from the letter, it seems that the three prominent Virginians were at least partially informed of the real nature of Clark's expedition, and it is likely that the source for the breach in secrecy may have been Clark himself. He and George Mason were very close friends, and he had spent the first few years of his life as young Thomas Jefferson's neighbor. More important than their apparent knowledge of at least some of Clark's orders was their justification for fighting in Kentucky and their plans for the land they believed would be gained in doing so. Their reasoning for supporting Clark's plans to carry the war to the Illinois country had nothing to do with British tyranny or with the creation of a nation of liberty. On the contrary, the reasons set forth in the letter from Wythe, Mason, and Jefferson to Clark are simply the destruction of the Native Americans of the Illinois country and the forceful acquisition of their lands. Their attitude represents a fundamental difference between the American Revolution in the east and its counterpart in the Old Northwest. Bloodshed over clashing ideals characterized the war in the east. In the west, hatred and fear dominated the minds of the combatants.

VIOLENCE COMMENCES IN THE OHIO VALLEY

At the same time, Ohio Valley Indian groups also went on the offensive. In January of 1778, Shawnee warriors, whose ranks had swollen after Cornstalk's murder, attacked the famous American frontiersman Daniel Boone's settlement of Boonesborough, capturing Boone. Later that spring, Shawnee warriors attacked Fort Randolph, the site of Cornstalk's death, as well as American settlements in the Kanawha Valley. These raids, which represented a continuation of an offensive begun in 1777, wrought considerable destruction to the area and forced many settlers in Kentucky to abandon settlements and huddle together amid disastrous living conditions in overcrowded forts.[31]

However, none of this violence stemmed the flow of settlers. New settlements cropped up almost weekly, but this of course made it that much more difficult for Kentuckians to protect all of their people. Almost daily, incidents of bloodshed and atrocity became the norm throughout the west during the late 1770s and early 1780s. According to Eric Hinderaker in his examination of a journal kept by Colonel William Fleming, a Virginian who made two separate trips to Kentucky, events that were originally occasion for disgust and revulsion eventually became "accepted as an unpleasant but inescapable reality." Furthermore Fleming's writings demonstrate, according to Hinderaker that "through repetition, the descriptions of violent death take on the character of a litany. The web of atrocity tales that runs through the pages of the journal also ran through the communities that Fleming visited." In addition to serving as a potent example of the constant violence occurring in the west during this period, Fleming's journal also demonstrates that the nature of the American Revolution in the West was fundamentally different than the struggle going on east of the Appalachians. According to Hinderaker, "there is not a single reference to the war against Great Britain. Nor are there expressed any musings on the wider implications of the revolutionary movement, or speculations about the capacity of Kentuckians for self-government." Rather, the American Revolution in the west, at least for whites, represented a continuation of the blood struggle for Indian land that had been raging for decades.[32]

Some Ohio Indians however, at least for a short while, held out hope that they might solve their differences with American settlers via diplomacy. For example, in early September of 1778, Daniel Boone, having recently escaped Indian captors, led an expedition against the Ohio Indian villages. Unfortunately for Boone, whose loyalties were already in question due to the closeness of the relationship he seems to have developed with his captors, the expedition experienced little to no success. Additionally, in depriving the settlements of the majority of their best defenders, the expedition left Kentucky vulnerable to attack. Such an attack materialized days later in the form of a combined force of over 350 Shawnees, Delawares, Miamis, Wyandots, Mingos, and British Loyalist militia who attacked Boonesborough at nearly the same time that Boone and his men were returning from their futile campaign. Despite catching the settlement off-guard, Blackfish, the leader of the war party, offered to allow the Kentuckians to surrender Boonesborough with the option of captivity at Detroit (from whence they would ultimately be ransomed) or adoption by local Indians. According to Kentucky historian Stephen Aron, such an offer represents a strong predisposition on the part of Ohio Valley Indians to "incorporate, not eradicate, their backcountry counterparts." For his part, Boone (further damaging his standing among the settlers) was willing to accept the offer, but his fellow Kentuckians outvoted him and signaled their preference for a fight. In the end, Blackfish and his warriors opted not to storm the fortification. After a ten-day siege in which 2 settlers and 37 Indians were killed as a result of sniper attacks, the Indians, anxious to return in time to assist with their villages' harvests, abandoned both the siege and the attempt to negotiate Boonesborough's surrender. In November of that year, a Kentucky militia attacked 2 prominent neutralist leaders, White Eyes of the Delaware and Moluntha, who had succeeded Cornstalk as the leading peace advocate among the Shawnee, as they traveled bearing messages from the Americans to the Ohio Valley villages. The Kentuckians' complete disregard for their status as neutralists and American couriers must have delivered a very strong message that all hope of negotiation was lost. Once again, in the words of Aron, "hatred and misunderstanding now overwhelmed any affinities between Kentucky pioneers and Shawnees."[33]

From that point on, the choice for Ohio Valley Indians was either to fight or flee, and their communities would remain divided between these two options throughout the rest of the war. The Shawnee community of Chillicothe provides an excellent illustration of this division. During the spring of 1779, nearly 400 Chillicothe Shawnees chose to move to Missouri in an effort to preserve their communities in another location rather than risk destruction to protect their current villages. Later that year, others moved to Tennessee for the same purpose; however, the approximately 100 warriors who chose to remain at Chillicothe represented the most resolute of the village, determined to fight to the last in defense of their homeland. According to Henry Hamilton, commanding at Detroit, these particular warriors were "inveterate against the Virginians." At the beginning of the summer they spurned a last-ditch effort by neutralist Delawares to mediate the dispute with the Americans. Later that month, the Kentuckians struck Chillicothe hard, burning several lodges, taking most of their possessions, and most importantly killing the war leader Blackfish. Over the next two years, raids across the Ohio by both Indians and settlers became commonplace.[34]

In October of 1779, one of the deadliest of these raids occurred. This time a large band of warriors led by Loyalist partisan Simon Girty attacked an American convoy returning from a supply trip to New Orleans. The attackers killed nearly all of the 70 men accompanying the supplies including the convoy's commander.[35] Subsequently, the so-called Hard Winter of 1779 to 1780 brought all activity to a stand still in Kentucky. For nearly three months, snow blanketed the west, and subzero temperatures froze rivers, animals, and settlers alike. Food became so scarce that the price of corn quadrupled in less than six months.[36]

By March of 1780, the weather moderated and settlement continued at the same rapid pace as before. Despite the privation of the Hard Winter, an estimated 20,000 people moved to Kentucky in 1779 and 1780. Several settlements were now thriving in Kentucky including Harrodsburg, Boonesborough, Logan's Station, Bryan's Station, and Lexington to name a few, but the increase in settlers only strengthened the determination of Ohio Valley Indians to resist the loss of their lands.

On March 10, 1780, the inhabitants of both Boonesborough and Bryan's Station sent George Rogers Clark petitions begging him to defend them against the attacks of the Shawnee.[37] Shortly after he received these petitions, Clark wrote John Todd, the civil commander of the district, expressing his suspicion that the British had more on their mind than just a few minor raids:

By the Acts from Every Post in the Illinois So nearly Corresponding I make no doubt of the English Regaining the Interest of Many Tribes of Indians and their designs agst the Illinois (Perhaps on Govr Hamiltons plan) and without some speady Check may prove Fatal to Kentucky and the Total loss of the Westn Cuntrey on the Mississippi.[38]

To counter this new threat, Clark began to plan and implement a defensive strategy. Both he and Jefferson believed that a fort at or near the junction of the Ohio and Mississippi rivers held the key to the entire western trade as well as the defense of the Kentucky settlements. In addition to the fort near the mouth of the Ohio, the Virginia legislature ordered Clark to construct four other forts—one each at the mouths of the Licking, Big Sandy, and Guyandotte rivers, as well as one at the eastern end of the Wilderness Road in an area known as Powell's Valley. Because of the scarcity of men, Clark and Todd decided that the best hope for an adequate defense of the Kentucky frontier lay in concentrating all of their approximately 150 men at the proposed fort near the mouth of the Ohio River. In mid-April, Clark began to survey that area for a suitable location. By the end of the first week in May, he had selected a site approximately five miles below the mouth of the river. Because nearly all the lands near the southern banks of the river flooded annually, Clark was forced to choose a location distant from the actual juncture of the two rivers.[39]

Unbeknownst to Clark or Todd, the British had decided that their best chance of ending the war lay in the western theater. According to historian James Alton James, this thorough British strategy called first for the capture of the Illinois country and the falls of the Ohio River and then Fort Pitt and Fort Cumberland. The British plan also called for simultaneous attacks on New Orleans and other posts in Spanish territory along the southern portion of the Mississippi River. In addition to cutting off supplies and communication between the west and the east, this strategy, if successful, would also allow British troops and their Native American allies in the west to augment British forces in the east.[40]

Various difficulties forced British officer Henry Bird to abandon the idea of attacking the falls of the Ohio in June of 1780. However, he and his force of 1,200 men, nearly 1,000 of whom were Ohio Valley warriors, were determined not to go back to Detroit empty-handed. During the march back to Detroit, Bird ordered his men to attack the Kentucky settlements of Ruddles and Martin's stations on the Licking River. The small stockaded posts fell easily in the face of Bird's two cannon. Ruddles Station capitulated first on June 24. Martin's Station suffered the same fate a few days later. Satisfied with his victories, Bird turned for Detroit. In addition to the usual plunder, Bird took nearly all 350 survivors as his prisoners. He gave 200 of the prisoners to his Indian allies as gifts while taking the rest with him to Detroit. Several of the captives did not survive the march north. According to one source, "Many of the women and children, unable to bear the strain of the march, were relieved of their sufferings through the use of the tomahawk."[41] Such a death, in the culture of most North American Indians including the Shawnees, would have been considered an act of mercy intended to spare prisoners a grueling trip they more than likely would not survive, as well as a way to eliminate the potential for sick and wounded captives to slow the party's escape. The Americans, needless to say, did not view the situation in this manner.[42]

RETALIATION AGAINST THE SHAWNEES

Upon learning of Bird's attack and the death of the prisoners, Clark immediately set about planning a retaliatory strike. For once, he had no trouble in recruiting volunteers. The attack had stirred the blood of practically every eligible male in Kentucky. In addition to the Kentucky militia, fresh troops had recently arrived from Virginia under the command of Colonel George Slaughter. By August 1, Clark's force had grown to nearly 1,000 men. Clark and his officers, including several prominent Kentucky settlers such as Daniel Boone, Levi Todd, and Benjamin Logan as well as Colonel Slaughter, decided to strike at the Shawnee villages on the north side of the Ohio River. The Shawnee, longtime enemies to settlement in the west had comprised a large portion of Bird's forces. In addition, many of the Kentuckians had not forgotten Lord Dunmore's War and the previous five years of intense raiding in the area. They craved an opportunity to finish the job they began in the summer of 1774.[43]

On August 6, Clark and his men arrived at the principal Shawnee town of Chillicothe. Aware of Clark's expedition, the Shawnee had deserted the town hours before. Clark ordered the town burned and marched his army northeast to the town of Piqua on the Miami River. All the while Clark suspected that the retreat by the Shawnee was only part of a strategy to lure his force to ground well suited for an ambush. Nevertheless, he pushed on.

Determined to exact revenge for the Bird raid, Clark and his force came within sight of Piqua on August 8. Clark barely had time to survey the situation when the Shawnee, along with Delaware, Mingo, and Wyandotte warriors amounting to a total strength of 300, sprang their trap. Confident in the abilities of his troops, Clark ordered them to meet the attackers head-on.[44]

> The confidence the enemy had of their own strength and certain victory, or the want of generalship, occasioned several neglects, by which those advantages were taken that proved the ruin of their army, being flanked two or three different times, drove from hill to hill in a circuitous direction, for upwards of a mile and a half; at last took shelter in their strongholds and woods adjacent, when the firing ceased for about half an hour, until necessary preparations were made for dislodging them. A heavy firing again commenced, and continued severe until dark, by which time the enemy were totally routed.[45]

According to Clark's report to Thomas Jefferson, the Shawnee and their allies had not counted on his bringing cannon along with him. Unable to find adequate shelter from Clark's artillery, their situation soon became untenable. At the end of the battle, Clark reported 14 dead and 13 wounded. The Shawnee carried off their dead and wounded during the night except for a few that lay too close to Clark's lines, but he estimated their casualties at approximately 50 warriors. While the American victory was a considerable one, Clark realized that it could have been much greater. The terrain had prevented him from employing his whole force, therefore allowing the Shawnee to escape once the battle was decided. Having set out with very few supplies, Clark had no choice but to turn the expedition back toward Kentucky.[46]

Despite the retreat of Clark's forces, and the relatively small amount of actual casualties taken by the Shawnees, Clark's campaign represented a major blow. The burning of their fields carried with it the potential for considerable suffering over the coming winter. Their only hope to avoid such an outcome lay with the ability of their British allies to resupply them. Unfortunately, Clark's campaign coincided with a marked decline in the availability of British military stores due to their funneling all available supplies to their overextended forces in Georgia and the Carolinas. Ohio Valley Indians began to grumble that the English, while preferable to the Americans, represented a poor substitute for their former French allies. This situation notwithstanding, the Shawnees and their allies continued their resistance despite the fact that Lord Cornwallis's surrender to the

Americans and their French allies at Yorktown in October of 1781 effectively brought the war to a close in the east.[47]

In the west, just as the war between American settlers and Ohio Valley
Indians had raged before Lexington and Concord, so it continued beyond
Yorktown. In March of 1782 an American militia from Pennsylvania, made
up of westerners who had recently suffered a series of devastating attacks at
the hand of British-allied Delawares, systematically massacred 96 pacifist
Delawares at the Moravian mission village of Gnadenhutten in Ohio. The
perpetrators of that attack engaged in the massacre despite knowing that
these Indians were not involved in the attacks on their settlements. In fact,
they had originally proposed wiping out the Moravian villages a year before
only to be rebuffed by their superiors at Fort Pitt. However, the attacks of the
British-allied Delawares in the western Pennsylvania, Virginia and Maryland
backcountries removed all barriers to their genocidal plan.[48] The details
remain some of the most chilling episodes of violence from the Ohio Valley
during the American Revolution:

> In the other house, Judith, an aged and remarkably pious and gentle
> widow was the first victim. Christina, before mentioned, fell on her
> knees and begged for life. In vain! In vain! The tigers had again tasted
> blood. In both houses men, women and children were bound by
> ropes in couples, and were thus led like lambs to the slaughter. Most
> all of them, I heard—for I only saw that part of the butchery which I
> was compelled to witness—marched cheerfully, and some smilingly
> to meet their death.[49]

In June of that year, another American expedition, comprised of some
400 untrained militia bent on visiting more revenge on the Indians of the
Ohio Valley, was surprised by a larger force of Indians, soon to be reinforced by British regulars on the Upper Sandusky River. As the Americans
attempted to retreat, their commander, General William Crawford, a notorious speculator in Indian land, was captured along with several others.[50]
On June 11, 1782, Crawford's Delaware captors took their revenge for the
massacre at Gnadenhutten:

> Crawford was stripped naked and ordered to sit down. . . . Crawford's
> hands were bound behind his back, and a rope fastened—one end to
> the foot of the post, and the other to the ligature between his wrists.
> The rope was long enough for him to sit down, or walk around the
> post once or twice and return the same way. Crawford then called to
> Girty and asked if they intended to burn him. Girty answered, "Yes."

He then replied he would take it all patiently. Upon this, Captain Pipe made a speech to the Indians, who, at its conclusion, yelled a hideous and hearty assent as sent to what had been said. their savage relations stepped forward in their stead. The fire was kindled, and poor Crawford was tied to the stake.[51]

The Delawares then shot Crawford and cut off both of his ears and taunted him fiercely. Eventually Crawford was scalped and finally breathed his last. The victims at Gnadenhutten had been avenged.[52]

When news of the defeat reached William Irvine, who was now commanding at Fort Pitt, he immediately began to plan a retaliatory campaign. Irvine directed George Rogers Clark to cross the Ohio River and attack the Shawnees from the south while he advanced west from Fort Pitt; however, word of their preparations reached Arent De Peyster, the commandant at Fort Detroit. He immediately assumed that the Americans intended to march against his post. Leaving nothing to chance, he ordered 1,100 loyalists and Indians under captains Alexander Caldwell, Alexander McKee, Joseph Brant, and Simon Girty to abandon a planned expedition against Wheeling and return to Detroit. Girty, a backcountry Loyalist who had betrayed the Americans a few years before, decided that they could not return from the expedition empty-handed and crossed the Ohio along with 300 warriors in mid-August and headed for the settlement of Bryan's Station.[53]

On the morning of August 16, 1782, Girty and his 300 warriors surrounded the settlement. The Indians intended to surprise the fort, but were unaware that during the night the inhabitants detected their presence. During the subsequent attack, the Kentuckians managed to sneak a few men safely past the Indians to go for help. Realizing that rescue parties were now on their way, the Indians and Girty withdrew on the morning of August 17. Taking their time destroying every field they came upon, Girty and his men encamped at a place on the north side the Licking River known as the Blue Licks on August 19. Unbeknownst to Girty, militia from Lincoln county as well as that of Fayette county under the command of colonels Benjamin Logan and Daniel Boone pursued them. By the morning of that day, the advance guard of this militia force spotted Girty's men across the river. At a hastily organized officers' council, Boone urged caution, but Major Hugh McGary, commander of the Lincoln county militia, would not listen. He ordered the militia to cross the river and attack. Within five minutes, Girty's men outflanked and routed the Americans. As the militiamen tried to retreat back across the river, the Indians poured volley after volley into them and tomahawked many of the Kentuckians as they tried to swim to safety. By the time the Americans made it back to Bryan's Station, they had lost 66 men including 2 colonels.[54]

Over the next several months, Clark invaded Ohio once again, but achieved nothing of importance while war parties of Shawnees, Mingos, Senecas and Cherokees joined to conduct devastating raids on American settlements in the area aided by British guns and Loyalist militias. The tide had turned. Ohio Valley Indians were winning the day in the West. But almost as quickly as it had come, their advantage disappeared. By the Fall of 1782, British officials had begun to chastise Ohio Valley Indians for spilling American blood. Major De Peyster at Detroit warned them that any further activities against the Americans would "be an affair of your own, as your Father can take no part in it."[55]

Sensing that the British might negotiate an end to the war with no consideration for their Indian allies, one Wyandot representative pleaded with the British that they "not allow your poor children to be crushed under the weight of their enemies. . . . Father! Should a Treaty of Peace be going on we hope your children will be remembered in the Treaty." In July of 1783, an American officer informed the Shawnees that the British had done exactly that. "Your Fathers the English have made Peace with us for themselves, but forgot you their Children, who fought with them, and neglected you like Bastards."[56]

8

"Like We Should Soon Become No People": The Assault on Indian Land in the Immediate Aftermath of the American Revolution

In 1787, Creek leader Alexander McGillivray remarked upon the tremendously difficult situation into which the American victory over the British had placed many native people. Specifically, the Creek leader feared that his people "may be forced to purchase a Shameful peace & barter our Country for a precarious Security."[1] In many respects, McGillivray's fears were prescient. As mentioned previously, the British willfully betrayed their Indian allies in the Treaty of Paris. Additionally, in the 20 years after the end of the conflict, the young American Republic demanded land cessions at an exorbitant rate and often resorted to fraud, coercion, and violence if their demands were not rapidly met with an affirmative response; however, while it might be easy to characterize Native Americans during this period as a conquered and subdued people, in reality during the last 20 years of the 18th century, Indian people continued to resist the disintegration of both their homelands and their sovereignty. Sometimes this resistance took the form of violence, but it as often as not manifested itself in diplomatic and cultural forms.

CHEROKEE FACTIONALISM INCREASES

For Cherokees the erosion of their traditional culture and their ties not only to one another but also to other native groups accelerated in the years following the war. The factionalism that the Revolution spawned among the Cherokees only increased after the cessation of hostilities. Accommodationist leaders regained firm control in the traditional Cherokee villages, but Dragging Canoe's Chickamauga followers continued to resist sporadically well into the 1790s. Another faction even considered emigrating to Spanish territory west of the Mississippi River; however, the majority of Cherokees opted for eliminating war altogether as an option for dealing with whites and instead turned to nonviolent paths of resistance. In an effort to preserve both their sovereignty and their land base, the Cherokees turned to métis, or mixed-race families, as cultural brokers to solidify peace with whites. These métis, together with accomodationist leaders, adopted a strategy of yielding on many outward and peripheral aspects of life in order to retain those aspects of Cherokee culture they considered most crucial. This new strategy consisted, among other things, of the adoption of pottery styles patterned more closely on European and American designs, of black slavery, and of some aspects of European gender norms while still resisting European agricultural methods and preserving a reciprocal exchange-based economy.[2]

Cherokee representatives attempted to implement this strategy in the negotiations leading to the Treaty of Hopewell (named for the plantation where the treaty negotiations took place) in 1785, which attempted to fix a final boundary between the lands of the Cherokees and the United States. According to Colin Calloway, the Treaty of Hopewell "confirmed Cherokee boundaries, but it did little to stop the encroachments on their lands." Additionally, what few provisions the Americans did adhere to initially were quickly discarded in later years if it suited their purposes. It was specifically in reference to their experience with the Treaty of Hopewell that Cherokee representatives complained to Virginia governor Patrick Henry in 1789 that they were "so Distrest by the No. Carolina People that it seems Like we sho'ld soon become no People. They have got all our Land from us. We have hardly as much as we can stand on, and they seem to want that little worse than the Rest." The failure of this strategy to protect their homeland from white land hunger only created more division among the Cherokees, and by the end of the 1790s many Cherokees who had earlier resisted joining the Chickamaugas were now fighting alongside them.[3]

THE RISE OF ALEXANDER MCGILLIVRAY AND INEQUALITY AMONG THE CREEKS

The Creek Confederacy ended the war as divided and factionalized as it had ever been. According to historian J. Leitch Wright, the fact that Creeks were surrounded on all sides by competing constituencies and powers made their situation all the more difficult:

> After 1783 the Muscogulges were surrounded by subjects of at least three powers—Americans in Georgia, Spaniards in the Floridas, and former British loyalists who lived among the Indians and in the Spanish Floridas. Britain had relinquished title to lands in the Southeast, but the British flag still flew over the nearby Bahamas, Detroit, and Canada. Meanwhile Frenchmen, one of whom was Napoleon, thought it was good idea to raise the French flag once again over Fort Toulouse. The Southeast was a hotbed of international intrigue and land speculation.[4]

Internal division only added to this difficult situation. Alexander McGillivray and those opposed to the Treaty of Hopewell (to which the Creeks were also a party) began to cultivate a relationship with the Spanish, now the possessors of Florida, rather than make peace with the newly independent Americans. McGillivray's leadership of these efforts marks a critical turning point in the postrevolutionary history of the Creeks. Over the next 10 years he would lead a movement that would both divide and fundamentally alter Creek society. According to Creek historian Claudio Saunt, "Before the Revolution, Creeks did not strive to accumulate significant amounts of material possession or to protect and defend their belongings from their neighbors." By the eve of the War of 1812, Creek society was marked by inequality and a sharp divide over those who believed in traditional Creek notion of communal property and those who had adopted a more materialistic and European conception of wealth and possessions.[5]

McGillivray, the wealthy son of a Scottish plantation owner and a Creek woman, had spent the majority of his formative years living on his father's plantation. Forced to remove to Creek country to escape the wrath of American revolutionaries bent on punishing his family for their loyalism, McGillivray came to live among his mother's people at the age of 25 with little to no knowledge of their culture and religion, as well as with only a rudimentary knowledge of their language. Despite these tenuous connections to the Creeks, he parlayed his status as a British Indian agent during the war to obtain the Creek title of Most Beloved Man, yet lived on a European style plantation replete with slaves and a house that rivaled those of the wealthiest southern white planters. At one point McGillivray entered into an agreement with the Spanish government that named him their commissary in Creek country, yet at the same time he was a secret partner in the British trading firm of Panton, Leslie, and Company, which eventually obtained a monopoly on trade with the Creeks. Due to the conflicting loyalties such a collection of attachments created, he always seemed to subordinate the overall interests of the Creeks to those of his colonial masters.[6]

The U.S. government increasingly came to see him as empowered to speak for all of Creek country, though in reality he held no traditional position of power in the Creek leadership structure. As such the American government wasted no opportunity available to them to co-opt McGillivray with various presents, titles, and land bounties. On one occasion the Americans even went so far as to make him a brigadier general in the U.S. army. McGillivray's stated desire to transform the Creeks into "cultivators and herdsmen instead of Hunters," fell right in line with the civilization paradigm that dominated Indian policy in the early republic. Therefore the U.S. government was more than happy to encourage his efforts.[7]

Traditional Creek leaders such as Hoboithle Mico of the Upper Creek town of Tallassee distrusted McGillivray and actively opposed many of his schemes. Eventually, his self-serving activities caught up with him and by the time of his death in 1793, Alexander McGillivray had been largely rejected by most if not all of the major factions in Creek society; however, once again according to Saunt, the damage had been done:

> McGillivray's rise to power challenged many of the long-held beliefs of Creeks about property and power. Though an extraordinary figure in Creek country, McGillivray nevertheless marked the entrance of other mestizos [métis], albeit less powerful and less visible than the Scots-Indian into leadership positions in the region.[8]

In the late 1780s and early 1790s, acculturated Creeks, many of them mestizos, but some not, began to force a centralized governing system patterned after those of Europe and the young United States on the rest of the Creek people. This faction increasingly wrested political and judicial power from the hands of the local clans and placed it in a supreme body whose primary purpose was to protect private property and enforce a hierarchical conception of society. By the late 1790s, those who supported this movement toward centralization and hierarchy imposed a National Council on their fellow kinsmen empowered to pass laws applicable to all Creeks. Included among the enactments of the National Council were laws creating harsh punishments for infractions of the National Council's statutes.[9]

By 1813, those Creeks who refused to accept the authority of the National Council had reached their limit and struck back violently. Calling themselves "Redsticks" after the Creek emblem of justice, they engaged in a yearlong war both against their brethren who supported the National Council and the U.S. government. They were eventually defeated by militias under the command of Andrew Jackson at Horseshoe Bend in March of 1814. The Americans forced a treaty on the Creeks that gave away not only large swaths of Redstick territory, but also that of the acculturated Creeks who had remained loyal to the United States. By this time, what had once been an exceptionally egalitarian and communal society had become wracked by inequality. Evidence indicates that by the end of the Redstick War, the top 20 percent of Creek society held more than 60 percent of the wealth in Creek country. Such divisions, which as we have seen, traced their roots back to the dilemmas created by the American victory in the Revolution, played right into the hands of an American government and citizenry eager to deprive all Creeks, loyal or rebellious, of their lands.[10]

CHICKASAWS IN A CHAOTIC WORLD

Making up for the loss of British trade goods represented the primary issue facing the Chickasaws after the British surrender in 1781. Since the Chickasaws had always operated as a polity in which individual villages made their own decisions concerning with whom to trade and ally, there had always been differences of opinion regarding what European powers to favor. But those differences of opinion had actually strengthened group cohesion, as no one group or central authority ever tried to force its will on the others. In the wake of the loss of British trade, the Chickasaws fell back on these same principles. Those who had always favored the French sought to ally with the Spanish, while those, such as Paya Mataha who had generally advocated strong ties with the British, now looked to a future relationship with the newly independent United States. In the immediate aftermath of the war, whichever trading partner looked as if it could supply the most goods trumped any pre-existing tendencies or jealousies either faction may have had. In the end, the Chickasaws were completely dependent upon trade for their survival.[11]

Due to this need for trade, the Chickasaw response during this postwar period was rather chaotic and confused. After some initial flirtations with a group of Loyalist rebels who resisted Spanish control of West Florida, the Chickasaws eventually came to accept the Spanish presence in the area. Specifically, the lack of an alternative trading partner as well as attacks by their Kickapoo and Mascouten enemies left them with little choice but to welcome the Spanish. According to one observer, "the Chickasaws are poor and there are no other white people except the Spaniards who can supply their needs." By July of 1782, they were actively engaged in negotiations with representatives of the United States as well. Additionally, individual American states such as Georgia and Virginia were also actively courting diplomatic and economic relationships with the Chickasaws. All of this added up to an extremely confusing situation for Chickasaw leaders, which they summed up in a letter to Congress in 1783:[12]

> When our great father the King of England called away his warriors, he told us to take your People by the hand as friends and brothers . . . It makes our hearts rejoice to find that our great father, and his children the Americans have at length made peace . . . And to find that our Brothers the Americans are inclined to take us by the hand . . . Not-withstanding the Satisfaction all these things give us we are yet in confusion & uncertainty. The Spaniards are sending talks amongst us, and inviting our young Men to trade with them. We also receive talks from the Governor of Georgia to the same effect- We have had Speeches from the Illinois inviting us to a Trade and Intercourse with them- Our Brothers, the Virginians Call upon us to a Treaty, and want part of our land, and we expect our Neighbors who live on Cumberland River, will in a Little time Demand, if not forcibly take part of it from us, also as we are informed they have been marking Lines through our hunt-ing grounds: we are daily receiving Talks from one Place or other, and from People we Know nothing about.[13]

The signing of the Treaty of Nashville between Virginia and the Chickasaws in November of 1783 finally brought at least some degree of clarity to the future direction of Chickasaw foreign relations. According to the terms of the agreement, the Chickasaws agreed to return all captives taken during the war and expel from their territory any other Indians and Loyalists still hostile to the United States. In return they received a clear delineation of their lands and promises that white encroachment would stop.[14]

The treaty, however, was negotiated primarily by leaders already predis-posed to the Americans and given the nonbinding nature of such agreements in Chickasaw politics, those who favored an alliance with Spain freely disre-garded it and continued to court the Spanish. By January of 1786, both parties had granted conflicting trade monopolies to the Americans and the Spanish. These conflicting moves not only created distrust among the both the Spanish and the Americans, but also created conflicts between the Chickasaws and their Creek neighbors, as well as the Kickapoos, Piankashaws, Miamis, and Illinois, to name just a few. Despite the tremendous difficulties they produced, none of these trade relationships bore the long-term sustained trade sufficient to replace the Chickasaws' former relationship with the British. The Chickasaws still found themselves in want of many of the items necessary for survival, not to mention the luxury items to which they had grown accustomed over several years of lucrative trade with the British. According to American army major John Doughty, even after the trade agreements with the Americans and the Spanish, the Chickasaws "never before were in such Distress for want of Powder, Lead, Blanketts, Strouds, etc."[15]

This confusing and potentially catastrophic situation would continue for the Chickasaws into the 1790s. Then, in 1795, the Spanish signed the Treaty of San Lorenzo, or Pinckney's Treaty, which fixed the boundaries between the United States and the Spanish colonies and thus commenced a Spanish retreat from the Mississippi Valley. This change had the effect of clarifying the future direction of Chickasaw trade and foreign policy. Now no longer caught between the vice grip of two powers, they would have to forge a lasting relationship with the Americans. Of course the pro-Spanish faction remained uneasy about the eventual outcome of such a relationship. According to one pro-Spanish Chickasaw leader, "we perceive in them [the Americans] the cunning of the Rattle snake who caresses the Squirrel he intends to devour." In the end, this leader's fears proved prophetic. With the Spanish now out of the picture, the United States no longer felt the need to negotiate with the Chickasaws but instead began to dictate terms of trade and land cessions. They also encouraged Chickasaws to indebt themselves at government trading posts, which in the words of Thomas Jefferson, led them to "cede their lands to rid themselves of debts." The strategy paid dividends rather quickly. In 1805, the Chickasaws ceded all their lands north of the Tennessee River in large part to settle debts incurred at the trading posts. In a series of land cessions the United States steadily deprived the Chickasaws of the majority of their traditional land base during the early years of the 19th century. Devoid of sufficient trade and rapidly losing their grip on their own territory, the Chickasaws were the smallest of the five groups removed from the southeast as part of Andrew Jackson's Indian Removal Act in the 1830s, but for the disastrous consequences wrought by the American Revolution their fate might have been different.[16]

THE PRESERVATION OF CHOCTAW SOVEREIGNTY

Much like the Chickasaws, the Choctaws' overwhelming priority after the war was to replace the trade lost by the departure of the British.[17] Unlike the Chickasaws, however, the Choctaws managed to preserve the autonomy of individual villages and divisions while not splitting into factions that favored trade with either the Americans, the Spanish, or a particular state. Instead, according to historian Greg O'Brien, "Choctaw chiefs responded to the post-Revolutionary situation by seeking to increase trade with all of these groups." Additionally, even in treaty making and in land cessions, the Choctaws found ways to resist the imposition of complete American control over their lives and lands.[18]

In 1785, delegations from both Georgia and the U.S. government arrived in Choctaw country to settle issues of land and trade. For Choctaws this was actually a welcome sign. The possibility of triangulating this trade with that of the Spanish spawned the hope that the end of the Revolution might still allow them to continue playing the major powers in the region against one another as they had done for years with rival European powers. The Americans, however, had other ideas.[19]

The representatives from both Georgia and the U.S. government took the opportunity to dictate to the Choctaws. At Hopewell, in late December and early January, the Choctaws met U.S. government representatives for the first time, and things went poorly from the start. The Americans, who had never understood the role of gift exchange in native diplomacy were insulted by Choctaw expectations of gifts before formal negotiations could begin. One of the representatives referred to the Choctaws as "the greatest beggars and the most indolent creatures we ever saw."[20]

In the end, despite Choctaw insistence that they would agree to no land cessions and despite their belief when they left the conference that they had not, they were surprised later to find out that they had ceded a small amount of land to the United States for the establishment of a trading post. No doubt that trading post was intended to further the design of indebting the Choctaws for the purpose of extracting future land cessions from them. Additionally, the relatively low-ranking chiefs sent to Hopewell were not authorized to cede land. Therefore by agreeing to the cession with these minor leaders the United States was also employing a strategy it would continue to use throughout its dealings with Native Americans, which was to weaken the power of traditional leaders by empowering individuals outside the traditional power structure and then using these people's newly granted status as a means of co-opting them.[21]

Hopewell also failed to produce the increased trade that lie at the heart of Choctaw willingness to enter into the agreement in the first place. But by refusing to blindly accept the imposition of U.S. control of their lands, the Choctaws did manage to alter the future course of federal Indian policy in the southeast. The United States had come into the Treaty of Hopewell expecting to place those Indians present under the complete and total jurisdiction of the United States, and they assumed that groups like the Choctaws would, according to Greg O'Brien "realize—if not fully accept—their subordinate role in the new North American order." That did not happen, and continued Choctaw resistance made certain that it would not happen in the years to come either. Once again, O'Brien has characterized the situation with exceptional clarity:

> By 1789 the United States had renounced its claims of absolute sovereignty over the territory it had acquired from Great Britain, thus converting Indian affairs from a domestic problem to a foreign policy issue.

In other words, even in the limited form the U.S. government recognizes today, the concept of native sovereignty, which represents in many cases the most important tool that modern Indian nations possess for protecting their culture, lands, and resources, can be traced back to the resistance of Southern Indians in general and the Choctaws specifically in the years immediately following the American Revolution.[22]

FROM ALLIES TO SYMBOLS: THE POSTWAR CATAWBA EXPERIENCE

Their status as American allies created for the Catawbas a somewhat unique experience in the immediate postwar years. Though their lands were devastated and their people starving, they were largely spared from the most immediate instances of white encroachment because of the role they had played in the American victory. In February of 1782, the South Carolina legislature sent 500 bushels of corn to help them survive the winter. The 1784 legislature went even further and voted to compensate the Catawbas £299 for their support during the war as well as to reimburse £125 for livestock the Catawbas had supplied the Continental Army. The South Carolina legislature also, at least temporarily, acted as a check on the land acquisition schemes of powerful individuals including Governor William Moultrie when they threatened the Catawbas.[23]

As time passed, however, South Carolinians began to devote increasingly less thought to their former Catawba allies. Once useful for their military prowess, the Catawbas were now only needed for their ability to serve as symbols that could assuage the guilt of the majority of South Carolina's record in Indian affairs. In a fashion similar to the role Pocahontas played for early Americans as an example of a "good Indian," the Catawbas operated as a justification for the often self-serving Indian policies of South Carolina's leading men.[24]

For their part the Catawbas endeavored to use their symbolic status to their advantage. They never missed an opportunity to remind both their kinsmen and their white neighbors of their service to South Carolina and the new nation. According to Catawba historian James Merrell, "patriotism became one more tool—along with pottery, land leases, and a less threatening countenance—Indians could use to carve a niche for themselves in the social landscape of the Carolina piedmont." But these strategies could only do so much. Increasingly, Catawba leaders grew so concerned over the security of their lands that they attempted unsuccessfully to convince the South Carolina legislature to ban the sale of any Catawba land even with tribal consent.[25]

By the 1790s their worst fears were coming to fruition. By that time their original 144,000-acre reservation had shrunk to less than 8,000 acres and they were barred from hunting off the reservation without special permission. Corrupt trustees assigned by the state to oversee Catawba land transactions only exacerbated this decline. When the Catawbas complained, local settlers intent on gaining Catawba land resorted to intimidation and subterfuge to get it. Yet, despite these obstacles, the Catawbas endured.[26] Once again according to Merrell:

> Once proprietors of the piedmont, they now existed only on the sufferance of people inclined to cheat them as often as protect them, mock them as readily as befriend them. It was a sad state, requiring more quiet resignation than open resistance. . . . Had Catawbas chosen another path, had they opted for something other than a life as potters and patriots, they would not have survived the century.[27]

Such was the price of survival in the new American world for many native groups.

THE POSTWAR COMPLICATIONS OF ABENAKI AMBIGUITY

While their strategy of ambiguity allowed the Abenaki to avoid the pitfalls experienced by those native groups who supported one of the combatants or attempted to remain neutral, it created considerable difficulties for them in the postwar period. In fact, according to Colin Calloway the Western Abenakis became "exiles in their own land" during this period. Those who had supported the British removed to Canada; however, New England Loyalists, who had also removed north of the border, avariciously groped for their lands and treated the Catholic Abenakis with disdain and outright antagonism.[28]

New England Loyalists of Puritan stock were not the only offenders. In 1784, an illegal settlement of Loyalist New Yorkers also encroached upon Abenaki land in Canada. When the New Yorkers disobeyed British orders to disperse, the authorities simply gave up trying to force them to respect the Abenakis' claim to the area, thus abandoning the Indians to the designs of the settlers.[29]

South of the Canadian border in the newly minted United States, things were just as bleak, or possibly worse, for the Abenakis. Having yearned for Abenaki land since the days before the American Revolution, the Vermont frontiersmen and land speculators Ethan and Ira Allen used the Abenakis' wartime strategy of dispersal and decentralization against them. The Allens undertook a campaign that painted the Abenakis as shiftless nomads who could not possibly hold title to land. They compounded this claim with reminders of joint French-Abenaki raids during the Imperial Wars of the first half of the 18th century.[30]

By the early 1790s the strategy seems to have paid dividends as the relationship between the Vermont Abenakis and American settlers had become extremely contentious. Both American and Indian alike promulgated accusations, threats, and occasional violence during this period. Eventually for most Abenakis the situation became untenable. Many decided to leave their traditional homeland rather than continue to resist a growing white population that considered them "trespassing nomads with no present rights and no legitimate historical claim to the country they had inhabited and continued to inhabit." While the strategy of ambiguity had spared them many of the ravages of war, it ultimately cost them their unity and their lands when the peace that ended that war once again unleashed upon the Abenakis the insatiable land hunger of American settlers.[31]

THE DEMISE OF THE STOCKBRIDGE INDIANS

By war's end, when the Stockbridge Indians began to return home from their service to the American cause, they too found their lands in jeopardy. Their prolonged absence from home, combined with the Continental Congress's inability to pay them, left the majority of them completely destitute. Furthermore, the war made widows of many Stockbridge women who along with their children would have to be supported by the community, thus adding to the financial difficulties facing the group.[32]

Even before the war officially ended, the Stockbridge were forced to beg for assistance from their American neighbors, reminding them both of their service during the war and of the fact that much of the land that settlers in Vermont and New York were now settling had never been either sold or given to them by the Stockbridge. In the end, these petitions fell on deaf ears and the Stockbridge were forced to relocate to lands offered them in 1783 by the Oneidas of New York, themselves one of the Americans' other prominent Indian allies. As they prepared to leave for New York, they sent one last petition to the government of Massachusetts which stated, among other things, "in this late War we have suffered much, our Blood has been spilled with yours and many of our Young Men have fallen by the Side of your Warriors. . . . Now we who remain are become very poor." The petition went on to inform their Massachusetts neighbors of their intentions to accept the Oneida offer. Finally, the Stockbridge petition voiced the hope that in their new home "instead of being further burdensome we hope to be of some advantage to the United States."[33]

Additionally, the Stockbridge requested that the small amount of land they still retained in the town of Stockbridge be looked after for them. Instead, within weeks the last piece of Stockbridge-owned land was sold, and by February of 1785 so few Indian people remained in Stockbridge that there was no reason to continue holding the Indian proprietors meeting, which had, up to that time, been conducted regularly for the purpose of handling town business and issuing new land grants. At this same time, the non-native population of Stockbridge skyrocketed. By 1810 the remaining Stockbridge Indians signed over title to their Indian burial ground in order to discharge their last remaining debts.[34]

Those who moved to New York to live among the Oneidas were successful in creating a new life, at least in the short-term; however, the Americans' voracious appetite for land could only be held at bay for so long. By 1785, the Oneida country, which the Americans had promised their former allies would always be theirs, was under pressure from all sides. Despite repeated attempts to force both the governments of New York and the United States to live up to their promises, by the end of the War of 1812, what few Stockbridge Indians remained in New York had decided to move to locations as far from their original homeland as Indiana and Wisconsin. Once again, in the words of Colin Calloway, "Indian patriotism did not earn Indian people a place in the nation they helped to create."[35]

THE FATE OF THE SIX NATIONS

Or course, those Iroquois who had allied with the British faced an even more difficult situation than their Oneida kinsmen. Not only did they likewise face the prospect of unchecked pressures on their land base from settlers, but this was also compounded by American anger at their having chosen to support the British. Those closest to the Iroquois knew even before the official end of the war that a British withdrawal would leave their Iroquois allies at the mercy of Americans determined to punish them harshly for their decision fight against the Patriot cause. When the British officers who worked with the Iroquois heard that their leaders had completely abandoned their Indian allies in the preliminary Articles of Peace agreed to on November 30, 1782, they attempted to conceal the news from the Iroquois.[36] Upon learning of the preliminary agreement, Sir Frederick Haldimand, then governor of Quebec, expressed his shock at the betrayal of the Iroquois. "The Indians have been entirely forgotten in the preliminaries," he wrote. These developments left Haldimand "heartily ashamed," and it was he who ordered his department not to breathe a word of it to the Iroquois themselves.[37] The Oneidas, themselves allied to the Americans, did not hesitate to inform those Iroquois who had sided with the British that their allies had abandoned them.[38]

Upon learning this news, Joseph Brant was incensed. He and other Iroquois representatives immediately informed the post commander at Fort Niagara that they "were a free people subject to no power on Earth," as well as "faithful allies of the King of England, but not his subjects." Therefore, the King had no authority to dispose of their lands in this way. While Brant and the other Iroquois leaders' protestations ultimately mattered little to the British diplomats hammering out the final treaty, they did convince Haldimand to refuse to surrender the British frontier posts as a bulwark against complete American domination of Iroquois lands. One of the other lasting effects of Indian anger at the terms of the peace agreement was the creation of the Western Confederacy led by the Shawnees, which would continue to resist the westward advance of American settlement well into the 19th century. In the end, however, none of this mattered to the politicians charged with debating the final settlement of the war. Indians were scarcely mentioned in the parliamentary debates over the Treaty of Paris in 1783.[39]

Brant, sensing that he had little chance of changing the outcome of the treaty negotiations, began to consider a move to Canada. Within weeks, British officials granted this request and Brant and his Mohawks as well as other Indian people who had remained loyal to the crown relocated to Grand River in March of 1784. By 1785, nearly 2, 000 Indians had settled there. Brant would live the rest of his life there as the leader of an exiled people.[40]

Those members of the Six Nations who remained in America faced ever-intensifying pressure from both settlers and their governments to cede large portions of their land. Almost immediately after hostilities ended the Americans embarked upon a concerted policy of encircling Iroquois reservations from all sides, thus cutting them off from one another and limiting their access to the British frontier posts. On September 5, 1784, representatives of what remained of the Six Nations met with New York officials at Fort Stanwix to begin the process of delineating the future course of their relationship. While both sides expressed a desire for peace and goodwill, the Six Nations representatives vehemently asserted their sovereignty and sternly expressed their resistance to any land cessions to New York or the newly independent United States. A few weeks later, they met with negotiators appointed by Congress at Fort Stanwix as well. At that meeting, the Iroquois diplomats present were less strident in their opposition to a negotiated settlement involving land. Rampant factionalism and outright shock at the giveaway of their lands by the English, combined with the realization that without the active military support of the British resistance to the Americans represented an iffy proposition at best, led the Iroquois negotiators to eventually accept the agreement the Americans were trying to force upon them.[41]

When early on in the proceedings, some Iroquois representatives attempted to force the Americans to accept Six Nations independence, the Congressional representatives denied that any such status existed. In an address that directly responded to the Iroquois claim of sovereignty the U.S. negotiators left little doubt as to what place they envisioned for native people in their new republic. "You are a subdued people," the commissioners lectured the Indians present, "you have been overcome in a war which you entered into with us, not only without provocation, but in violation of most sacred obligations."[42] Such a position on the part of the U.S. government, now the only power in reach of a large majority of Indians, represents a watershed moment for the native people of North America. Whereas, before the American Revolution they had largely been treated as allies by the European nations jockeying for influence and position in Colonial America, they were now considered vanquished peoples by the only power left. In previous conflicts, even those groups that had supported one European power over another and lost could usually count on the desire of the victor to win them to their side of the conflict and keep them there as a check upon this kind of hubris; however, the fundamental difference between the primary goals of European colonial regimes and those of the United States completely changed the equation. The British, French, Dutch, Spanish, and others valued North America for its potential to enrich their empires through trade, which as often as not required native trading partners, guides, and allies. The newly created United States envisioned a future in which access to land for farming and commercial purposes represented the key strategy for success. The sanctity of native land claims had no place in such a vision.

The Iroquois now agreed to a treaty in which they promised to return all prisoners taken during the war, ceded a large swath of their home territory, relinquished all claims to lands in Ohio, and promised to respect the lands of the Oneidas and Tuscaroras. As difficult as each of the stipulations were to the Iroquois, what was even more damaging was the fact that the agreement set a precedent in which the various states that bordered Iroquois territory now all began to demand separate treaties.[43]

Not long after the negotiations with the Americans, Pennsylvania representatives arrived in Iroquois country and demanded their own land cession. In this case, the Pennsylvanians argued that Great Britain had already given the land to the state in the peace agreement. So they presented themselves as desirous of giving the Six Nations a say in the matter, all the while intimating to the Indian negotiators that they in reality had no real choice but to agree to the cession. For their part, the Six Nations negotiators demanded $1,000 on top of the $4,000 in trade goods the Pennsylvanians offered. The Pennsylvanians readily agreed. From their perspective, for $1,000 in worthless Continental currency they had just scored a massive tract of land in northwestern Pennsylvania roughly equal to one-third the size of the entire state. Such agreements not only served to deprive the Six Nations of their precious land base and disrupt their subsistence cycle, but also create more factionalism within the group.[44]

In light of the various experiences outlined above, those Iroquois who had chosen exile over negotiation, while not without their own hardships, seemed to have made the right decision. Even the Oneidas and Tuscaroras, allies of the Americans, eventually found U.S. guarantees of perpetual title to their lands fleeting. Despite this, the experience of the Mohawk Grand River refugees clearly demonstrates that Indian people were still capable of exercising agency over their own lives. While the decision to remove to Canada might be seen in one sense as another example of how the Iroquois were a defeated and subdued polity in this period, this is far from the case. Rather, it represents a perfect example of the way that they and other native communities had managed to adapt for centuries both before and after the arrival of whites. The fact that the Mohawks relocated to Grand River and not another site in Canada constitutes just one piece of the proof. Originally, Governor Haldimand had pushed for them to relocate to a spot encircled by Loyalist settlements and cut off from contact with the rest of the Six Nations. Brant flatly refused and demanded the Grand River location and in so doing created an opportunity for the Six Nations to reconstitute itself as a political entity. Almost immediately after they relocated at Grand River, representatives of all Six Nations reestablished the League of Peace and Friendship along the lines that had existed since the time of Hiawatha and

Deganawidah. Although the American Revolution brought hardship and defeat, the Iroquois League, however diminished, had survived.[45]

THE ONGOING WAR IN THE OHIO VALLEY

For Ohio Valley Indians, the American Revolution truly was the worst possible scenario, and as they had during the war, the Shawnees would prove throughout the immediate postwar era to be a stubborn antagonist of the newly independent United States. Much like they did with the groups to the east and south, the Americans attempted to force their interpretation that all of the Indians in the territories surrendered by Great Britain were conquered peoples, and they continued to demand that they surrender large portions of their land. At the Treaty of Fort McIntosh in January of 1785, U.S. representatives pushed for large land cessions from the Wyandots, Ottawas, and Delawares. Conspicuously absent, however, were the Shawnees who alone refused to settle with the Americans. For them, the war spawned by the American Revolution had not ended.[46]

Realizing that a peace agreement that did not include the Shawnees would accomplish very little, the Americans tried again at Fort Finney one year later in January of 1786. The American commissioners sent to the conference boasted long records of Indian-hating and were completely recalcitrant in their dealings at Fort Finney. Shawnee leaders, weary of warfare and cognizant of the fact that many of their allies had already made peace with the Americans, felt they had no choice but to give in at least temporarily and ignored the pleas of their warriors to continue resistance. In the end, the Shawnee representatives at Fort Finney were forced to agree to a treaty ceding nearly all of their lands in eastern and southern Ohio. Younger Shawnee warriors, however, refused to accept the agreement.[47]

When it became clear to the Americans that a significant portion of the Shawnees were openly refusing to abide by the terms of the Treaty of Fort Finney they reacted with violence. Later that year, Benjamin Logan, a settler who had risen to a position in the high command of the Kentucky militia, led a scorched earth offensive into Shawnee territory, leaving a trail of burned out villages and corpses in his wake. Even Moluntha, one of the Shawnee chiefs most instrumental in bringing about the Fort Finney agreement, did not escape the wrath of Logan's men. When they attacked his village, the aged leader confronted them with the copy of the treaty he had been provided. When asked by one of the expedition's leaders if he had participated in the Battle of Blue Licks, Moluntha nodded his head even though he had not in fact taken part in the battle. According to Colin Calloway, the Shawnee chief, who understood very little

English, more than likely misunderstood the question. In any event, upon Moluntha's apparent affirmative answer to his question, the American split the Shawnee's head open with a hatchet and then ordered the town burned. With Moluntha's death, even Shawnees who had counseled peace now joined their young men in resolving to resist the Americans to the last. Shortly after Moluntha's murder, the Shawnees formally joined the confederacy of Western tribes then being assembled by Joseph Brant, which they would ultimately lead in a sporadic war against the United States over the next 30 years.[48]

When the Americans called another conference in 1789 in an attempt to reassert the land cessions made at Fort McIntosh, Shawnees (as they had at Fort McIntosh) refused to participate. In 1790, a force of 1,500 militia under the command of General Josiah Harmar set out to force the Shawnees to abide by the agreements made at Fort McIntosh and Fort Finney. Harmar and his force were instead themselves attacked by a group of Shawnee and other Ohio Indian warriors under the leadership of the Shawnee war leader Blue Jacket. Harmar's force was so damaged by Blue Jacket's attacks that he was forced to withdraw from the area.[49]

Fresh off this victory, Blue Jacket and the Shawnees began to call upon the British for material and logistical support, which the British were often willing to provide via the frontier posts they still refused to surrender to the Americans. While they would not commit to supplying actual British troops to Blue Jacket's resistance, their contributions of supplies and ammunition played a key role in many Shawnee victories over the next several years, such as that which occurred at the Battle of the Wabash in late 1791. On November 4 of that year, a combined force of Ohio Indians led by Blue Jacket and the Miami war leader Little Turtle scored the greatest victory ever won by American Indians against the United States. The Americans, under the command of Arthur St. Clair, suffered well over 900 total casualties while Blue Jacket and Little Turtle's forces lost fewer than 50 men. According to Shawnee historian Colin Calloway, the Battle of the Wabash "effectively destroyed the new nation's only army. Compared with St. Clair's defeat, George Custer's disaster at the Battle of the Little Big Horn eighty-five years later was a skirmish and a minor setback."[50]

Such a victory paid dividends almost immediately for the Western Confederacy as new recruits began to flock to the area known as the Glaize, a multicultural Indian community located on the Maumee River near present-day Defiance, Ohio, where they had made their headquarters. In 1792, the Americans, now in a seriously weakened position, offered to renegotiate the previous agreements made at Fort Finney and Fort McIntosh. They were met at Fort Knox by a large and for the most part, unified, delegation consisting of

Shawnees, Miamis, Wyandots, Ottawas, Ojibwas, Potawatomis, Sauks and Foxes, Creeks, Cherokees, Conoys, Nanticokes, Mahicans, and Mingos. Unfortunately, the Americans had absolutely no intention of actually renegotiating anything. The talks were simply intended to buy time for the newly appointed commander of U.S. forces in the west, General Anthony Wayne, to rebuild his army.[51]

By June of 1794, Wayne had largely succeeded in his efforts and had advanced to the site of St. Clair's defeat on the Wabash River. There, he constructed a new fort, deliberately aiming to provoke a new round of hostilities. When Wayne's forces repelled an attack on his fort shortly thereafter, the Western Confederacy's momentum suffered and many warriors began to head for their home villages. Divergent tribal agendas and traditional animosities between some of the member groups combined to drain the confederacy of as much as half of its fighting strength throughout 1794. By the time they met Wayne in open battle at Fallen Timbers along the Maumee River in Northwest Ohio in late summer, they were nowhere near the force that had defeated St. Clair three years earlier. In the Battle of Fallen Timbers on August 20, Wayne's forces prevailed. When the retreating warriors of the confederacy sought to take shelter among the British at Fort Miami, the commanders of the fort ordered the doors barred. Wayne followed up his victory with another scorched earth campaign throughout the Ohio Valley.[52]

In the face of the daily depredations of Wayne's army, the crumbling strength of the confederacy, and the reluctance of the British to provide actual troops, Blue Jacket decided to give up the fight. At the Treaty of Greenville in the summer of 1795, he and other like-minded Ohio Indian leaders signed away nearly the entire southern and eastern sections of Ohio to the Americans and now professed their loyalty to the new American state; however, among the Shawnee leaders not present at Greenville was a man who would die leading his people in a legendary resistance movement alongside his brother, the Shawnee prophet Tenskwatawa, that would not only nearly dislodge the Americans from the Ohio Valley but would also restore his people's pride and honor. The Shawnee man's name was Tecumseh and the conditions created as a result of Blue Jacket's capitulation in the Treaty of Greenville would lead directly to his rise to power. Thus the war between Ohio Valley Indians and the Americans so intent on possessing their lands had not ended in the faraway palaces of Paris, but would continue well into the next century. However, armed confrontations and religious revitalization movements such as that of Tecumseh and Tenskwatawa represent only one of the many ways in which native people continued to resist the imposition of American domination of both their lives and their lands. In fact, armed resistance eventually ceased, but other forms of resistance continue to this day and it is to those struggles that we must now turn to for they, more than any other aspect of the Native American experience in the American Revolution, demonstrate that for them the struggle never truly ended.[53]

Conclusion:
The Struggle Continues

By the beginning of the 20th century, violent Indian resistance to white land encroachment had ended, and for many nonnative Americans, Indians receded into a mythical past, which only served to reinforce American nationalism and buttress white assumptions of superiority and modernity. Unless they lived near a reservation or in some other situation that brought them into direct contact with native people, most nonnative Americans gave Indians very little thought. When Indians appeared in modern America, they did so as stock characters. When confronted with the word "Indian," nonnatives conjured up ideas of buckskins, painted faces, and throbbing drumbeats. Throughout most of the 20th century, Americans viewed Indians who appeared outside this mold as anomalies. Then, out of the turbulence of the 1960s and the multitude of failures that constituted the varying directions of U.S. Indian policy throughout the first 70 years of the century, arose the Red Power movement. Arguably its most famous manifestation, the 1973 siege at Wounded Knee, South Dakota, in which a group of activists from the American Indian Movement (AIM) and local Lakotas engaged in a tense and violent confrontation with the U.S. government, reverberated throughout not only the United States but the world. For many, the siege was noteworthy simply because it appeared to be a reprisal of the kind of Indian versus white confrontations that characterized the original American conquest of the plains and the far west. That conquest figured largely into their mythic conceptions of their own past. For them, Wounded Knee represented another chapter in the cowboys' and Indians' struggle over Indian land. Certainly, elements of the siege at Wounded Knee lent itself to this interpretation. In the words of Madonna Thunderhawk, one of the activists involved in the siege, land was at the forefront of the rage expressed by the members of AIM and the residents of the Pine Ridge reservation that spring; however, there was another part of the equation that has been overlooked. In an interview for the PBS documentary *William Kunstler: Disturbing the Universe,* Thunderhawk pondered the meaning of the siege for the native people involved, "You're fighting for your land and your identity, you know, and you don't know what you can do when your back is against the wall," she stated.[1] In other words, while land has represented a crucial issue in the struggle between native and nonnative people since the arrival of Europeans in the late 15th century, the American Revolution opened up a new arena of conflict. Those who survived both the Revolution and the onslaught of white settlement in its wake found themselves forced to watch as Americans appropriated the artifacts, names, and symbols of now dispossessed native peoples to carve out a national identity.

According to Native American historian Philip Deloria, "Playing Indian is a persistent tradition in American culture, stretching from the very instant of the national big bang into an ever-expanding present and future."[2] Deloria further argues that its purpose is "the creative assembling of an ultimately unassemblable American identity."[3] In other words, portraying one's self as Indian, whether accurately or not, has over the years served as a vehicle for defining what white America is by the process of presenting what it is not. This process began even before Lexington and Concord. Those Bostonians disguised as Mohawks who dumped the tea into Boston harbor on a cold December night in 1773 fooled absolutely no one. That was not the intent of the famous Boston Tea Party. Instead, they were aiming to establish a new identity by committing an act that was decidedly anti-British so as to mark the event as a complete break with their British past. What better figure to express that break than that of an Indian, who had from the very beginning stood in opposition to the colonialism of Great Britain and the other European powers? This choice was made all the easier by the fact that for the most part New England had largely been devoid of Indians (with the exception of praying Indians, such as the Stockbridge) for nearly a century by that point. In short, Indians were both the antithesis of Britishness and no longer a threat to the colonists of Boston. Their likeness could therefore be appropriated without hindrance.[4]

Perhaps nothing epitomizes the penchant of New Englanders in particular to appropriate and manipulate Indian images for their own purposes than the case of Metacom or "King Philip." According to historian Jill Lepore, as late-17th-century New England Puritans grew increasingly intertwined with native culture, they came to fear that they were the ones being colonized due to the necessity of adopting so many Indian lifeways in order to survive. According to Lepore, this fear then led them to seek the annihilation of the Wampanoags and their leader, King Philip. Philip's increasing resistance to English colonists in Massachusetts provided the pretext for the Puritans to declare war on the Wampanoags. In order to defeat Philip and his people, the New England colonists engaged in an extremely ferocious and ruthless war of extirpation against them. King Philip's War, as it came to be known, created a disturbing paradox in the minds of Puritan leaders and thinkers. In order to prevent themselves from descending into supposed savagery, Puritans had been forced to adopt tactics they considered fit only for savages. According to Lepore, Puritans dealt with this reality by producing an extremely voluminous amount of printed rationalizations for it. These writings told a story that justified New England's destruction of Indian savages, yet went to considerable lengths to differentiate Puritan methods from those of the Spanish conquistadors of the black legend such as Hernando Cortes and Francisco Pizarro; however, once New England had been largely emptied of the Indians who had struck such fear in the hearts of late-17th-century Puritans, they became symbolically useful. By the dawn of the American Revolution, New England, now largely devoid of native inhabitants, looked to none other than Philip himself for inspiration in their fight against the oppression of the British government. For Revolutionary Era New Englanders, Philip was useful as a metaphor for British tyranny in that he could be employed to depict "the British as more savage enemies than the Indians of King Philip's War."[5]

By the 1830s, the strange saga of Philip's symbolic power had taken an even stranger turn when his life and death became the subject of one of the most popular stage plays of the day. John Augustus Stone's *Metamora: or, The Last of the Wampanoags* (1829) depicted Philip as a tragic hero, whose death caused audiences to weep uncontrollably. Yet at this very same time actual living Indians in the American southeast were dying in large numbers at the hands of the U.S. government's Indian removal policy and with very few tears falling in response. According to Lepore, the difference is that one Indian, King Philip as portrayed in *Metamora,* was imagined while the other, the dying Cherokees and their Southeastern Indian brethren, were all too real:

> Peel back all the layers—the play's origins, its actors, its audiences, its critics—and what remains is a struggle for American and Indian identity. Through plays like *Metamora,* white Americans came to define themselves in relation to an imagined Indian past. That definition however, required that there be no Indians in the present, or at least not anywhere nearby.[6]

Since at least the days of the Imperial Crisis between Great Britain and the colonies that ultimately flared into a revolution, Americans engaged in a process by which they defined themselves as a people wholly separate from their actual European roots by manipulating an imagined "Indianness," which, at times, they appropriated for their own and at others manipulated to justify their conquests of actual Indian people. From Tammany Hall, to 19th-century poets, to the hippies of the 1960s and the modern New Age movement, "the Indian has," once again in the words of Philip Deloria, "skulked in and out of the most important stories various Americans have told about themselves."[7] The American Revolution is of course no exception to this, yet as the event in which this particular pattern of cultural misrepresentation began, it seems as good a place as any to begin the process of setting the record straight. Perhaps by doing so, we can achieve a society in which caricatures parading as college mascots will no longer be defended as "patriotic."[8] It is largely thanks to the efforts of Native Americans themselves over the years that society has begun to recognize and in some cases address issues such as insensitive mascots, movie stereotypes, repatriation of remains and sacred artifacts, as well as the issues of alcohol abuse and violence toward native women. There exists no better proof therefore that, though the American Revolution certainly represented "a great blow" to paraphrase that emissary from 1784, Native Americans refused to let it be a fatal one.

NOTES

INTRODUCTION

1. "Don Francisco Cruzat to Estevan Miró," 23 August 1784, Lawrence Kinnaird, ed., *Spain in the Mississippi Valley,* vol. 3, pt. 2 (Washington, D.C.: U.S. Government Printing Office, 1946), 117.

2. Gregory Evans Dowd, "Insidious Friends: Gift Giving and the Cherokee-British Alliance in the Seven Years War," Andrew R. L. Cayton and Fredrika J. Teute eds., *Contact Points: American Frontiers from the Mohawk Valley to the Mississippi, 1750–1830* (Chapel Hill: University of North Carolina Press, 1998), 144–145.

3. "Governor Lyttelton to Board of Trade," CO 5/376/55-57; John Echols, "An Extract of a Journal—'Concerning a March That Capt: Robt. Wade took to the New River—In Search of Indians,'" 12 August 1758, *Virginia Calendar of State Papers,* vol. 1, ed., William P. Palmer (Richmond, VA: Superintendent of Public Printing, 1875), 254–257; Tom Hatley, *The Dividing Paths: Cherokees and the South Carolinians through the Revolutionary Era* (New York: Oxford University Press, 1995), 100–101.

4. Hatley, *The Dividing Paths,* 109–115, Lyttelton quotation pg. 115.

5. Ibid., 120–214; Colin Calloway, *The American Revolution in Indian Country: Crisis and Diversity in Native American Communities* (New York: Cambridge University Press, 1995), 182.

6. The reasons for this change of allegiance on the part of Ohio River groups are multifaceted. Groups such as the Delawares had never been united in their support of the British from the beginning. Many scholars have argued that the Delawares' ultimate objective in participating in the war had always been the removal of both the French and the English from the Ohio country. Additionally, by 1757–1758, the British naval blockade had so damaged the ability of the French to

supply gifts and supplies to the Ohio River groups that they were no longer power-ful enough to aid them against the British and they therefore concluded that their position would be strengthened by aligning themselves with the winning side of the conflict. Finally, the French commander in chief, the Marquis de Montcalm had so alienated many of his Alqonquian allies by that point that he drove them into the British camp. See Richard White, *The Middle Ground: Indians, Empires, and Republics in the Great Lakes Region, 1650-1815* (New York: Cambridge University Press, 1991), 242-248; Michael N. McConnell, *A Country Between: The Upper Ohio Valley and Its Peoples, 1724-1774* (Lincoln, NE: University of Nebraska Press, 1992), 120-129.

7. Ibid., 208-209; Post, *Two Journals of Western Tours*, 282-285; White, *The Middle Ground*, 250; McConnell, *A Country Between*, 128-141.

8. Calloway, *Scratch of a Pen*, 54-55.

9. Ibid.,

10. "Address of the Six Nations to Jeffrey Amherst, May 22, 1763," in Milton Hamilton, ed., *The Papers of Sir William Johnson*, vol. 10 (Albany: The University of the State of New York, 1951), 680.

11. Calloway, *American Revolution in Indian Country*, xxii.

12. Woody Holton, "American Revolution and Early Republic," *American History Now*, Eric Foner and Lisa McGirr, eds.(Philadelphia: Temple University Press, 2011), 26.

13. See for example, Mary Beth Norton *Liberty's Daughters: The Revolutionary Experience of Early American Women, 1750-1800* (Ithaca, NY: Cornell University Press, 1986), Carol Berkin, *Revolutionary Mothers: Women in the Struggle for America's Independence* (New York: Viking, 2006), Sylvia Frey, *Water from the Rock: Black Resistance in a Revolutionary Age* (Princeton, NJ: Princeton University Press, 1993), Gary Nash, *The Urban Crucible: The Northern Seaports and the Origins of the American Revolution* (Cambridge, MA: Harvard University Press, 1986) and Woody Holton, *Forced Founders: Indians, Debtors, Slaves and the Making of the American Revolution in Virginia* (Chapel Hill, NC: University of North Carolina Press, 1999).

14. Thomas Bender, "Wholes and Parts: The Need for Synthesis in American History," *The Journal of American History*, vol. 73, no. 1 (Jun., 1986), 126.

15. James H. Merrell, "Some Thoughts on Colonial Historians and American Indians," *The William and Mary Quarterly*, Third Series, vol. 46, no. 1 (Jan., 1989), 118.

16. Vine Deloria Jr., "The American Revolution and the American Indian: Problems in the Recovery of a Usable Past," *Spirit and Reason: The Vine Deloria Jr., Reader* (Golden, CO: Fulcrum Publishing, 1999), 206.

CHAPTER 1

1. "James Hamilton to Sir William Johnson, February 1761," in Milton Hamilton, ed., *The Papers of Sir William Johnson*, vol. 10 (Albany: The University

of the State of New York, 1951), 212; "Journal of James Kenny, 1761–1763," John Jordan, ed., *Pennsylvania Magazine of History and Biography,* vol. 37, no. 1 (1913), 171–173; "Journal of James Gorrell, 12 July 1762 and May 18, 1763," *The Papers of Sir William Johnson,* vol. 10, 706, 713; Gregory Evans Dowd, *War under Heaven: Pontiac, The Indian Nations, & the British Empire* (Baltimore, MD: Johns Hopkins University Press, 2002), 125–126.

2. "James McDonald to George Croghan, 12 July 1763," *The Papers of Sir William Johnson,* vol. 10, 744.

3. Ibid., 744.

4. "George Etherington to Henry Gladwin, 12 June 1763," *William Johnson Papers,* vol. 10, 695

5. Dowd, *War under Heaven,* 124–126.

6. Richard White, *The Middle Ground: Indians, Empires, and Republics in the Great Lakes Region, 1650–1815* (New York: Cambridge University Press, 1991), 269–271.

7. Ibid., x.

8. Ibid., 76–77.

9. Ibid., 76–77, 92–93.

10. Ibid., 95.

11. Colin G. Calloway, *One Vast Winter Count: The Native American West Before Lewis and Clark* (Lincoln, NE: University of Nebraska Press, 2003), 225–228; White, *The Middle Ground,* 1–17.

12. Reuben G. Thwaites, ed., *The Jesuit Relations and Allied Documents: Travels and Explorations of the Jesuit Missionaries in New France 1610–1791,* 73 vols. (Cleveland: Burrows Brothers, 1896–1901), 34: 98–99.

13. White, *Middle Ground,* 1–3, 10–23. For the connection between Native warfare and disease epidemics, see Paul Kelton, *Epidemics and Enslavement: Biological Catastrophe in the Native Southeast* (Lincoln: University of Nebraska Press, 2007).

14. For more on this process see Gary Clayton Anderson, *The Indian Southwest, 1580–1830: Ethnogenesis and Reinvention* (Norman: University of Oklahoma Press, 1999).

15. White, *Middle Ground,* 23–33.

16. Ibid., 142–145.

17. Calloway, *One Vast Winter Count,* 314.

18. Ibid., 314–316; Daniel Richter, *Facing East from Indian Country: A Native History of Early America* (Cambridge, MA: Harvard University Press, 2001), 184–185; White, *The Middle Ground,* 223–227.

19. Richter, *Facing East,* 184–185; White, *Middle Ground,* 241. See also Fred Anderson, *The Crucible of War: The Seven Years' War and the Fate of Empire in British North America, 1754–1766* (New York: Vintage Press, 2000), 29–32.

20. Richter, *Facing East,* 185–186; White, *Middle Ground,* 245–248; Calloway, *One Vast Winter Count,* 340–345.

21. See White, *Middle Ground;* David Dixon, *Never Come to Peace Again: Pontiac's Uprising and the Fate of the British Empire in North America* (Norman:

University of Oklahoma Press, 2005); Gregory Evans Dowd, *War under Heaven: Pontiac, the Indian Nations and the British Empire* (Baltimore, MD: Johns Hopkins University Press, 2002); Idem, *A Spirited Resistance: The North American Indian Struggle for Unity, 1745-1815* (Baltimore, MD: Johns Hopkins University Press, 1992); Colin Calloway, *The Scratch of a Pen: 1763 and the Transformation of North America* (New York: Oxford University Pres, 2006).

22. White, *Middle Ground*, 256–257; Calloway, *One Vast Winter Count*, 349.

23. "Lord Jeffrey Amherst to Sir William Johnson, February 22, 1761," *Papers of Sir William Johnson*, vol. 3, 345. For more examples of Amherst's views on Native Americans see also "Amherst to Johnson, June 24, 1761," "Amherst to Johnson, August 9, 1761" and "Amherst to Johnson, August 11, 1761," *Papers of Sir William Johnson*, Vol. 3, 421, 515 and 517.

24. White, *Middle Ground*, 262–262; James Axtell, "The White Indians of Colonial America," *The European and the Indian: Essays in the Ethnohistory of Colonial North America* (New York, Oxford University Press, 1981), 170–173; Ethnohistorian Daniel Richter, a specialist on the Iroquois, has referred to the Iroquois practice of going to war for the purpose of taking captives with which to replace lost members as "mourning war." James F. Brooks, in examining captivity among the native groups of the Southwest borderlands considers captivity "one extreme expression along a continuum of exchange." While historians of other areas of colonial America might not describe the phenomenon of captive taking to replace lost population using the exact terms of Richter and Brooks, there is widespread agreement that it was commonly practiced throughout colonial America. See Daniel Richter, *The Ordeal of the Longhous: The Peoples of the Iroquois League in the Era of European Colonization* (Chapel Hill: University of North Carolina Press, 1992), 32–38; James F. Brooks, *Captives and Cousins: Slavery, Kinship, and Community in the Southwest Borderlands* (Chapel Hill: University of North Carolina Press, 2002), 17; see also, John Demos, *The Unredeemed Captive: A Family Story from Early America* (New York: Vintage Books, 1994).

25. "Benjamin Franklin to Peter Collinson, May 9, 1753," *The Benjamin Franklin Papers*. Available on-line at http://franklinpapers.org/franklin/. Accessed September 24, 2010.

26. "Journal of James Kenny," 7.

27. "Henry Bouquet to Jeffrey Amherst, March 20, 1762," Jeffery Amherst papers, William L. Clements Library, The University of Michigan; White, *Middle Ground*, 263; Calloway, *One Vast Winter Count*, 349.

28. Anderson, *Crucible of War*, 329.

29. Dowd, *War under Heaven*, 53–53; Calloway, *One Vast Winter Count*, 349; White, *Middle Ground*, 263–268.

30. "George Washington to Francis Fauquier, December 2, 1758," *Official Papers of Francis Fauquier*, George Reese, ed., (Charlottesville: University Press of Virginia, 1980), 117–118.

31. Michael N. McConnell, *A Country Between: The Upper Ohio Valley and Its Peoples, 1724-1744* (Lincoln, NE: University of Nebraska Press, 1992), 150–151;

Calloway, *One Vast Winter Count,* 347–349; Anderson, *The Crucible of War,* 474–475; White, *Middle Ground,* 266–268.

32. "Journal of James Kenny," 171–172.

33. Dowd, *A Spirited Resistance,* 33.

34. Ibid., 30–32; "Otsineky Indian Response to Conrad Weiser," quoted in Paul A. W. Wallace, *Conrad Weiser, 1696–1760, Friend of Colonist and Mohawk* (Philadelphia: University of Pennsylvania Press, 1945), 88.

35. White, *The Middle Ground,* 279–280.

36. Dowd, *A Spirited Resistance,* 35–36; Idem, *War under Heaven,* 274–275; Calloway, *One Vast Winter Count,* 351–353.

37. T. C. Barrow, ed., "A Project for Imperial Reform 'Hints Respecting the Settlement of our America Colonies,' 1763," *William and Mary Quarterly,* 3 series, 24 (1967), 116.

38. Calloway, *The Scratch of a Pen: 1763 and the Transformation of North America* (New York: Oxford University Press, 2006), 91–94. For American anger over the Proclamation and its enforcement, see Woody Holton, *Forced Founders: Indians, Debtors, Slaves and the Making of the American Revolution in Virginia* (Chapel Hill, NC: University of North Carolina Press, 1999).

CHAPTER 2

1. "Henry Stuart to John Stuart August 25th, 1776," in William L. Saunders, *The Colonial Records of North Carolina,* vol. 10 (Raleigh, NC: Joseph Daniels, 1890), 778.

2. Ibid.

3. "The Deposition of Samuel Wilson, etc., Taken Before Arthur Campbell and William Campbell Gentlemen Commissioners etc., relative to a purchase of Land by Richard Henderson and Company, etc.," *Calendar of Virginia State Papers and Other Manuscripts, 1652–1781 preserved in the Capitol at Richmond,* William P. Palmer, editor. (Richmond, R. F. Walker, Superintendent of Public Printing, 1875) vol. 1, 283.

4. John Oliphant, *Peace and War on the Anglo-Cherokee Frontier, 1756–1763* (Baton Rouge: Louisiana State University Press, 2001), 191–207; Tom Hatley, *The Dividing Paths: Cherokees and South Carolinians through the Revolutionary Era* (New York: Oxford University Press, 1995), 217.

5. Hatley, *The Dividing Paths,* 217–218.

6. "Henry Stuart to John Stuart Aug. 25th, 1776," *The Colonial Records of North Carolina,* vol. 10, 764.

7. Colin Calloway, *The American Revolution in Indian Country: Crisis and Diversity in Native American Communities* (New York: Cambridge University Press, 1995), 246–247.

8. *South Carolina Gazette,* June 4, 1763. Quoted in Steven C. Hahn, *The Invention of the Creek Nation, 1670–1763* (Lincoln: University of Nebraska Press, 2004), 2.

9. David H. Corkran, *The Creek Frontier, 1540–1783* (Norman: University of Oklahoma Press, 1967), 234–235; "John Stuart to Jeffery Amherst, May 31, 1763,"

Jeffery Amherst papers, William L. Clements Library, The University of Michigan.

10. Corkran, *The Creek Frontier,* 238–240.

11. Ibid., 241–248.

12. Ibid., 247–250.

13. Ibid., 248–252.

14. Ibid., 253–254.

15. Kenneth Coleman and Milton Ready, *Colonial Records of Georgia* vol. 38 (Athens: University of Georgia Press, 1989), pt. 1, 255–256.

16. Colin Calloway, *The Scratch of a Pen: 1763 and the Transformation of North America* (New York: Oxford University Press), 109–110.

17. Ibid., 110; *Colonial Records of Georgia,* vol. 28, pt. 2, 50–52.

18. Corkran, *The Creek Frontier,* 257–262; Calloway, *The Scratch of a Pen,* 110–111; See also J. Russell Snapp, *John Stuart and the Struggle for Empire on the Southern Frontier* (Baton Rouge: Louisiana State University Press, 1996).

19. Corkran, *The Creek Frontier,* 262–263.

20. "Stuart to Gage, November 27, 1767," Thomas Gage Papers, William L. Clements Library, The University of Michigan; Corkran, *The Creek Frontier,* 263.

21. "McIntosh to Gage, Nov. 27, 1767," Thomas Gage Papers, William L. Clements Library, The University of Michigan; Corkran, *The Creek Frontier,* 264, 266–268.

22. Corkran, *The Creek Frontier,* 268–269; "Representation of the Lords of Trade, 7 March 1768," in E. B. O'Callaghan, *Documents Relative to the Colonial History of the State of New York* vol. 8 (Albany, NY: Weed, Parsons and Company, 1857), 24; Lord Hillsborough to the governors in America, 15 April 1768, in O'Callaghan, *Documents Relative to the Colonial History of the State of New York* vol. 7, 55–56; "Hillsborough to Tryon, 15 April 1768," in *The Colonial Records of North Carolina,* vol. 7, 707.

23. Corkran, *The Creek Frontier,* 281.

24. Ibid., 282–285.

25. Calloway, *The American Revolution in Indian Country,* 213–216.

26. James Adair, *The History of the American Indians* (London: Edward and Charles Dilly, 1775), 255.

27. Calloway-*American Revolution in Indian Country,* 213.

28. Paul Kelton, *Epidemics and Enslavement: Biological Catastrophe in the Native Southeast* (Lincoln: University of Nebraska Press), 106–143; Calloway, *The American Revolution in Indian Country,* 219–220.

29. Seymour Feiler, ed. and trans., *Jean-Bernard Bossu's Travels in the Interior of North America, 1751–1762* (Norman: University of Oklahoma Press, 1962), 172.

30. Calloway, *The American Revolution in Indian Country,* 221.

31. Arell M. Gibson, *The Chickasaws* (Norman: University of Oklahoma Press, 1972), 64–65.

32. Ibid., 221–222.

33. Greg O'Brien, *Choctaws in a Revolutionary Age, 1750–1830* (Lincoln: University of Nebraska Press, xv–xvii.

34. Ibid., xviii.

35. Greg O'Brien, "Protecting Trade through War: Choctaw Elites and British Occupation of the Floridas," *Pre-Removal Choctaw History: Exploring New Paths,* Greg O'Brien, ed. (Norman: University of Oklahoma Press, 2008), 103–104.

36. Ibid., 104.

37. Ibid., 104–105. See also, Richard White, *Roots of Dependency: Subsistence, Environment, and Social Change among the Choctaws, Pawnees and Navajos* (Lincoln: University of Nebraska Press, 1983).

38. Ibid., 105–106.

39. Ibid., 106–107.

40. Ibid., 107–115.

41. James H. Merrell, *The Indians' New World: Catawbas and Their Neighbors from European Contact through the Era of Removal* (Chapel Hill, NC: University of North Carolina Press, 1989), 8–9.

42. Ibid., 10. For more on the connection between disease epidemics and the native slave trade see Kelton, *Epidemics and Enslavement.*

43. Merrell, *The Indians New World,* 135.

44. Ibid., 135–139, 143–44, 150.

45. Ibid., 171; Charles Woodmason, *The Carolina Backcountry on the Eve of the American Revolution: The Journal and Other Writings of Charles Woodmason, Anglican Itinerant,* ed., Richard J. Hooker (Chapel Hill, NC: University of North Carolina Press, 1969), 14.

46. Merrell, *The Indians' New World,* 191.

47. Ibid., 192–195.

48. Ibid., 196.

49. Ibid., 197–200.

50. Ibid., 202; see also, Woody Holton, *Forced Founders: Indians, Debtors, Slaves and the Making of the American Revolution in Virginia* (Chapel Hill: University of North Carolina Press, 1999), and Kelton, *Epidemics and Enslavement.*

51. Merrell, *The Indians' New World,* 214–216.

52. Hatley, *The Dividing Paths,* 216–226.

CHAPTER 3

1. William N. Fenton, *The Great Law of the Longhouse: A Political History of the Iroquois Confederacy* (Norman: University of Oklahoma Press, 1998), 564; Barbara Graymont, *The Iroquois in the American Revolution* (Syracuse, NY: Syracuse University Press, 1972), 48–50; Isabel Thomson Kelsay, *Joseph Brant, 1743–1807: Man of Two Worlds* (Syracuse, NY: Syracuse University Press, 1972), 135–138.

2. Colin G. Calloway, *The Western Abenakis of Vermont, 1600–1800: War, Migration, and the Survival of an Indian People* (Norman: University of Oklahoma Press, 1990), 7, 46; Calloway, *The American Revolution in Indian Country: Crisis and Diversity in Native American Communities* (New York: Cambridge University Press, 1995), 65–66.

3. Calloway, *The American Revolution in Indian Country*, 66–69, and *The Western Abenakis of Vermont*, 188–189.

4. Peter Force, *American Archives*, series 4, vol. 2 (Washington, D.C., 1837–1846), 621.

5. John Adams, *Papers of John Adams, Vol. 2, 1773–1775*. Robert J. Taylor, ed. (Cambridge, MA.: Harvard University Press, 1977), 300.

6. Robert Middlekauff, *The Glorious Cause: The American Revolution, 1763–1789* (New York: Oxford University Press, 1982), 230–235; Woody Holton, *Forced Founders: Indians, Debtors, Slaves, and the Making of the American Revolution in Virginia* (Chapel Hill: University of North Carolina Press), 1999.

7. Calloway, *The American Revolution in Indian Country*, 68–70; Calloway, *The Western Abenakis of Vermont*, 204–208; see also Paul Lawrence Stevens, "His Majesty's Savage Allies: British Policy and Northern Indians during the Revolutionary War. The Carleton Years, 1774–1778," PhD diss., State University of New York at Buffalo, 1984.

8. Calloway, *The American Revolution in Indian Country*, 90–92. For more on the experience of communities other than Stockbridge see Daniel Mandell, "'To Live More Like My Christian English Neighbors': Natick Indians in the Eighteenth Century," *William and Mary Quarterly* Third Series, vol. 48, no. 4 (Oct., 1991), pg. 552–579.

9. Daniel Mandell, *Behind the Frontier: Indians in Eighteenth-Century Massachusetts* (Lincoln: University of Nebraska Press, 1996), 202; Calloway, *The American Revolution in Indian Country*, 89–92; see also, Jean M. O'Brien, " 'Divorced' from the Land: Resistance and Survival of Indian Women in Eighteenth-Century New England," in *After King Philip's War: Presence and Persistence in Indian New England*, ed., Colin Calloway (Hanover, NH: University Press of New England, 1997), 144–161. The experience of the Narragansett People during the Imperial Crisis mirrors that of the New England Praying Indians in many ways. For an analysis of the Narragansetts see Ruth Wallis Herndon and Ella Wilcox Sekatau, "The Right to a Name: The Narragansett People and Rhode Island Officials in the Revolutionary Era," in *After King Philip's War*, 114–143.

10. Richter, *The Ordeal of the Longhouse*, 30–32. For a discussion of the different origin points of the league see Elizabeth Tooker, "The League of the Iroquois: Its History, Politics, and Ritual," in *Handbook of North American Indians*, vol. 15, ed., Bruce Trigger (Washington, D.C.: Smithsonian Institution, 1978), 418–422; and Fenton, *The Great Law of the Longhouse*, 51–98; See also Barbara A. Mann and Jerry L. Fields, "A Sign in the Sky: Dating the League of the Haudenosaunee," *American Indian Culture and Research Journal* 21:2(1997):105–163

11. Richter, *The Ordeal of the Longhouse*, 32–39.

12. Reuben Gold Thwaites, ed., *The Jesuit Relations and Allied Documents: Travels and Explorations of the Jesuit Missionaries in New Franc, 1610–1791*, vol. 15 (Cleveland, OH: The Burrows Brothers, 1899), 237.

13. Fenton, *The Great Law of the Longhouse*, 330–331.

14. Richter, *The Ordeal of the Longhouse*, 137

15. Ibid., 134–137; see also, Francis Jennings, *The Ambiguous Iroquois Empire: The Covenant Chain Confederation of Indian Tribes with English Colonies* (New York: W. W. Norton, 1990).

16. Fenton, *The Great Law of the Longhouse*, 464; Graymont, *The Iroquois in the American Revolution*, 30; Jeptha Root Simms, *History of Scoharie County and Border Wars of New York* (Albany, NY: Munsell and Tanner, 1846), 127.

17. Simms, *History of Scoharie County*, 128.

18. Fenton, *The Great Law of the Longhouse*, 472–477.

19. "Sir William Johnson to Edmund Atkin, 21 June 1757," in Almon Lauber, ed., *The Papers of Sir William Johnson*, vol. 9 (Albany: The University of the State of New York, 1939), 785.

20. Graymont, *The Iroquois in the American Revolution*, 32; Fenton, *The Great Law of the Longhouse*, 512–513.

21. Richard White, *The Middle Ground: Indians, Empires, and Republics in the Great Lakes Region, 1650–1815* (New York: Cambridge University Press, 1991), 245.

22. Ibid., 248; Fenton, *The Great Law of the Longhouse*, 496–499.

23. Fenton, *The Great Law of the Longhouse*, 509.

24. Ibid., 509–513.

25. Ibid., 520.

26. Ibid., 520–521.

27. Anderson, *The Crucible of War*, 529–532; see also Fenton, *The Great Law of the Longhouse*, 522–530.

28. "John Forbes to Jeffrey Amherst, February 7, 1759," *Writings of General John Forbes Relating to His Service in North America*, Alfred Proctor James, ed. (Menasha, WI: The Collegiate Press, 1938), 290.

29. Anderson, *The Crucible of War*, 404–405.

30. Fenton, *The Great Law of the Longhouse*, 517–519.

31. Gregory Evans Dowd, *War under Heaven: Pontiac, the Indian Nations & The British Empire* (Baltimore, MD: Johns Hopkins University Press, 2002), 2.

32. Sir William Johnson, "Journal of Indian Affairs, July 4 to August 4, 1763," in Milton W. Hamilton, ed., *The Papers of Sir William Johnson*, vol. 10 (Albany: The University of the State of New York, 1951), 769–770.

33. Dowd, *War Under Heaven*, 137.

34. Ibid., 149–153; see also, Anderson, *The Crucible of War*, 551–552.

35. Graymont, *The Iroquois in the American Revolution*, 33; Fenton, *The Great Law of the Longhouse*, 529.

36. Fenton, *The Great Law of the Longhouse*, 533–535, quoted material appears on page 535.

37. Ibid., 535.

38. Graymont, *The Iroquois in the American Revolution*, 33–34.

39. Ibid., 34–40; see also Fenton, *The Great Law and the Longhouse*, 548–555.

40. Graymont, *The Iroquois and the American Revolution*, 39.

41. Fenton, *The Great Law and the Longhouse*, 536–540.

42. Ibid., 539, 555; see also Graymont, *The Iroquois in the American Revolution,* 43.

43. Graymont, *The Iroquois in the American Revolution,* 44–47.

44. Ibid., 47.

CHAPTER 4

1. Christian Frederick Post, *Two Journals of Western Tours* (London, 1759), 274. (available on-line via the Library of Congress American Memory Web site. http://memory.loc.gov).

2. Ibid., 282.

3. James Merrell, *Into the American Woods: Negotiators on the Pennsylvania Frontier* (New York: W. W. Norton, 1999), 209.

4. "George Washington to Francis Fauquier, December 2, 1758," *Official Papers of Francis Fauquier,* George Reese, ed., (Charlottesville: University Press of Virginia, 1980), 117–118.

5. Patrick Griffin, *American Leviathan: Empire, Nation, and Revolutionary Frontier* (New York: Hill and Wang, 2007), 43; Greg Dowd's *War under Heaven* argues along similar lines that what motivated Pontiac Rebellion in the Ohio Valley was less a failure to adhere to the Middle Ground relationship as out-lined by Richard White or the religious movement fostered by Neolin as it was a lack of respect for Indian sovereignty on the part of Great Britain and her colonist. See Gregory Evans Dowd, *War under Heaven: Pontiac, The Indian Nations and the British Empire* (Baltimore, MD: The Johns Hopkins University Press, 2002).

6. Griffin, 43.

7. "Gage to Shelburne, 13 June 1767," quoted in Griffin, *American Leviathan,* 44.

8. Anderson, *Crucible of War,* 611–613; Dowd, *War under Heaven,* 192–199.

9. Dowd, *War under Heaven,* 197–200.

10. "William Penn to Sir William Johnson, 17 February 1764," in Milton Hamilton, ed., *The Papers of Sir William Johnson,* vol. 4 (Albany: The University of the State of New York, 1925), 324

11. Wilbur R. Jacobs, ed., *The Appalachian Frontier: The Edmund Atkin Report and Plan of 1755* (Lincoln: University of Nebraska Press, 1967), 65.

12. Colin Calloway, *The Shawnees and the War for America* (New York: Viking, 2007), 3–6; Kent, *Susquehanna's Indians,* 80; see also, John Witthoft and William A. Hunter, "The Seventeenth-Century Origins of the Shawnee," *Ethnohistory* vol. 2, no. 1 (Winter 1955), 42–57; James H. O'Donnell III, *Ohio's First Peoples* (Athens: Ohio University Press, 2004), 4, 31; Martha Potter Otoe, *Ohio's Prehistoric Peoples* (Columbus: Ohio Historical Society, 1980), 63–72.

13. Calloway, *The Shawnees and the War for America,* 7–9; Howard, *Shawnee!,* 6–8; Kent, *Susquehanna's Indians,* 78; White, *The Middle Ground,* 30–31; Calloway, "We have Always been the Frontier," 39–40; Noel Schutz, "The Study of Shawnee Myth in an Ethnographic and Ethnohistorical Perspective," (PhD Diss., Indiana University, 1975).

14. Calloway, *The Shawnees and the War for America*, 10–14, 21; Howard, *Shawnee!*, 6–9; White, *The Middle Ground*, 31; Kent, *Susquehanna's Indians*, 78–91.

15. Michael N. McConnell, *A Country Between: The Upper Ohio Valley and Its Peoples, 1724–1774* (Lincoln: University of Nebraska Press 1992), 5–15.

16. Ibid., 54–55.

17. Daniel Richter, *The Ordeal of the Longhouse: The Peoples of the Iroquois League in the Era of European Colonization* (Chapel Hill: University of North Carolina Press, 1992), 105–137.

18. McConnell, *A Country Between*, 57.

19. Ibid., 59–60.

20. Ibid., 14–20, Hamilton letter quoted on p. 20.

21. Howard, *Shawnee!*, 9–12; Dowd, *Spirited Resistance*, 30–31.

22. Anderson, *Crucible of War*, 327–329.

23. Griffin, *American Leviathan*, 42.

24. "George Croghan to William Johnson, 22 December 1759," in Milton Hamilton, ed., *The Papers of Sir William Johnson*, vol. 10 (Albany: The University of the State of New York, 1951), 131.

25. Dowd, *War under Heaven*, 80.

26. Griffin, *American Leviathan*, 43.

27. Holton, *Forced Founders*, 23.

28. "Henry Gladwin to William Johnson, 28 July 1764," George Croghan to William Johnson, 26 May 1766," and "John Bradstreet to Williams Johnson, 14 August 1764," Thomas Gage Papers, William L. Clements Library, The University of Michigan.

29. Woody Holton, *Forced Founders: Indians, Debtors, Slaves & the Making of the American Revolution in Virginia* (Chapel Hill: University of North Carolina Press, 1999), 26–27, 32.

30. "Continental Association of 20 October 1774," "Virginia Resolutions on Lord North's Conciliatory Proposal, 10 June 1775," "Resolutions of Congress on Lord North's Conciliatory Proposal Jefferson's Draft Resolutions, 25 July 1775," "The Resolutions as Adopted by Congress, Philadelphia, July 31, 1775," *The Papers of Thomas Jefferson*, Julian P. Boyd, ed. (Princeton, NJ: Princeton University Press, 1950), 149–154, 170–174, 225–233.

31. "Benjamin Franklin to Jonathan Shipley, March 10, 1774," *Papers of Benjamin Franklin*, William Wilcox, ed. (New Haven, CT: Yale University Press, 1978), 138–140; "Notes for Discourse with Lord Chatham on his Plan, Tuesday, Jan. 31, 1775," *Papers of Benjamin Franklin*, William Wilcox, ed. (New Haven, CT: Yale University Press, 1978), 461–462.

32. Matthew C. Ward, "'The Indians Our Real Friends': The British Army and the Ohio Indians, 1758–1772," in *The Boundaries between Us: Natives and New-comers along the Frontiers of the Old Northwest Territory, 1750–1850*, ed. Daniel P. Barr (Kent, OH: The Kent State University Press, 2006), 73; Richard White, *The Middle Ground: Indians, Empires, and Republics in the Great Lakes Region,*

1650–1815 (New York: Cambridge University Press, 1991), 264; Gregory Evans Dowd, *War under Heaven: Pontiac, the Indian Nations & the British Empire* (Baltimore, MD: The Johns Hopkins University Press, 2002), 79.

33. "Thomas Gage to Francis Fauquier, 2 July 1766," Thomas Gage Papers, William L. Clements Library, The University of Michigan; Fred Anderson, *Crucible of War: The Seven Years' War and the Fate of Empire in British North America, 1754–1766* (New York: Vintage Books, 2000), 637; Ward, "'The Indians Our Real Friends,'" 77–78.

34. See Holton, *Forced Founders.*

35. See Ethan A. Schmidt, *The Divided Dominion: Social Conflict and Indian Hatred in Early Virginia* (Boulder: University Press of Colorado, 2014).

36. Colin G. Calloway, *The American Revolution in Indian Country* (New York: Cambridge University Press, 1995), 189.

37. C. Hale Sipe, *The Indian Wars of Pennsylvania* (Harrisburg, PA: The Telegraph Press, 1931), 479–505.

38. "George Rogers Clark to Samuel Brown, 17 June 1798," in James Alton James, ed., *George Rogers Clark Papers, 1771–1781* (Springfield: Illinois State Historical Library, 1912), 3–9.

39. Sipe, *The Indian Wars of Pennsylvania*, 479–505.

40. "George Rogers Clark to Samuel Brown, 17 June 1798," in James, ed., *George Rogers Clark Papers, 1771–1781*, 3–9; L. Edward Purcell, *Who Was Who in the American Revolution,* (New York: Facts on File, 1993), 118.

41. "George Rogers Clark to Samuel Brown, 17 June 1798," in James, ed., *George Rogers Clark Papers, 1771–1781*, 3–9.

42. Ibid.

43. John Murray, the fourth Earl of Dunmore, was born in Scotland in 1732. His father, the third Earl of Dunmore, had actually participated in the Jacobite rebellion of 1745, but George II later pardoned him. Dunmore, a descendant of the House of Stuart on his mother's side, inherited his title upon his father's death in 1756. In 1761, he became a representative Scottish peer to the House of Lords and moved to London, where he engaged in a vigorous official and social life. Appointed royal governor of New York in 1770, he came to the colonies in October of that year.

44. Draper MSS 3 D 81–86 (Wisconsin Historical Society, Madison; microfilm copy at the University of Kansas, Lawrence, KS).

45. Sipe, *The Indian Wars of Pennsylvania*, 479–505.

46. "George Rogers Clark to Samuel Brown, 17 June 1798," in James, ed., *George Rogers Clark Papers, 1771–1781*, 3–9.

47. Ibid.; Sipe, *The Indian Wars of Pennsylvania*, 479–505; Charles McKnight, *Our Western Border* (Philadelphia: J. C. McCurdy, 1876), 161–169.

48. "George Rogers Clark to Samuel Brown, 17 June 1798," in James, ed., *George Rogers Clark Papers, 1771–1781*, 1912), 3–9.

49. Sipe, *The Indian Wars of Pennsylvania*, 479–505.

50. Reminiscences of Judge Henry Jolly in Reuben Gold Thwaites and Louise Phelps Kellogg, eds., *Documentary History of Dunmore's War, 1774* (Madison: State Historical Society of Wisconsin, 1905), 9–14.

51. Dunmore's Account in Thwaites and Kellog, eds., *Documentary History of Dunmore's War, 1774,* 368–395.

52. Dunmore's Account in Thwaites and Kellog, eds., *Documentary History of Dunmore's War, 1774,* 368–395; Sipe, *The Indian Wars of Pennsylvania,* 479–505; McKnight, *Our Western Border,* 161–169.

CHAPTER 5

1. C. Ford Worthington, ed., *Journals of the Continental Congress* (Washington, D.C.: Government Printing Office, 1905–1937), 2: 182.

2. "Talk of John Stuart to the Creeks, August 15, 1775," The National Archives (TNA): Public Record Office (PRO), CO5/76, 181.

3. "Talk of John Stuart to the Cherokees, August 30, 1775," CO5/76, 179.

4. See David H. Corkran, *The Creek Frontier, 1540–1783* (Norman: The University of Oklahoma Press, 1967), 291–295; James H. Merrell, *The Indians New World: Catawbas and Their Neighbors from European Contact through the Era of* Removal (Chapel Hill: The University of North Carolina Press, 1989), 216; James H. O'Donell, III, *Southern Indians in the American Revolution* (Knoxville: The University of Tennessee Press, 1973), 42–43, 72; Colin Calloway, *The American Revolution in Indian Country: Crisis and Diversity in Native American Communities* (New York: Cambridge University Press, 1995), 194–196, 222.

5. O'Donnell, *Southern Indians in the American Revolution,* 30

6. "Thomas Gage to Lord Dartmouth, June 12, 1775," *The Correspondence of Thomas Gage,* vol. 1 (North Haven, CT: Archon Books, 1969), 404.

7. "Gage to John Stuart, Sept. 12, 1775," CO5/76, 187.

8. O'Donnell, *Southern Indians in the American Revolution,* 31.

9. Calloway, *The American Revolution in Indian Country,* 194–195.

10. "Henry Laurens to John Laurens, August 14, 1776," David R. Chestnutt, ed., *The Papers of Henry Laurens,* January 5, 1776–November 1, 1777 (Columbia: University of South Carolina Press, 1988), II: 229.

11. "James Creswell to William Henry Drayton, July 27, 1776," in Robert W. Gibbes, ed., *Documentary History of the American Revolution* (New York: D. Appleton, 1853–1857), 2:31.

12. "William Sharpe to Cornelius Harnett, July 27, 1776," cited in Jim Piecuch, *Three Peoples, One King: Loyalists, Indians, and Slaves in the Revolutionary South, 1775–1782* (Columbia, S.C.: 2008), 69.

13. "Creswell to Drayton, July 27, 1776," in Gibbes, ed., *Documentary History of the American Revolution,* 2:30–31.

14. See Calloway, *The American Revolution in Indian Country,* 197.

15. O'Donnell, *Southern Indians in the American Revolution,* 43.

16. Ibid., 43–44; see also Tom Hatley, *The Dividing Paths: Cherokees and South Carolinians through the Revolutionary Era* (New York: Oxford University Press, 1995), 218–219.

17. "Andrew Williamson to Griffith Rutherford, August 14, 1776," William Saunders, ed., *The Colonial Records of North Carolina*, vol. 1 (Raleigh: P. M. Hale, Printer to the State, 1886), 159–160; *Documenting the American South*, University Library, The University of North Carolina at Chapel Hill, 2007, http://docsouth.unc.edu/csr/index.html/document/csr01-0061.

18. O'Donnell, *Southern Indians in the American Revolution*, 45–59; Hatley, *The Dividing Paths*, 219–226; Calloway, *The American Revolution in Indian Country*, 198–201.

19. Piecuch, *Three Peoples, One King*, 132–139.

20. Calloway, *The American Revolution in Indian Country*, 203; O'Donnell, *Southern Indians in the American Revolution*, 84.

21. Calloway, *The American Revolution in Indian Country*, 203–205.

22. O'Donnell, *Southern Indians in the American Revolution*, 118–119.

23. Ibid.

24. Raymond E. Evans, "Notable Persons in Cherokee History: Dragging Canoe," *Journal of Cherokee Studies*, vol. 2, no. 2, 176–189 (Cherokee: Museum of the Cherokee Indian, 1977); Calloway, *The American Revolution in Indian Country*, 204–205; Hatley, *The Dividing Paths*, 226–227; Samuel Cole Williams, *Tennessee during the Revolutionary War* (Nashville: Tennessee Historical Commission, 1944), 182.

25. Evans, "Notable Persons in Cherokee History: Dragging Canoe," 176–189.

26. Calloway, *The American Revolution in Indian Country*, 201.

27. Corkran, *The Creek Frontier*, 289.

28. Ibid., 290–291.

29. Ibid., 291; Kenneth Coleman and Milton Ready, *Colonial Records of Georgia* vol. 38 (Athens: University of Georgia Press, 1989), pt. 2, 18.

30. Corkran, *The Creek Frontier*, 291–292.

31. Ibid., 291.

32. Calloway, *The American Revolution in Indian Country*, 257.

33. "Gage to Stuart, Sept. 12, 1775," CO5/76, 187; see also, O'Donnell, *Southern Indians in the American Revolution*, 30.

34. "Gage to Dartmouth," 404; see also, *Southern Indians in the American Revolution*, 30.

35. O'Donnell, *Southern Indians in the American Revolution*, 30–31, 49.

36. Corkran, *The Creek Frontier*, 294–295.

37. CO 5/77, 255.

38. Corkran, *The Creek Frontier*, 295.

39. Ibid., 296–297.

40. Ibid., 297–298.

41. Ibid., 298–300.

42. Ibid., 301–302.

43. "Taitt to Tonyn, May 22, 1777," CO5/77, 599.

44. "Stuart to Howe, Apr. 13, 1777," CO5/94, 567.

45. Corkran, *The Creek Frontier*, 305–308.

46. Corkran, *The Creek Frontier,* 309–311.

47. Ibid., 311–314.

48. Ibid., 316–320.

49. Ibid., 320–325.

50. Calloway, *The American Revolution in Indian Country,* 222.

51. Ibid., 222; K. G. Davies, *Documents of the American Revolution* (Shannon: Irish University Press, 1972), vol. 12: 277.

52. Davies, *Documents of the American Revolution,* vol. 14, 50, 69; O'Donnell, *Southern Indians in the American Revolution,* 63; Calloway, *The American Revolution in Indian Country,* 222.

53. Calloway, *American Revolution in Indian Country,* 213.

54. See chapter 2 for a discussion of the incident with the Illinois country Indians.

55. Davies, *Documents of the American Revolution,* vol. 14: 79–82, 112–115, 147–148; see also Calloway, *The American Revolution in Indian Country,* 223.

56. O'Donnell, *Southern Indians in the American Revolution,* 72; Calloway, *The American Revolution in Indian Country,* 223.

57. Davies, *Documents of the American Revolution,* vol. 13: 246.

58. Calloway, *The American Revolution in Indian Country,* 223.

59. Davies, *Documents of the American Revolution,* vol. 15: 183–184; Calloway, *The American Revolution in Indian Country,* 224.

60. Calloway, *The American Revolution in Indian Country,* 224; Davies, *Documents of the American Revolution,* vol. 13: 351, 395, vol. 15: 187–188, 212; James Alton James, *George Rogers Clark Papers, 1781–1784* (Springfield: Illinois Historical Society, 1926), 136.

61. Calloway, *The American Revolution in Indian Country,* 225; Davies, *Documents of the American Revolution,* vol. 17: 29–30.

62. Calloway, *The American Revolution in Indian Country,* 225.

63. *Papers of the Continental Congress, 1774–1789.* National Archives Microfilm, no. M247, reel 65, item 51, vol. 2, 41–42.

64. Ibid., 226.

65. Ibid., 226–227.

66. Ibid., 227–228; Davies, *Documents of the American Revolution,* vol. 18: 219–221.

67. Calloway, *The American Revolution in Indian Country,* 228.

68. Ibid., 222; O'Donnell, *Southern Indians in the American Revolution,* 6.

69. Davies, *Documents of the American Revolution,* 28.

70. Greg O'Brien, "The Choctaw Defense of Pensacola in the American Revolution," *Pre-Removal Choctaw History: Exploring New Paths,* Greg O'Brien, ed. (Norman: University of Oklahoma Press, 2008), 125.

71. O'Brien, "We Are behind You: The Choctaw Occupation of Natchez in 1778," *Journal of Mississippi History,* vol. 64 (2002), 107–124.

72. Calloway, *The American Revolution in Indian Country,* 224–225; O'Brien, "The Choctaw Defense of Pensacola in the American Revolution," 125–126.

73. O'Brien, "The Choctaw Defense of Pensacola in the American Revolution," 127.

74. Ibid.

75. Ibid., 128.

76. Ibid.

77. "Choctaw Chiefs to James Colbert," quoted in O'Brien, *Choctaws in a Revolutionary Age,* 129.

78. Ibid., 129–130.

79. Ibid., 133–134.

80. Ibid., 135–138.

81. Ibid., 138–143.

82. *Papers of the Continental Congress, 1774–1789* (Washington D.C: National Archives Microfilm, no. M247, reel 65, item 51, vol. 1, 56

83. James Merrell, *The Indians' New World: Catawbas and Their Neighbors from European Contact through the Era of Removal* (Chapel Hill: University of North Carolina Press, 1989), 215.

84. Ibid., 216.

85. Ibid., 217.

CHAPTER 6

1. William N. Fenton, *The Great Law of the Longhouse: A Political History of the Iroquois Confederacy* (Norman: University of Oklahoma Press, 1998), 211.

2. Colin Calloway, *The Western Abenakis of Vermont, 1600–1800: War, Migration, and the Survival of an Indian People* (Norman: University of Oklahoma Press, 1990), 207–209.

3. Calloway, *The American Revolution in Indian Country: Crisis and Diversity in Native American Communities* (New York: Cambridge University Press, 1995), 69.

4. Calloway, *Western Abenakis of Vermont,* 209.

5. Ibid., 209–214.

6. Calloway, *The American Revolution in Indian Country,* 72.

7. Calloway, *The Western Abenakis of Vermont,* 210.

8. Ibid.

9. Ibid., 213.

10. Ibid., 219, Calloway, *The American Revolution in Indian Country,* 78.

11. Calloway, *The Western Abenakis of Vermont,* 216–220.

12. Calloway, *The American Revolution in Indian Country,* 92–93.

13. Ibid., 94.

14. Ibid., 96.

15. Ibid., 96–97.

16. Carl Leopold Baurmeister, *Revolution in America: Confidential Letters and Journals 1776–1784 of Adjutant General Major Baurmeister of the Hessian Forces,* Bernard A. Uhlendorf, trans. (Westport, CT: Greenwood Press, 1973), 205.

17. Calloway, *The American Revolution in Indian Country,* 98–100.

18. Barbara Graymont, *The Iroquois in the American Revolution* (Syracuse, NY: Syracuse University Press, 1972), 48–50; Alan Taylor, *The Divided Ground: Indians, Settlers, and the Northern Borderland of the America Revolution* (New York: Vintage, 2006), 69–70.

19. "Thomas Gage to Lord Dartmouth, July 18, 1774," *The Papers of Sir William Johnson*, vol. 8 (Albany: The University of the State of New York, 1933), 1185.

20. William N. Fenton, *The Great Law of the Longhouse: A Political History of the Iroquois Confederacy* (Norman: University of Oklahoma Press, 1998), 570–571; Taylor, *The Divided Ground*, 70–71.

21. Taylor, *The Divided Ground*, 72; Fenton, *The Great Law of the Longhouse*, 572–573.

22. Graymont, *The Iroquois in the American Revolution*, 53; Taylor, *The Divided Ground*, 75.

23. Fenton, *The Great Law of the Longhouse*, 578–579; Graymont, *The Iroquois in the American Revolution*, 53.

24. Fenton, *The Great Law of the Longhouse*, 582–583.

25. Ibid., 583; Taylor, *The Divided Ground*, 74–75.

26. Graymont, *The Iroquois in the American Revolution*, 55; "Samuel Kirkland to the Committee of Albany, June 9, 1775," in Pomroy Jones, *Annals and Recollections of Oneida County* (New York: Pomroy Jones, 1851), 853.

27. Fenton, *The Great Law and the Longhouse*, 583.

28. Graymont, *The Iroquois in the American Revolution*, 58; Fenton, *The Great Law and the Longhouse*, 585.

29. Graymont, *The Iroquois in the American Revolution*, 59–63; Fenton, *The Great Law and the Longhouse*, 585–586.

30. Fenton, *The Great Law and the Longhouse*, 586; Graymont, *The Iroquois in the American Revolution*, 62–63; Taylor, *The Divided Ground*, 75–77.

31. Taylor, *The Divided Ground*, 78.

32. Fenton, *The Great Law of the Longhouse*, 587.

33. Ibid., 587; Taylor, *The Divided Ground*, 81–82.

34. Taylor, *The Divided Ground*, 78; Graymont, *The Iroquois in the American Revolution*, 64–66; Fenton, *The Great Law and the Longhouse*, 588.

35. Taylor, *The Divided Ground*, 80; Graymont, *The Iroquois in the American Revolution*, 69–74; Fenton, *The Great Law and the Longhouse*, 589; Calloway, *The American Revolution in Indian Country*, 122.

36. Graymont, *The Iroquois in the American Revolution*, 69–74; Fenton, *The Great Law and the Longhouse*, 589.

37. E. B. O'Callaghan, *Documents Relative to the Colonial History of the State of New York*, vol. 8 (Albany, NY: Weed, Parsons, 1857), 619.

38. Taylor, *The Divided Ground*, 83.

39. Fenton, *The Great Law and the Longhouse*, 593–594: Taylor, *The Divided Ground*, 84–85.

40. "Extract from the Journal of James Deane, Interpreter to tile Six Nations from March 21to April 3," *American Archives*, series 4, vol. 5, 1100, available

on-line at http://lincoln.lib.niu.edu/cgi-bin/amarch/documentidx.pl?doc_id=S4-V5-P01-sp17-D0071&showfullrecord=on; Fenton, *The Great Law and the Longhouse,* 597.

41. Fenton, *The Great Law and the Longhouse,* 598, Graymont, *The Iroquois and the American Revolution,* 87–90; Taylor, *The Divided Ground,* 85–86.

42. Graymont, *The Iroquois in the American Revolution,* 104–105; Taylor, *The Divided Ground,* 87.

43. Taylor, *The Divided Ground,* 89.

44. Ibid., 88.

45. Ibid., 89; Graymont, 106.

46. Taylor, *The Divided Ground,* 90.

47. Ibid., 91; Graymont, *The Iroquois in the American Revolution,* 115–117.

48. Taylor, *The Divided Ground,* 91; Graymont, *The Iroquois in the American Revolution,* 117–128; Isabel Thompson Kelsay, *Joseph Brant, 1743-1807: Man of Two Worlds* (Syracuse, NY: Syracuse University Press, 1984), 195–199.

49. Taylor, *The Divided Ground,* 92.

50. Ibid.; Graymont, *The Iroquois in the American Revolution,* 130–144.

51. Taylor, *The Divided Ground,* 92–93.

52. Graymont, *The Iroquois in the American Revolution,* 165–166.

53. Ibid., 146–147.

54. *Papers of the Continental Congress, 1774-1789* (Washington D.C: National Archives Microfilm, no. M247, item 153, vol. 3, 286–290.

55. Taylor, *The Divided Ground,* 93; Graymont, *The Iroquois in the American Revolution,* 167–174.

56. Graymont, *The Iroquois in the American Revolution,* 181–183; Taylor, *The Divided Ground,* 93–94.

57. Graymont, *The Iroquois in the American Revolution,* 183–191; Taylor, *The Divided Ground,* 94.

58. Taylor, *The Divided Ground,* 95.

59. Ibid., 96–97.

60. Graymont, *The Iroquois in the American Revolution,* 192–193.

61. Ibid., 192–222; Taylor, *The Divided Ground,* 97–102.

62. Graymont, *The Iroquois in the American Revolution,* 223–235; Taylor, *The Divided Ground,* 100.

63. Taylor, *The Divided Ground,* 101.

64. Ibid., 102–105; Graymont, *The Iroquois in the American Revolution,* 240–241, 252.

CHAPTER 7

1. Clark's Memoir in James, ed., *George Rogers Clark Papers 1771-1781* (Springfield: Illinois State Historical Society, 1926), 288.

2. The Journal of Henry Hamilton, 1778-1779, in Barnhart, ed., *Henry Hamilton and George Rogers Clark in the American Revolution,* 102–205.

3. Ibid., 75; "The Journal of Henry Hamilton, 1778–1779," in Barnhart, ed., *Henry Hamilton and George Rogers Clark in the American Revolution*, 102–205.

4. Patrick Griffin, *American Leviathan: Empire, Nation and Revolutionary Frontier* (New York: Hill and Wang, 2007), 123; see also, Eric Hinderaker, *Elusive Empires: Constructing Colonialism in the Ohio Valley, 1673–1800* (New York: Cambridge University Press, 1997), 201; Richard White, *The Middle Ground: Indians, Empires and Republics in the Great Lakes Region, 1650–1815* (New York: Cambridge University Press, 1991), 384; Stephen Aron, *How the West Was Lost: The Transformation of Kentucky from Daniel Boone to Henry Clay* (Baltimore, MD: Johns Hopkins University Press, 1996), 20.

5. Colin Calloway, *The American Revolution in Indian Country: Crisis and Diversity in Native American Communities* (New York: Cambridge University Press, 1995),164.

6. Robert L. Scribner, *Revolutionary Virginia, The Road to Independence: A Documentary Record*, vol. 7 (Charlottesville: University Press of Virginia, 1973), 770; Colin Calloway, *The American Revolution in Indian Country: Crisis and Diversity in Native American Communities* (New York: Cambridge University Press, 1995), 164.

7. Randolph Downes, *Council Fires on the Upper Ohio* (Pittsburgh, PA: University of Pittsburgh Press, 1969), 180.

8. Calloway, *The American Revolution in Indian Country*, 158.

9. Ibid., 160; See also, Thomas Wildcat Alford, *Civilization and the Story of the Absentee Shawnees, as told to Florence Drake* (Norman, OK: University of Oklahoma Press, 1936), 8; and James H. Howard, *Shawnee!: The Ceremonialism of a Native American Tribe and its Cultural Background* (Athens, OH: University of Ohio Press, 1981), 25–30, 213–222.

10. Calloway, *The American Revolution in Indian Country*, 158–166.

11. Clark's memoir in James Alton James, ed., *George Rogers Clark Papers 1771–1781*, (Springfield: Illinois State Historical Library, 1912), 208–209.

12. Ibid.; "June 15, 1776 West Fincastle County Legislative Petition" in Seineke, ed., *The George Rogers Clark Adventure in the Illinois and Selected Documents of the American Revolution at the Frontier Posts*, 180–81.

13. Ibid.

14. Clark's memoir in James, ed., *George Rogers Clark Papers 1771–1781*, 214–215.

15. Gary B. Nash, *The Unknown American Revolution: The Unruly Birth of Democracy and the Struggle ot Creat America* (New York: Penguin, 2006), 260.

16. Hinderaker, *Elusive Empires*, 207–209.

17. David Zeisberger, *The Moravian Missionary Diaries of David Zeisberger: 1772–1781*, Herman Wellenreuther and Carola Wessel, eds. (University Park: Pennsylvania State University Press, 2005), 358.

18. Calloway, *The American Revolution in Indian Country*, 166; *The Shawnees and the War for America* (New York: Penguin, 2008), 63–64.

19. Calloway, *The Shawnees and the War for America*, 64–65.

20. Reuben Gold Thwaites and Louis Phelps Kellogg, eds., *Frontier Defense on the Upper Ohio, 1777–1778* (Madison: Wisconsin Historical Society, 1912), 157.

21. Ibid., 150.

22. James H. O'Donnell, *Ohio Valley Indians* (Athens: Ohio University Press, 2004), 56.

23. Thwaites and Kellogg, *Frontier Defense on the Upper Ohio,* 159–160.

24. Ibid., 188.

25. Ibid., 206.

26. George Rogers Clark, *Campaign in the Illinois* (Cincinnati, OH: Robert Clarke, 1869), 22.

27. "Two Letters of Patrick Henry Authorizing Clark Expedition, 2 January, 1778," in Seineke, ed., *The George Rogers Clark Adventure in the Illinois and Selected Documents of the American Revolution at the Frontier Posts,* 214–215.

28. Ibid.

29. Seineke, *The George Rogers Clark Adventure in the Illinois and Selected Documents of the American Revolution at the Frontier Posts,* 215.

30. "George Wythe, George Mason, and Thomas Jefferson to George Rogers Clark, 3 January, 1778," in Kathrine Wagner Seineke, ed., *The George Rogers Clark Adventure in the Illinois and Selected Documents of the American Revolution at the Frontier Posts* (New Orleans, LA: Polyanthos, 1981), 216.

31. Calloway, *The Shawnees and the War for America,* 67–68; Hinderaker, *Elusive Empires,* 220–221.

32. Hinderaker, *Elusive Empires,* 222.

33. Aron, *How the West Was Lost,* 45–49.

34. Ibid., 48.

35. Lowell Henry Harrison, *George Rogers Clark and the War in the West* (Lexington: University Press of Kentucky, 1976), 68–69.

36. James, *The Life of George Rogers Clark,* 185.

37. Petition from the Inhabitants of Boonesborough to Clark, 10 March 1780, in James, ed., *George Rogers Clark Papers, 1771–1781,* 398–400.

38. "Clark to John Todd, Jr., March 1780," in James, ed., *George Rogers Clark Papers, 1771–1781,* 404–407.

39. "Clark to Thomas Jefferson 23 September 1779," in James, ed., *George Rogers Clark Papers, 1771–1781,* 335–36; James, *The Life of George Rogers Clark,* 197; "Clark to John Todd, Jr., March 1780," in James, ed., *George Rogers Clark Papers, 1771–1781,* 404–407.

40. James, *The Life of George Rogers Clark,* 198–99; "Pierre Prevost to Clark, 20 February 1780," in James, ed., *George Rogers Clark Papers, 1771–1781,* 394–395.

41. James, ed., *George Rogers Clark Papers, 1771–1781,* cxxxvii.

42. Harrison, *George Rogers Clark and the War in the West,* 73; John Bakeless, *Background to Glory: The Life of George Rogers Clark* (Philadelphia: J. B. Lippincott, 1957), 253; James, *The Life of George Rogers Clark,* 209.

43. Draper MSS 50 J 7; "Clark to Jefferson, 22 August 1780", in James, ed., *George Rogers Clark Papers, 1771–1781,* 451.

44. "Clark to Jefferson, 22 August 1780," in James, ed., *George Rogers Clark Papers, 1771–1781,* 451.

45. Ibid.

46. Ibid.

47. Aron, *How the West Was Lost,* 48–49; Calloway, *The Shawnees and the War for America,* 71–72.

48. Gregory Evans Dowd, *A Spirited Resistance: The North American Indian Struggle for Unity, 1745–1815* (Baltimore, MD: The Johns Hopkins University Press, 1992), 85–86.

49. Charles McKnight, *Our Western Border in Early Pioneer Days* (Chicago, IL: The Educational Company, 1902), 413–414.

50. Downes, *Council Fires on the Upper Ohio,* 273–274.

51. C. W. Butterfield, *An Historical Account of the Expedition Against the Sandusky under Colonel William Crawford in 1872* (Cincinnati, OH: Robert Clarke, 1873), 380–382.

52. Ibid., 387–391.

53. Ibid., 268–69.

54. Ibid. 270–72; Draper MSS 52 J 37; "The Battle of the Blue Licks 19 August 1782," in James, ed., *George Rogers Clark Papers, 1781–1783,* 89–93.

55. Calloway, *The Shawnees and the War for America,* 73–74.

56. Downes, *Council Fires on the Upper Ohio,* 279–280; Calloway, *The Shawnees and the War for America,* 75.

CHAPTER 8

1. Colin Calloway, *The American Revolution in Indian Country: Crisis and Diversity in Native American Communities* (New York: Cambridge University Press, 1995), 284.

2. Tom Hatley, *The Dividing Paths: Cherokees and South Carolinians Through the Era of Revolution* (New York: Oxford University Press, 1995), 227–235.

3. Calloway, *The American Revolution in Indian Country,* 209, 284; James Mooney, *Myths of the Cherokee* (New York: Dover Publications, 1996), 61

4. J. Leitch Wright, *Creeks and Seminoles: The Destruction and Regeneration of the Muscogulge People* (Lincoln, NE: University of Nebraska Press, 1986), 115.

5. Claudio Saunt, *A New Order of Things: Property, Power, and the Transformation of the Creek Indians, 1733–1833* (New York: Cambridge University Press, 1999), 1.

6. Ibid., 67–78.

7. Ibid., 76–81, Alexander McGillivray quote p. 81.

8. Ibid., 89.

9. Ibid., 90–91, 179–183.

10. Ibid., 249–250, 272.

11. Calloway, *The American Revolution in Indian Country,* 228–230; Edward J. Cashin, *Guardians of the Valley: Chickasaws in Colonial South Carolina and*

Georgia (Columbia: University of South Carolina Press, 2009), 142, 147; James R. Atkinson, *Splendid Land, Splendid People: The Chickasaw Indians to Removal* (Tuscaloosa: University of Alabama Press, 2004), 120–121, 137–139; Arell M. Gibson, *The Chickasaws* (Norman: University of Oklahoma Press, 1971), 73.

12. Calloway, *The American Revolution in Indian Country*, 230–232.

13. *Papers of the Continental Congress, 1774–1789,* National Archives Microfilm, No. M247, reel 104, item 78, vol. 24, 445–449.

14. Gibson, *The Chickasaws*, 75–76; Atkinson, *Splendid Land, Splendid People*, 122–123; Cashin, *Guardians of the Valley*, 142–145, Calloway, *The American Revolution in Indian Country*, 234.

15. Atkinson, *Splendid Land, Splendid People*, 123–124, 128–129, 134–137, 145; Calloway, *The American Revolution in Indian Country*, 235–238.

16. Gibson, *The Chickasaws*, 90–95; Calloway, *The American Revolution in Indian Country*, 241–242.

17. Greg O'Brien, *Choctaws in a Revolutionary Age, 1750–1830* (Lincoln: University of Nebraska Press, 2002), 51.

18. Greg O'Brien, "The Conqueror Meets the Unconquered: Negotiating Cultureal Boundaries on the Post-Revolutionary Southern Frontier," *Pre-Removal Choctaw History* (Norman: University of Oklahoma Press, 2008), 150.

19. Ibid., 151–152.

20. Ibid., 155–156.

21. Ibid., 166–168.

22. Ibid., 170–171.

23. James Merrell, *The Indians New World: Catawbas and Their Neighbors from European Contact through the Era of Removal* (Chapel Hill: University of North Carolina Press, 1989), 217.

24. Ibid., 217–218.

25. Ibid., 219–223.

26. Ibid., 224.

27. Ibid., 225.

28. Colin Calloway, *The Western Abenakis of Vermont, 1600–1800: War, Migration, and the Survival of an Indian People* (Norman: University of Oklahoma Press, 1990), 224–225.

29. Ibid.

30. Ibid., 225–226.

31. Ibid., 234–237.

32. Calloway, *The American Revolution in Indian Country*, 100–101.

33. Ibid., 101–102.

34. Ibid., 103.

35. Ibid., 104–107.

36. Barbara Graymont, *The Iroquois in the American Revolution* (Syracuse, NY: Syracuse University Press, 1972), 258–259: Alan Taylor, *The Divided Ground: Indians, Settles and the Northern Borderland of the American Revolution* (New York: Vintage Press, 2006), 111–112.

37. William Leete Stone, *Memoirs, and letters and journals of Major General Riedesel during his residence in America* (Albany, NY: J. Munsell, 1868), 169.

38. Taylor, *The Divided Ground*, 112.

39. Graymont, *The Iroquois in the American Revolution*, 260–262; Taylor, *The Divided Ground*, 114–115.

40. Graymont, *The Iroquois in the American Revolution*, 264, 284.

41. Taylor, *The Divided Ground*, 118–119; Graymont, *The Iroquois in the American Revolution*, 270–281.

42. Graymont, *The Iroquois in the American Revolution*, 281.

43. Ibid., 282.

44. Ibid., 283–284.

45. Ibid., 284–285; Taylor, *The Divided Ground*, 120–121.

46. Colin Calloway, *The Shawnees and the War for America* (New York: Viking, 2007), 76–78.

47. Ibid., 82–83.

48. Ibid., 83–84.

49. Ibid., 89–90.

50. Ibid., 92–94.

51. Ibid., 95–98.

52. Ibid., 103–105.

53. Ibid., 106–108.

CONCLUSION

1. Madonna Thunderhawk, "Extended Interview," *William Kunstler: Disturbing the Universe.* http://www.pbs.org/pov/disturbingtheuniverse/interview_thunderhawk .php#.UbYJkL-UC4h

2. Philip J. Deloria, *Playing Indian* (New Haven, CT: Yale University Press, 1998), 7.

3. Ibid., 5.

4. Ibid., 1–9.

5. Jill Lepore, *The Name of War: King Philip's War and the Origins of American Identity* (New York: Vintage, 1999), 187.

6. Lepore, *The Name of War*, 193.

7. Deloria, *Playing Indian*, 5.

8. Sara Garlick, "Ban Criteria Largely Flawed," *University Daily Kansan.* August 19, 2005, The University of Kansas.

BIBLIOGRAPHIC ESSAY

What follows is a bibliographical essay designed to provide readers with an overview of some of the most relevant scholarly literature concerning the experience of Native Americans in the American Revolutionary Era as well as the immediate postwar period and the continuing struggle over control of native identities.

While most general studies of the American Revolution tend to either ignore Native Americans completely or portray them simply as ancillary figures of marginal importance to the outbreak and outcome of the struggle, the following works provide more comprehensive coverage: James L. Stokesbury, *A Short History of the American Revolution* (1991); Edward Countryman, *The American Revolution* (1985); Robert Middlekauff, *The Glorious Cause: The American Revolution, 1763–1789* (1982); and Don Higginbotham, *The War for American Independence* (1983).

Gary B. Nash's, *The Unknown American Revolution: The Unruly Birth of Democracy and the Struggle to Create America* (2005), however, exceeds all of the above in its presentation of American Indians as full-fledged participants in the conflict and agents of its origins, progress, and eventual conclusion.

Beyond the more general histories of the American Revolution mentioned above, there are a few that focus primarily or solely on Native Americans. Though none of these offer a comprehensive synthesis or treatment, Colin Calloway's *The American Revolution in Indian Country: Crisis and Diversity in Native American Communities* (1995) stands as one of the best researched and most important books on the subject and is invaluable to anyone interested in either learning more about the topic or embarking upon research in this area. Other works in this vein include S. F. Wise, "The American Revolution and Indian History," in John S. Moir, ed., *Character and Circumstance: Essays in Honour of Donald Grant Creighton* (1970); Francis Jennings, "The Indians' Revolution," in Alfred F. Young, ed., *Explorations in the History of American Radicalism* (1976); Kenneth M. Morrison, "Native Americans and the American Revolution: Historic Stories and Shifting Frontier Conflict," in Frederick E. Hoxie, ed., *Indians in American History* (1988); as well as Bernard Sheehan, "The Problem of the Indian in the American Revolution," in Phillip Weeks, ed., *The America Indian Experience* (1988). Vine Deloria Jr.'s "The American Revolution and the American Indian: Problems in the Recovery of a Usable Past," *Spirit and Reason: The Vine Deloria, Jr., Reader* (1999) offers a pointed critique of the tendency of Americans (particularly during the bicentennial period of the mid-1970s) to continue to create whitewashed narratives of the American Revolution for the purpose of providing the American public with a history concerned more about making Americans feel good about themselves rather than getting at the actual historical truths.

One cannot understand the American Indian experience in the American revolution without a firm background in the literature regarding Indians in Colonial America. The following general studies of Indians in pre-revolutionary America to 1754 represent some of the best avenues for gaining such knowledge. They include Daniel Richter, *Facing East from Indian Country: A Native History of Early America* (2001); James Axtell, *The European and the Indian: Essays in the Ethnohistory of Colonial North America* (1981), *The Invasion Within: The Contest of Cultures in Colonial North America* (1986) and *Beyond 1492: Encounters in Colonial North America* (1992); Colin Calloway, *New Worlds for All: Indians, Europeans and the Remaking of Early America* (1998) and *White People, Indians, and Highlanders: Tribal Peoples and Colonial Encounters in Scotland and America* (2008); Gary Nash, *Red, White and Black: The Peoples of Early North America* (1974); Peter Mancall, *Deadly Medicine: Indians and Alcohol in Early America* (1995); as well as Alden T. Vaughan, *Transatlantic Encounters: American Indians in Britain, 1500–1776* (2006).

Likewise, the literature on specific Indian communities and groups prior to the outbreak of the Seven Years' War in 1754 is an extremely active and growing area of scholarship that must be consulted if one is to fully understand Indian country on the eve of the American Revolution. Below,

I have organized the literature for this period into the same geographic divisions utilized in the main body of this volume.

Studies that focus primarily on particular Indian peoples prior to 1754 in the colonial south consist of Tom Hatley, *The Dividing Paths: Cherokees and the South Carolinians through the Revolutionary Era* (1995) and with Peter H. Wood and Gregory A. Waselkov, eds. *Powhatan's Mantle: Indians in the Colonial Southeast* (1989); Paul Kelton, *Epidemics and Enslavement: Biological Catastrophe in the Native Southeast* (2007); John Oliphant, *Peace and War on the Anglo-Cherokee Frontier, 1756–1763* (2001); Steven C. Hahn, *The Invention of the Creek Nation, 1670–1763* (2004); David H. Corkran, *The Creek Frontier, 1540–1783* (1967) and *The Cherokee Frontier: Conflict and Survival, 1740–1762* (1962); James H. Merrell, *The Indians' New World: Catawbas and Their Neighbors from European Contact through the Era of Removal* (1989); Ethan A. Schmidt, *The Divided Dominion: Social Conflict and Indian Hatred in Early Virginia* (2014); J. Leitch Wright, *Creeks and Seminoles: The Destruction and Regeneration of the Muscogulge People* (1986); Claudio Saunt, *A New Order of Things: Property, Power, and the Transformation of the Creek Indians, 1733–1833* (1999); Edward J. Cashin, *Guardians of the Valley: Chickasaws in Colonial South Carolina and Georgia* (2009) and *Lachlan McGillivray, Indian Trader: The Shaping of the Southern Colonial Frontier* (1992); James R. Atkinson, *Splendid Land, Splendid People: The Chickasaw Indians to Removal* (2004); Arell M. Gibson, *The Chickasaws* (1971); Theda Perdue, *Cherokee Women: Gender and Culture Change: 1700–1835* (1998); John T. Juricek, *Colonial Georgia and the Creeks: Anglo-Indian Diplomacy on the Southern Frontier, 1733–1763* (2010); Alan Gallay, *The Indian Slave Trade: The Rise of the English Empire in the American South, 1670–1717* (2002); Michelene Pesantubbee, *Choctaw Women in a Chaotic World: The Clash of Cultures in the Colonial Southeast* (2005); Patricia Galloway, "Choctaw Factionalism and Civil War," *Journal of Mississippi History* 44 (1982); Daniel H. Usner, *Indians, Settlers, and Slaves in a Frontier Exchange Economy: The Lower Mississippi Valley before 1783* (1992); Robbie Ethridge, *Creek Country: The Creek Indians and Their World* (2004) and *From Chicaza to Chickasaw: The European Invasion and the Transformation of the Mississippian World, 1540–1715* (2010); Greg O'Brien, *Choctaws in a Revolutionary Age, 1750–1830* (2005) and as editor, *Pre-Removal Choctaw History: Exploring New Paths* (2008); and Louis De Vorsey Jr., *The Indian Boundary in the Southern Colonies, 1763–1777* (1966).

The most salient scholarship on the Indian peoples of the colonial north to 1754 includes Daniel Richter, *The Ordeal of the Longhouse: The Peoples of the Iroquois League in the Era of European Colonization* (1992);

Paul A. W. Wallace, *Conrad Weiser, 1696–1760, Friend of Colonist and Mohawk* (1945); William N. Fenton, *The Great Law of the Longhouse: A Political History of the Iroquois Confederacy* (1998); Colin G. Calloway, *The Western Abenakis of Vermont, 1600–1800: War, Migration, and the Survival of an Indian People* (1990) and as editor, *Dawnland Encounters: Indians and Europeans in Northern New England* (1991); Daniel Mandell, "'To Live More Like My Christian English Neighbors': Natick Indians in the Eighteenth Century," *William and Mary Quarterly* Third Series, vol. 48, no. 4 (Oct., 1991) and *Behind the Frontier: Indians in Eighteenth-Century Massachusetts* (1996); Jean M. O'Brien, "'Divorced' from the Land: Resistance and Survival of Indian Women in Eighteenth-Century New England," in *After King Philip's War: Presence and Persistence in Indian New England,* ed., Colin Calloway (1997).

Francis Jennings, *The Ambiguous Iroquois Empire: The Covenant Chain Confederation of Indian Tribes with English Colonies* (1990); Jack Campisi and Laurence M. Hauptman, *The Oneida Indian Experience: Two Perspectives* (1988); Patrick Frazier, *The Mohicans of Stockbridge* (1992); and Anthony F. C. Wallace, *The Death and Rebirth of the Seneca* (1972).

Some of the very best scholarship in the field of colonial Native American history over the past 25 years can be found within that which examines the Ohio Valley and beyond during the years before the Seven Years' War. Specifically, Richard White, *The Middle Ground: Indians, Empires, and Republics in the Great Lakes Region, 1650–1815* (1991) and James Merrell, *Into the American Woods: Negotiators on the Pennsylvania Frontier* (1999) represent some of the most influential writing on the subject during that time. Other works of note that focus on the Ohio Valley during this period include Michael N. McConnell, *A Country Between: The Upper Ohio Valley and Its Peoples, 1724–1774* (1992); James H. O'Donnell III, *Ohio's First Peoples* (2004); Martha Potter Otoe, *Ohio's Prehistoric Peoples* (1980); John Witthoft and William A. Hunter, "The Seventeenth-Century Origins of the Shawnee," *Ethnohistory* vol. 2, no. 1 (Winter 1955); Eric Hinderaker, *Elusive Empires: Constructing Colonialism in the Ohio Valley, 1673–1800* (1997); Gunlög Fur, *A Nation of Women: Gender and Colonial Encounters Among the Delaware Indians* (2009); Susan Sleeper-Smith, *Indian Women and French Men: Rethinking Cultural Encounter in the Western Great Lakes* (2001); Colin Calloway, *One Vast Winter Count: The Native American West Before Lewis and Clark* (2003); Stephen Aron, *How the West Was Lost: The Transformation of Kentucky from Daniel Boone to Henry Clay* (1996); and Randolph C. Downes, *Council Fires on the Upper Ohio* (1969).

Studies of the Seven Years' War, Pontiac War, and the Imperial Crisis of the 1760s that offer significant coverage of Native Americans include David Dixon, *Never Come to Peace Again: Pontiac's Uprising and the Fate of the British Empire in North America* (2005); Gregory Evans Dowd, *A Spirited Resistance: The North American Indian Struggle for Unity, 1745–1815* (1992) and *War under Heaven: Pontiac, the Indian Nations and the British Empire* (2002); and "Insidious Friends: Gift Giving and the Cherokee-British Alliance in the Seven Years War," Andrew R. L. Cayton and Fredrika J. Teute eds., *Contact Points: American Frontiers from the Mohawk Valley to the Mississippi, 1750–1830* (1998); Fred Anderson, *The Crucible of War: The Seven Years' War and the Fate of Empire in British North America, 1754–1766* (2000); Matthew C. Ward, *Breaking the Backcountry: The Seven Years' War in Virginia and Pennsylvania, 1754–1765* (2004) and "'The Indians Our Real Friends': The British Army and the Ohio Indians, 1758–1772," in *The Boundaries Between Us: Natives and Newcomers along the Frontiers of the Old Northwest Territory, 1750–1850*, ed. Daniel P. Barr (2006); Ian K. Steele, *Betrayals: Fort William Henry and the "Massacre"* (1990); Colin Calloway, *The Scratch of Pen: 1763 and the Transformation of North America* (2006); and Woody Holton, *Forced Founders: Indians, Debtors, Slaves and the Making of the American Revolution in Virginia* (1999).

Colin Calloway, *The American Revolution in Indian Country: Crisis and Diversity in Native American Communities* (1995) still constitutes the pre-eminent work on the native experience in the revolutionary era and is required reading for anyone seeking to gain a clearer understanding of the topic. The book was ahead of its time in that it placed Indian people at the heart of the analysis and inspired much of the scholarship that has been published since. Likewise, Calloway's article "'We have Always Been the Frontier': The American Revolution in Shawnee Country," *American Indian Quarterly* 16 (1992) is also a very important piece of scholarship on this topic. If any earlier work exerted an influence similar to that of Calloway's it would have to be Barbara Graymont's, *The Iroquois in the American Revolution* (1972), as one of the very first, if not the first book to focus solely on the experience of a particular native group in the American Revolution; Graymont's book is still considered a must-read for anyone investigating this subject. Additionally, Alan Taylor, *The Divided Ground: Indians, Settlers, and the Northern Borderland of the American Revolution* (2006) represents one of the very best entries into the field to come along since Calloway's work from the mid-1990s. Other examples of American Revolutionary scholarship that include a focus on Native Americans include Isabel Thomson Kelsay, *Joseph Brant, 1743–1807: Man of Two Worlds* (1972); Patrick Griffin, *American Leviathan: Empire, Nation, and*

Revolutionary Frontier (2007); James H. O'Donnell III, *Southern Indians in the American Revolution* (1973) and *The Cherokees of North Carolina in the American Revolution* (1976); Jim Piecuch, *Three Peoples, One King: Loyalists, Indians, and Slaves in the Revolutionary South, 1775–1782* (2008); Greg O'Brien, "We Are Behind You: The Choctaw Occupation of Natchez in 1778," *Journal of Mississippi History*, vol. 64 (2002); Paul Lawrence Stevens, "His Majesty's Savage Allies: British Policy and Northern Indians During the Revolutionary War. The Carleton Years, 1774–1778," PhD dissertation (1984); Ruth Wallis Herndon and Ella Wilcox Sekatau, "The Right to a Name: The Narragansett People and Rhode Island Officials in the Revolutionary Era," in Colin Calloway, ed., *After King Philip's War: Presence and Persistence in Indian New England* (1997); David Levinson, "An Explanation of the Oneida-Colonist Alliance in the American Revolution," *Ethnohistory* 23 (1976); Robert S. Allen, *His Majesty's Indian Allies: British Policy in the Defence of Canada, 1774–1815* (1992); William T. Hagan, *Longhouse Diplomacy and Frontier Warfare: The Iroquois Confederation in the American Revolution* (1976); David A. Armour and Keith R. Widder, *At the Crossroads: Michilimackinac during the American Revolution* (1986); and Wiley Sword, *President Washington's Indian War* (1986).

Colin Calloway has likewise contributed some of the most significant scholarship on Native Americans in the immediate postwar period to 1815. His *The Shawnees and the War for America* (2007) and *Crown and Calumet: British-Indian Relations, 1783–1815* (1987) stand as some of the best work in the field. Other prominent scholarship that covers the post-war period includes Reginald Horsman, *Expansion and American Indian Policy, 1783–1815* (1967); Edward J. Cashin, "'But Brothers, It is Our Land We Are Talking About': Winners and Losers in the Georgia Backcountry," in Ronald Hoffman, Thad W. Tate, and Peter J. Albert, eds., *An Uncivil War: The Southern Backcountry during the American Revolution* (1985); Randolph C. Downes, "Creek-American Relations, 1782–1790," *Georgia Historical Quarterly* 29 (1937); Helen Hornbeck Tanner, "The Glaize in 1792: A Composite Indian Community," *Ethnohistory* 25 (1978); William G. McLoughlin, *Cherokee Renascence in the New Republic* (1986); R. David Edmunds, *The Shawnee Prophet* (1983); as well as Joel Martin, *Sacred Revolt: The Muskogees Struggle for a New World* (1993).

Philip J. Deloria, *Playing Indian* (1998) represents the gold standard of recent works on the on going struggle between whites and native people over who controls Indian identity while Robert F. Berkhofer, *The White Man's Indian: Images of the American Indian from Columbus to the Present* (1979) is for most scholars of Native American history the origin point of such investigations. Other prominent examples of scholarship in this vein are Jill Lepore, *The Name of War: King Philip's War and the Origins of American Identity* (1999); Roy Harvey Pearce, *Savagism and Civilization: A Study of the Indian and the American Mind* (1965); June Namias, ed., *Narrative of the Life of Mary Jemison. By James E. Seaver* (1992) and "Jane McCrea and the American Revolution," in *White Captives: Gender and Ethnicity on the American Frontier* (1993); Robert W. Venables, "The Iconography of Empire: Images of the American Indian in the Early Republic, 1783–1835" (1992); Donald A. Grinde and Bruce E. Johansen, *Exemplar of Liberty: Native America and the Evolution of Democracy* (1991); and Bruce E. Johansen and Elisabeth Tooker, "Commentary on the Iroquois and the U.S. Constitution," *Ethnohistory* 37 (1990).

INDEX

Abraham, 55
accommodation, 13, 14, 16;
 Cherokees, 158
acculturation, 13
Adair, James, 36
Adams, John ("Novanglus"), 50
Adams, Samuel, 50
African Americans: intermarriage with
 Native Americans, 52; slavery,
 158, 159
agricultural methods, 158
AIM (American Indian Movement),
 177–178
Albany Congress (1754), 54–55,
 56, 131
Algonquian nations, 57–58
American Indian Movement (AIM),
 177–178
American Revolution: historiography
 of, 5–6, 8; nature of in the East
 and West, 139–141, 147, 148;
 role and experience of Native
 Americans in, 1–2; roles of forts
 in, 77
American Revolution immediate
 aftermath, 157–175; Catawbas
 from allies to symbols, 165;

Cherokee factionalism increases,
 158; Chickasaws in a chaotic
 world, 161–163; Choctaw
 sovereignty, 163–165; fate of the
 Six Nations, 168–172; ongoing
 war in the Ohio Valley, 172–175;
 rise of Alexander McGillivray and
 inequality among the Creeks,
 159–161; Stockbridge Indians,
 167–168; Western Abenakis,
 166–167
*The American Revolution in Indian
 Country: Crisis and Diversity in
 Native American Communities*
 (Calloway), 5, 6
American Revolution in the North:
 Praying Indians as Patriot
 soldiers, 118, 121–123; splintering
 of the Six Nations, 118, 124–138;
 Western Abenaki survival,
 118–121
American Revolution in the South,
 87–115; British government's
 position on role of Native
 Americans in the conflict, 88;
 Catawba participation in, 114–115;
 Cherokee civil war, 88–94;

American Revolution (*continued*)
Chickasaw war for autonomy,
103–109; Choctaw calculations,
109–113; Creek Confederacy,
94–103; and John Stuart, 87–110;
Second Continental Congress
address to principal Indian
nations, 87
American Revolution in the West,
139–155; Clark's expedition to
Illinois country, 139–140,
145–147; death of Cornstalk and
end of Shawnee neutrality,
143–145; initial Ohio Indian
neutrality, 141–143; nature of,
139–141, 147; Ohio Valley Indians
on the offensive, 147–151;
retaliation against the Shawnees,
151–155
Americans: colonists desire for western
Indian land, 5; Indian policy in
early republic, 160, 164; and
McGillivray, 160
Amherst, Lord Jeffrey, 4, 18, 19, 21; and
Sir William Johnson, 59–60, 61
Anderson, Fred, 69–60, 80
Andros, Sir Edmund, governor of
New York, 54, 74
Anglican Church, 62, 63, 64, 65, 125
Anglican Mohawk Mission, 125
Anglo-Cherokee War, 26
Appalachian Mountains, 75, 79, 124;
Pontiac's War west of the, 13;
Royal Proclamation of 1763, 24
Arbuckle, Captain Matthew, 144
Arnold, Benedict: invasion from
Canada, 118; Valcour Bay, 122
Aron, Stephen, 148, 149
artifacts, names, and symbols of Native
Americans, 178–180
Atkin, Edmund, Superintendent of
Indian Affairs, 44, 55, 71
Atlantic Ocean, British control of, 132
Attakullakulla (Little Carpenter), 2,
26, 27
Augusta Conference (1763), 26;
Choctaws at, 29

Bacon's Rebellion, 74
baggatiway game, 11, 12
Bahamas, British in, 159
Baker's Bottom, 85
Battle of Augusta (1780), 103
Battle of Blue Licks, 172
Battle of Fallen Timbers, 174
Battle of Oriskany, 134, 136
Battle of Point Pleasant, 85, 144
Battle of the Bluff, 93
Battle of the Little Big Horn, 173
Battle of the Wabash (1791),
173, 174
Beaver Wars, 15, 75
Bender, Thomas, 7
Bird, Henry, 150 152
Blackfish, 148, 149
black slavery, 158, 159
Blue Jacket, Shawnee leader, 173, 174
Boone, Daniel, 147, 148, 151, 154
Boonesborough, 147, 148, 149, 150
Bossu, Jean-Bernard, 37
Boston Harbor, 50
Boston Port Bill, 83
Boston Tea Party, 178
Bouquet, Colonel Henry, 30, 68
Braddock, Edward, British General, 17,
54, 55, 56
Bradstreet, Colonel John, 78
Brant, Joseph (Thayendanegea in
Mohawk), 64, 125–126, 137, 138,
154; and the British, 133;
commissioned as captain, 136;
confederacy of Western tribes,
173; and Johnson, Sir Guy, 126,
129, 130; at Kanonwalohale, 138;
languages and kinship
connections, 125, 136; move to
Grand River, Canada, 169;
reputation for savagery, 134–136;
wife Catherine Croghan, 136
British: attempts to limit western
settlement, 79–81; in Bahamas,
159; in Canada, 159; in Detroit,
159; goals in North America, 170;
and McGillivray, 160; position on
role of Native Americans in the

conflict, 88; unilateral control of North America, 1–2, 5

British Indian policy, 13, 18, 24; collapse in the North, 47–65; collapse in the South, 25–45; collapse in the West, 67–86

Brown, Thomas, successor as Indian Superintendent, 93–94

Bryan's Station, 149, 150, 154, 155

Bull, Captain, 4

Burgoyne, General John, campaign in Saratoga, New York, 119, 122, 133

Butler, Colonel John, 131, 135, 136

Butler, Lieutenant Colonel William, 136

Butler, Walter, 136, 137

Cahokia, 145

Caldwell, Alexander, 154

Calloway, Colin, 81, 94, 109, 121, 122, 141, 158, 166, 168, 172, 173; *The American Revolution in Indian Country*, 5, 6

Calvinist missionaries, 62–63

Cambridge, Massachusetts, Washington's headquarters, 118, 121

Cameron, Alexander, 113

Campbell, General John, 108–109, 112, 113

Canada: American invasion of (1775), 51; Benedict Arnold's invasion from, 118; British in, 159; Indians of, 121, 122, 132, 134; and the Western Abenakis, 167

Canajoharie meeting (1759), 57

Captina Creek, 82, 84, 85

Carleton, Guy, governor of Quebec, 119, 132, 136

Carolina colony founding, 41

Carolinas: English settlements, 2, 3; myth of the revolution in the, 114–115

Catawba Nation, 41–45

Catawba Old Town, 115

Catawbas: from allies to symbols, 165; in American Revolution, 88, 114–115; and South Carolina, 165

Catholicism, 50, 80; and the Western Abenakis, 48

Cavendish, Lord, 138

Cayugas, 53, 54, 61; Battle of Oriskany, 134

Champlain Valley, 119

Charles I, beheading of, 64

Charleston Committee of Safety, 114

Chatham, Lord, 80

Cherokees, 25–28, 45, 76, 155; at Augusta Congress (1763), 29; civil war, 88–94; confederacy of, 2–3; disease epidemics, 3; factionalism increases, 158; Indian emissary for, 1; meeting at Fort Knox (1792), 173–174; and Six Nations of the Iroquois Confederacy, 42; South Carolina defeat of the, 21

Cherokee War (1761), 3

Cherokee War (1776), 88, 91, 99

Chester, Peter, governor of Florida, 106

Chickamaugas, 91–94, 158

Chickasaws, 45; in a chaotic world, 161–163; allied to the British, 36–38; at Augusta Congress (1763), 29; and Creeks, 162; independence of, 36–38; Indian emissary for, 1; patrolling Mississippi River, 88, 104–106, 110; war for autonomy, 103–104

Chillicothe village, 149, 151

Choctaw-Creek War, 40–41

Choctaws, 45, 109–113; at Augusta Congress (1763), 29; cultural transformation among, 38–41; Indian emissary for, 1; patrolling Mississippi River, 88, 104, 105, 110; sovereignty of, 163–165

Christianity, 51; converts to, 70

Christian, William, 91

Clark, General George Rogers, 82–83, 84, 106; defense of the Kentucky frontier, 150–152; delegate to Virginia Assembly, 152–143; expedition to Illinois country, 139–140, 145–147; invading Ohio, 155

Claus, Daniel, 125, 132–133
Clinton, George, governor of
    New York, 54
Columbian landing in the Caribbean, 52
communal property, Creek
    Confederacy, 159
Concord, 51, 128, 142, 153
Conestogas, 69–70
Congregational Church, 51, 52;
    New England, 122
Connecticut: Susquehana Company,
    21; Wyoming Valley, 58
Connecticut River settlements, 120
Connolly, John, 84, 141
Conoys, meeting at Fort Knox (1792),
    173–174
Continental Congress, 121, 127, 167;
    Cornstalk at, 143; Indian
    Committee, 128–129
Corkran, David, 98
Cornplanter, Seneca leader, 133, 137
Cornstalk, Shawnee leader, 83, 85, 141,
    144–145
Cornwallis, Lord Charles, 115, 138,
    152–153
Cortes, Hernando, 179
Covenant Chain, 47, 48, 54, 58, 61;
    Mohawks in, 122; origin of,
    73–74; protocols of, 124, 130
covert operations, 145–146
Cowetas, 99
Crawford, General William, 153–154
Creek Confederacy, 94–103
Creeks: Augusta Congress (1763), 29;
    communal property, 159;
    divisions between young and old,
    28, 34; end of Seven Years' War,
    28; Georgia settlements, 28;
    Houmahta, 33; and the imperial
    crisis, 28–36, 45; land cessions, 31,
    35; Latchaway Creeks, 30, 96, 99;
    Lower Creeks, 28, 29, 31, 35; and
    McGillivray, 160; meeting at Fort
    Knox (1792), 173–174; National
    Council, 160–161; Oconee Creeks,
    28; Oconee River incident (1767),

33; Pensacola Congress (1765), 30;
    Picolata Treaty (1765), 31; private
    property, 160; Redsticks, 161;
    Seminoles, 28, 30, 31, 96, 98;
    Stuart on role in American
    Revolution, 88, 89, 94–95; Treaty of
    Augusta, 29; Upper Creeks, 29, 35
Cresap, Captain Michael, 82–83, 84, 85
Crofts, Lieutenant Will, 120, 121
Croghan, Cathrine, wife of Brant,
    Joseph (Thayendanegea in
    Mohawk), 136
Croghan, George, 68, 69, 77, 78, 136
cultural misrepresentation and
    stereotypes of Native Americans,
    180
cultural transformation among
    Choctaws, 38–41
Custer, General George, 173

Dartmouth, Lord, 79
Dean, James, 132
Deganawidah epic, 52–53, 65, 172
Delawares, 3–4, 20, 172; and
    Conestogas, 69; refugees, 22,
    70–76; and Shawnees, 141; and
    Sir William Johnson, 59;
    Treaty of Easton, 58, 67
Deloria, Philip, 178, 180
Deloria, Vine, Jr., 8
De Peyster, Arent, 154, 155
DeSoto expedition (1540), 41
Detroit, 145, 148, 149, 151; British in,
    159
disease epidemics, 23, 52; Catawba
    Nation, 41–42, 43–44; Cherokees,
    3; Onondagas, 117; and refugee
    villages, 15; smallpox, 17, 23,
    43, 75, 92
Doughty, Major John, 163
Dowd, Gregory, 22, 60, 61
Dragging Canoe (Tsi.yu Gansi. Ni),
    26–28, 45; in American
    Revolution, 88–94, 158
Draper's Meadows, 3
Drayton, William Henry, 44

Dunmore, John, governor of Virginia, 83, 84, 85. *See also* Lord Dunmore's War
Dutch, goals in North America, 170
Dutch colonists, 52

Echols, John, 3
economy, reciprocal exchange-based, 158
Egremont, Lord, Secretary of State, 4, 24
Emisteseguo, Upper Creek leader, 98, 101, 103
English settlements: Carolinas, 2; Virginia, 2
English settlements of the Carolinas and Virginia, 2, 3
Escochabey (Cherokee headman), 35, 95
Etherington, George, at Michilimackinac (fort), 11–12
ethnogenesis, cultural borrowing and adaptation, 15–16
ethnohistory, 5, 7
European gender norms, 158
European powers, Native Americans playing them against one another, 1
Evans, John, 42, 43

Fauquier, Francis, governor of Virginia, 21, 80
Fee, Thomas, 99
Fenton, William, 57, 126, 127
Five Nations of the Iroquois Confederacy, and Ohio Valley peoples, 71–72, 76. *See also* Six Nations of the Iroquois Confederacy
Fleming, Colonel William, 147–148
Floridas, Spanish in, 159, 161
Forbes, John, British General, 2, 21, 56, 59, 67, 68
Fort Ancient complex of the Ohio Valley, 71
Fort Cumberland, 150
Fort Detroit, 12, 23, 78, 154
Fort Dunmore, 84

Fort Duquesne, 2, 4, 17, 18, 21, 54, 55, 59, 67–68, 77
Fort Finney, 172, 173
Fort Frontenac, 56
Fort Hunter, 135
Fort Jefferson, 108
Fort Knox, meeting of delegation of Indian tribes, 173–174
Fort Lévis, 60
Fort Loudon, 3
Fort McIntosh, 173
Fort Miami, 174
Fort Michilimackinac, 11–12, 23
Fort Niagara, 21, 57, 60, 61, 131, 169
Fort Ontario, 129
Fort Oswego, 54
Fort Pitt, 12, 20–21, 22, 23, 68, 77–78, 84, 150, 153
Fort Randolph, 144, 147
forts, roles in the American Revolution, 77
Fort Schuyler, 117, 138
Fort Stanwix, 21, 81, 117; conference (1768), 63–64, 81–82; meeting of Six Nations of the Iroquois Confederacy (1784), 170
Fort St. Louis, 72
Fort Toulouse, 159
Fort Vincennes, 139
Fort William-Henry, 54
Foxes, meeting at Fort Knox (1792), 173–174
Franchimastabe, Choctaw leader, 113
Franklin, Benjamin, 19–20, 70, 80
Freemasons, 125
French: departure from North America, 1, 5, 17, 18, 30; goals in North America, 170; and the Middle Ground, 13–18
French and Indian War, 20, 21. *See also* Seven Years' War
French settlements in Louisiana and Illinois, 2
fur trade, 14, 16; Beaver Wars, 15; decline of, 49

Gage, General Thomas, 40, 69, 80, 89, 96; and John Connolly, 141; letter to John Stuart, 121; and Sir Guy Johnson, 128; and Sir William Johnson, 124

Galphin, George, 98, 100, 101, 102

Gates, Horatio, 122

Genesees, 60–61

George III, King of England, 24, 45, 48, 79. *See also* Royal Proclamation (1763)

Georgia: Americans in, 159; at Augusta Congress (1763), 29; and the Chickasaws, 162; and the Choctaws, 164

German Flats meeting (1763), 61

gift-giving and reciprocity, 17, 18, 19, 21; cessation of, 31; Choctaws, 39; restoring, 24; Western Abenakis, 49

Gill, Joseph Louis, chief of village of St. Francis, 120

Girty, Simon, 149, 153–154

Gladwin, Major Henry, 78

Glaize multicultural Indian community, 173

Glen, James, South Carolina governor, 42

Gnadenhutten in Ohio, 153, 154

Gordon, Patrick, governor of Pennsylvania, 73, 74

Grand River, Canada, Mohawks move to, 169, 171

Graymont, Barbara, 65, 126

Great Council Fire, Six Nations of the Iroquois Confederacy, 117

Greathouse, Daniel, 84–85

Great Lakes Indians, 12, 13, 15, 16, 17, 18

Great League of Peace and Power, Iroquois Confederacy, 53, 65

great war for empire, 1

Greene, Nathanael, 115

Griffin, Patrick, 68

Guilford Courthouse, 115

Haldimand, Sir Frederick, 136, 138; governor of Quebec, 169, 171

Hamilton, General Henry, 103, 107, 139–140, 149, 150

Hamilton, James, governor of Pennsylvania, 75

Hand, General Edward, 144–145

Handsome Fellow of the Okfuskee Creeks, 97

"Hard Winter" (1779–1780), 149

Harmar, General Josiah, 173

Harrodsburg, 149

Harrods Town, Kentucky, 142

Haudenosanee, 52. *See also* Iroquois Confederacy

Henderson, Richard, 26

Hendrick (Mohawk leader), 54–55

Henry, Patrick, 83; "Give Me Liberty or Give Me Death" speech, 50; governor of Virginia, 143, 145–146, 158

Herkimer, General Nicholas, 133

Hiawatha, 52–53, 65, 171

Hillsborough, Lord, 34, 79

Hinderaker, Eric, 147–148

historiography, 5, 8

Hoboithle Mico, Creek leader, 160

Holton, Woody, 5–6

Hopewell. *See* Treaty of Hopewell

Horsehead Bottom, 82

horse raiding, 33

Howe, General William, 97, 109, 133, 134

Hurons, 15, 54; Battle of Oriskany, 134

identity, Indian struggle for, 8

Illinois, French settlements in, 2

Illinois country Indians, 12, 16, 17; raiding south into Chickasaw territory, 37; and Revolutionary War, 140

Imperial Crisis, 12, 38, 41; effects on Christian Indians of New England, 51; and the Six Nations of the Iroquois Confederacy, 48

Indiana, 145

Indian burial grounds, 168

Indian Charity School, 63

Indian emissary for Ohio country Indians, 1, 5

Indian Proprietors, Stockbridge
Indians, 168
Indian Removal policy, Jackson,
Andrew, 163
internal conflict, Native Americans, 28
Iroquois Confederacy, 52–65;
Deganawidah epic, 52–53, 65;
diplomatic system of, 53–54;
Great League of Peace and Power,
53, 65; Hiawatha, 52–53, 65;
Treaty of Easton, 67; wampum-
based ritual of condolence and
diplomacy, 53. *See also* Covenant
Chair; Five Nations of the
Iroquois Confederacy; Six Nations
of the Iroquois Confederacy
Irvine, William, 154

Jackson, Andrew, 161; Indian Removal
policy, 163
James, James Alton, 150
Jefferson, Thomas, 146–147, 150, 152;
on the Chickasaws, 163; governor
of Virginia, 92–93, 108
Jesuit missionaries, 48, 50, 53
Johnson Hall meetings (1768 and
1762), 52, 58–59
Johnson, Mary Brant, wife of Sir
William, 64–65, 124
Johnson, Sir Guy: and Joseph Brant,
126, 129, 130; and the Mohawks,
131; replaced by Sir John Johnson,
138; and Samuel Kirkland,
126–127; as Superintendent of
Indian Affairs, 124–125, 133; trip
to England, 132–133
Johnson, Sir John, 125, 129, 134, 137;
replacing Sir Guy Johnson, 138:
Johnson, Sir William; at Albany
Congress (1754), 54, 55;
Canajoharie meeting (1759), 57;
death of, 124, 125; Fort Stanwix
conference (1768), 63–64, 81–82;
German Flats meeting (1763), 61;
Johnson Hall meeting (1762),
58–59; Johnson Hall meeting
(1768), 52; letter to Edmund

Atkin, 55–56; meeting with Indian
delegates (July 11, 1774), 47–48;
and Mohawks, 64, 131; and
northern boundary, 62, 63;
Superintendent of Indian Affairs, 4
Johnstone, George, governor of West
Florida, 30
Jones, John Gabriel, 142

Kanasha Valley, 147
Kaskaskia, 145, 146
Kenny, James, 20, 22
Kentucky, 145; settlements in, 149; and
Shawnees, 142, 149; and Virginia,
142–143
Kickapoos, 108, 161, 162
King Beaver (Tamaqua), 67
King George's War, 76
King Philip's War, 52, 74, 81, 179
Kirkland, Samuel, 63, 64, 125, 138;
official agent of the American
Revolutionary cause, 129–130;
and Six Nations, 126–128, 131
Kispoki division of Shawnees, 141–142
Kittaning, 72–73

lacrosse, 11
Lakotas, 177–178
land as capital for credit, 81
land speculators, 81
land squatters, 81
La Présentation mission, 60
Laurens, Henry, 90
Lee, General Arthur, 99
Lee, General Charles, 91
Lepore, Jill, 179
Leslie, Lieutenant, 11
Lewis, Colonel Andrew, 85
Lexington, 51, 128, 142, 149, 153
Lincoln county militia, 154
Little Carpenter (Attakullakulla), 2,
26, 27
Little Turtle, Miami war leader, 173
Logan, Benjamin, 151, 154, 172
Logan, Mingo chief, 82, 84, 85
Logan's Station, 149
Long Warrior, Seminole leader, 96

Lord Dunmore's War, 37–38, 81–86, 124, 125, 140; limits of American settlements, 141. *See also* Dunmore, John
Louisbourg on Cape Breton Island, 56
Louisiana, French settlements in, 2
Lyttelton, William Henry, South Carolina governor, 3

Macutte'Mong, Ottawa chief, 140
Mahicans, 54, 74; meeting at Fort Knox (1792), 173–174
Maquachake division of Shawnees, 141, 142
Martin's Station, 151
Mascoutens, 161
Mason, George, 146–147
Massachusetts: and Stockbridge Indians, 168;and Wampanoags, 54, 179
Massachusetts Provincial Congress, 121
Mathews, Captain Robert, 138
Mayo Fort, 3
McConnell, Michael, 74
McCrea, Jane, Indian murder of, 119
McGary, Major Hugh, 154
McGillivray, Alexander, 101, 102, 103; on American victory over the British, 157; background of, 159–160; and Dragging Canoe, 93
McIntosh, General William, 100, 101
McIntosh, Roderick, 34
McKee, Alexander, 154
medal chiefs, 30, 31
Merrell, James H., 7, 41, 43, 44, 114, 115, 166
Metacom ("King Philip"), 179
Metamora: or, The Last of the Wampanoags (Stone), 179–180
métis (mestizos), mixed-race families as cultural brokers, 158, 160
Miami, British fort at, 11
Miamis, 11, 162; meeting at Fort Knox (1792), 173–174; and Shawnees, 141
Middle Ground, 13–18, 24, 39. *See also* Pontiac's War

Mingo Pouscouche, Choctaw leader, 113
Mingos, 155; meeting at Fort Knox (1792), 173–174; refugees, 22, 70–76; and Shawnees, 141
Misisquoi, Abenaki village, 121
Mission of Saint Joseph, 15
Mohawks, 53, 54, 58, 59, 62; Battle of Oriskany, 134; Boston Tea Party, 178; and Mahican conflict, 74; move to Grand River, Canada, 169, 171; at Mussel Shoals, 25; and Oneidas and Tuscaroras, 117, 131; and Sir William Johnson, 64–65; and Wyoming Valley, 58
Moluntha, Shawnee chief, 172–173
Montcalm, Marquis de, 56
Montgomery, John, 92
Montour, Andrew, 68
Montreal, 18, 59; defeat of French at, 58
Moravian villages, 153
Morgan, George, 144
The Mortar (Yayatustenuggee), 30
Moultrie, William, governor of South Carolina, 165
murder, and the Middle Ground, 13–14
Muscogulges, 159
Mussel Shoals, 25, 27

Nanticokes, meeting at Fort Knox (1792), 173–174
Napoleon, 159
Natchez defense, 110
National Council, Creek Confederacy, 160–161
Native American history, 5–9; British attempts to limit western settlement, 79–81; imperial crisis, 12, 16
Native Americans: American Indian Movement (AIM), 177–178; appropriating artifacts, names, and symbols of, 178–180; cultural misrepresentation and stereotypes, 180; from domestic

problem to foreign policy issue, 165; intermarriage with African Americans, 52; internal conflict, 28; Pine Ridge reservation, South Dakota, 177–178; playing European powers against one another, 1; Red Power movement, 177; resistance in the West, 76–79; resisting American domination, 174–175; role and experience in the American Revolution, 1–2; sovereignty of, 165, 170; struggle continues, 175, 177–180; struggle for Indian identity, 8; symbolic status of, 165, 166; turbulence of the 1960s, 177; United States Indian policy, 177; World War II service in the armed forces, 122–123; Wounded Knee, South Dakota, 177–178

Native Americans in the American Revolution (Schmidt), 6–9
nativism, 22–23, 76
natural resources, competition for, 22, 37, 49
Neolin, Delaware holy man, 22, 23, 60, 76
New England: Congregational Church, 122; King Philip's War, 179; and the Western Abenakis, 167
New Jersey, 122
Newton, Sir Isaac, 6
New York, 122; and the Stockbridge Indians, 167–168; and the Western Abenakis, 167
New York City, Stockbridge Indian battle, 123
Nimham, Stockbridge Indian chief, 123
North Carolina, at Augusta Congress (1763), 29

O'Brien, Greg, 38, 39, 110, 111, 164, 165
Odanak, burning of, 49
Ogulki, 35, 36, 95
Ohio Company, 21

Ohio Valley peoples, 12, 15, 17, 23, 67–86; Delawares, 72–75, 86; Dunmore's War, 124; and Five Nations of the Iroquois Confederacy, 71–72; generation divide among, 143; Indian emissary for, 1; Mingos, 75, 86; on the offensive, 147–151; ongoing war after Revolution, 172–175; proposed alliance with, 27; and Revolutionary War, 140; Shawnees, 70–72, 86, 172; Treaty of Easton, 3–4
Ojibwas, 11; meeting at Fort Knox (1792), 173–174
Okfuskee Creeks, 97
Oneidas, 53, 54, 63, 64, 65; and the Americans, 137, 171; Battle of Oriskany, 134; and the Iroquois, 169; and Mohawks and Senecas, 117, 131; and Stockbridge Indians, 168; village of Kanonwalohale, 138
Onnontaé, 53
Onondaga Congress, 125
Onondagas, 23, 53, 54, 59; Battle of Oriskany, 134; disease epidemic, 117; Great Council Fire, 117
Onontio (Algonquian term), 16
Ontario, 56
Osages, 105
Oswego, 60
Ottawas, 1, 23, 60, 139, 172; meeting at Fort Knox (1792), 173–174; at Mussel Shoals, 25
Ouiatenon, British fort at, 11

pan-Indian theology, 22–23
Panton, Leslie, and Company, 160
Paxton boys, 69–70
Paya Mataha, Chickasaw leader, 106, 107, 161
PBS documentary, *William Kunstler: Disturbing the Universe,* 178
Penn family, 58
Penn, John, 70

Pennsylvania, 21; American militia
    from, 153; Delawares in, 3; and
    Iroquois country, 171
Penn, Thomas, 73
Pensacola, falling to the Spanish
    (1781), 109, 113
Pequots, 54
Petty, John, 85
Piankashaws, 162
Pinckney's Treaty (1795), 163
Pine Ridge reservation, South Dakota,
    177–178
Piomingo (Chickasaw chief), 36
Pipe, Captain, 154
Piqua division of Shawnees, 141, 142
Pitt, William, 56
Pizarro, Francisco, 179
Pluggy's Town, 143
Pocahontas, 165
Pontiac's Rebellion. See Pontiac's War
Pontiac's War, 1, 12, 18–24, 81; and the
    Conestogas, 69–70; end of, 62; war
    over status, 60. See also Middle
    Ground
Pontiac Uprising. See Pontiac's War
Post, Christian Frederick, 67–68
Potawatomis, 11; meeting at Fort Knox
    (1792), 173–174
pottery styles, 158, 166
Praying Indians of Massachusetts, 48,
    51–52, 65, 178; as Patriot soldiers,
    118, 121–123
Presbyterians, 63, 64; Scotch-Irish,
    69
Princeton University, 63
prisoners of war, 19–20
Pumpkin King, Seminole leader, 96
Puritan clergy, 51
Puritans, 64, 167

Quakers, 59
Quapaws, 105
Quebec, 18, 19; defeat of French at,
    58
Quebec Act (1774), 50, 79–80
Queen Anne's War, 75

Rae, Robert, 98, 101
Ragueneau, Father Paul, 15
Rawdon, Francis, 115
reciprocal exchange-based economy,
    158
Red Power movement, 177
Redsticks, Creek Confederacy, 161
refugees, 15, 22; Shawnees, Delawares,
    and Mingos, 70–76
reservation, Catawba Nation, 44
revolutionary scholars, 5
Richter, Daniel, 54
Rogers, Robert, 48–49, 120
Royal Proclamation (1763), 24, 32, 34,
    45, 48, 62; enforcement of, 78–79;
    northern boundary line, 63; and
    Ohio Valley, 68, 77; violations of,
    83, 85–86
Ruddles Station, 151
rules of warfare, European, 112
runaway slave catchers, Catawbas, 42, 45
Rutherford, General Griffith, 91

sachems, 47, 65
Sandusky, British fort at, 11
Saratoga, New York, Burgoyne, General
    John, 119
Sauks, meeting at Fort Knox (1792),
    173–174
Saunt, Claudio, 159, 160
Savannahs, 72
Schmidt, Ethan A., Native Americans in
    the American Revolution, 6–9
Schuyler, General Philip, 131–132, 134,
    135, 137
scouting parties, 120
Second Continental Congress address
    to principal Indian nations, 87
Seineke, Kathrine Wagner, 146
Seminoles, in American Revolution,
    88, 96
Senecas, 53, 54, 55, 57–58, 59, 117, 155;
    Battle of Oriskany, 134; and
    Calvinist missionaries, 63; and
    Conestogas, 69; and the French,
    60; Genesees, 60–61

Seven Years' War (1754–1763), 2, 37,
    38; and the Iroquois Confederacy,
    54; and loyalty of the Catawbas,
    43; and the Western Abenakis, 49.
    See also French and Indian War
Shawnees, 20, 172; end of neutrality,
    143–145; Indian emissary for, 1;
    meeting at Fort Knox (1792), 173–
    174; at Mussel Shoals, 25, 26;
    political organization of, 141–142;
    refugees, 22, 70–76; retaliation
    against the, 151–155; Western
    Confederacy, 169
Shelby, Evan, 92
Siouan-speaking groups, 41
Sipe, C. Hale, 82
Six Nations of the Iroquois
    Confederacy, 52–65, 124–138;
    after the American Revolution,
    168–172; Cayugas and Oneidas,
    126; and the Cherokees, 42;
    choosing exile over negotiation,
    171; and the Connecticut
    Assembly, 4–5; decline of, 48;
    Fort Stanwix meeting (1784), 170;
    Grand Council meeting at
    Onondaga, 129; Great Council
    Fire, 117; League of Peace and
    Friendship, 171–172; Longhouse,
    125; Mohawks and Senecas, 126;
    relationships with British
    government, 59; sovereignty of,
    170; and Treaty of Fort Stanwix
    (1768), 81–82, 124. *See also*
    Iroquois Confederacy
Six Towns Choctaws, 111–112
Skenandon, Oneida sachem, 133
Slaughter, Colonel George, 151
slave raids, 41–42
social history, 7
Solomon, Captain, 122
South Carolina: at Augusta Congress
    (1763), 29; and the Catawbas, 165;
    defeat of the Cherokees, 21
South Dakota: Pine Ridge reservation,
    177–178; Wounded Knee, 177–178

Sovereignty: of Choctaws, 163–165; of
    Native Americans, 165, 170; of Six
    Nations of the Iroquois
    Confederacy, 170
Spanish: allied to the Americans, 93;
    and the Chickasaws, 161, 162; and
    the Choctaws, 164; declaration of
    war against Britain (1779), 107,
    111; fall of Mobile to (1780), 112;
    fall of Pensacola to (1781), 109,
    113; in Floridas, 159, 161; goals in
    North America, 170; and
    McGillivray, 160; on the
    Mississippi River, 104; at New
    Orleans, 88; retreat from the
    Mississippi Valley, 163
Spanish Empire, in North America, 1
Stamp Act, 64, 80, 127
Starved Rock, 72
St. Clair, Arthur, 173, 174
stereotypes of Native Americans, 180
St. Francis, Quebec, 118, 120, 121
St. Joseph, British fort at, 11
St. Leger, Colonel Barry, 133–134
Stockbridge Indians, 51, 118, 121–123,
    178; demise of, 167–168; Indian
    Proprietors, 168; relationship with
    the Americans, 123
Stone, John Augustus, *Metamora: or,
    The Last of the Wampanoags*
    (1829), 179–180
Stuart, Captain, 144
Stuart, Charles, 104, 109
Stuart, Henry, 25, 27, 89
Stuart, John, 27, 29, 30–31, 32, 33; and
    American Revolution in the
    South, 87–110 ; on the Catawbas,
    114; on the Chickasaws and
    Choctaws, 103; and Creeks on role
    in American Revolution, 88, 89,
    94–95; death of (1779), 107, 110;
    and Drayton, William Henry,
    44–45; Mobile conference (1765),
    39; Mobile conference (1777),
    104–105; Pensacola conference
    (1776), 99–100

Stuart, John, Anglican missionary
    among the Mohawks, 65, 128
subsistence issues, 3, 23, 45; Catawba
    Nation, 42, 43;
    Western Abenakis, 121
Sullivan, General John, 123, 137
Sumter, Thomas, 115
Susquehanna Company, 4, 21
Susquehannocks: and Conestogas, 69,
    72; and Shawnees, 71
Swashan, Abenaki chief, 118
Sycamore Shoals Conference, 26, 27
symbolic status, of Native Americans,
    165, 166

Taitt, David, 95, 100, 101
Tallachea (Creek leader), 33
Tamaqua (King Beaver), 21, 67
Taylor, Alan, 124, 130, 132, 138
Tchoukafala (Chickasaw town), 36
Tecumseh, Shawnee leader, 174
Teedyuscung (Delaware leader), 4,
    21, 59
Tennessee, 149
Tenskwatawa, Shawnee Prophet, 174
Thawekila division of Shawnees, 141
Thunderhawk, Madonna, 178
Todd, John, 150
Todd, Levi, 151
Tonyn, Patrick, governor of Florida, 96,
    98, 99, 100
Toole, Matthew, 42
Townsend Duties, 64, 127
trading practices: and alcohol, 34, 40,
    47, 75; Choctaws, 38–39; fair, 24,
    31, 32; importance in American
    Revolution, 100, 101, 106;
    licenses, 34; unfair, 47;
    unregulated, 37
Treaty of Albany (1775), 121
Treaty of Aranjuez (1779), 111
Treaty of Dewitt's Corner (1777), 91
Treaty of Easton (1758): Delawares, 58,
    67; Ohio country Indians, 3–4, 56
Treaty of Fort Finney, 172
Treaty of Fort McIntosh (1785), 172

Treaty of Fort Stanwix, 48, 62, 81–82
Treaty of Greenville (1795), 174
Treaty of Hard Labor, 45, 79
Treaty of Hopewell (1785), 158, 159,
    164–165
Treaty of Nashville (1783), 162
Treaty of Paris, 8, 49, 94, 121; British
    and their Indian allies, 157;
    Parliamentary debates, 169
Treaty of San Lorenzo (1795), 163
triangular native diplomacy, 1
Trumbull, governor of Connecticut, 127
Tsi.yu Gansi. Ni (Dragging Canoe),
    26–28, 45
Tuscaroras, 45, 63, 64, 65; and the
    Americans, 137, 171; Battle of
    Oriskany, 134; and Mohawks and
    Senecas, 117, 131

United States: Indian policy, 177, 179;
    primary goals of versus European
    colonial goals, 170. See also
    Americans; American Revolution

Valcour Bay, Arnold, Benedict, 122
Vermont: and the Stockbridge Indians,
    167–168; Western Abenakis of,
    118–121, 167
Vincennes or St. Vincents, 145
Virginia: at Augusta Congress (1763),
    29; and the Cherokees, 2–3; and
    the Chickasaws, 162; conflict with
    Ohio Valley Indian groups,
    140–141; and Kentucky, 142–143;
    land as capital for credit, 81; and
    Shawnees, 25, 126; title to the
    Ohio country, 21
Virginia Anglo-Indian conflict. See
    Lord Dunmore's War

"Walking Purchase" (1737), 58
Wampanoags, 54, 179
wampum-based ritual of condolence
    and diplomacy, 53
war belts, 25, 27, 60, 89, 130
War of 1812, 159, 168

War of the Austrian Succession, 16
War of the Spanish Succession, 16
Washington, General George, 21, 68,
    118, 134; Cornwallis surrender at
    Yorktown, 138; expedition to
    western New York and
    Pennsylvania, 137; and
    Stockbridge Indians, 122, 123
Wayne, General Anthony, 174
Weiser, Conrad, 22–23, 59
Western Abenakis of New England and
    Canada, 48–51, 65, 118–121;
    burning of Odanak, 49;
    decentralization or avoidance
    strategy, 49, 50–51, 118, 120, 167;
    and Peace of Paris, 121; post-war
    complications of, 166–167;
    religious conflict, 48
Western Confederacy, 173, 174; and
    Joseph Brant, 173; Shawnees,
    169
West Fincastle Petitions, 142, 146
Westos, 45
Wheelock, Eleazar, 63, 64, 125, 128
Whitcomb, Major Benjamin, 120
White Eyes, 149

Whitehall, 18, 32, 34, 52, 89
White, Richard, 14, 16
William Kunstler: Disturbing the
    Universe, PBS documentary, 178
Williamsburg, 145, 147
Williamson, Colonel Andrew, 91
Willing, Captain James, 105, 106, 110
World War II, Native American service
    in the armed forces, 122–123
Wounded Knee, South Dakota,
    177–178
Wright, James, governor of Georgia, 29,
    31, 32, 33, 35
Wright, J. Leitch, 159
Wyandots, 11, 57, 155, 172; meeting at
    Fort Knox (1792), 173–174
Wyoming Valley, Connecticut, 58
Wythe, George, 146–147

Yamasees, 45
Yamasee War, 43, 72
Yayatustenuggee (The Mortar), 30
Yorktown, Virginia, surrender at, 138,
    152–153

Zeisberger, David, 143

About the Author

ETHAN A. SCHMIDT, PhD, is assistant professor of history at Delta State University in Cleveland, Mississippi. His published works include *The Divided Dominion: Social Conflict and Indian Hatred in Early Virginia* as well as articles in *Atlantic Studies, American Indian Quarterly,* and the *Historical Journal of Massachusetts*. He holds a doctorate in early American history and Native American history from the University of Kansas. He previously taught at Texas Tech University.